"Chandler provides a handle on what will be happening over the next couple of decades, and he lets the church know what it has to do about it. Others have tried to do this, but I think his effort may be the clearest and best. This book is going to be HOT!"

Tony Campolo, *Professor of Sociology*
Eastern College, St. Davids, Pennsylvania

"*Racing Toward 2001* with Russell Chandler at the wheel is an unforgettable ride. The man who wrote one of the two best books on the New Age has written again. This time he forces us to cope with the furious future. If we fail to cope, we cannot live. What David Halberstam did in the *New Century*, Russell Chandler has done for evangelicals. His may be the most significant book of the decade, for unless we understand the new millennium, the best part of our work may be left in the old one. Chandler's work is a paradox. It is not grandiose or self-important, yet its immense content trivializes so much of what is published these days. He says it is not about church growth, but surely no church will grow that refuses to take seriously the future he delineates. He says this book is not about leadership, yet any would-be evangelical leader who ignores it will be leading somewhat in the dark. He says it is not about prophecy, yet I predict that this will be the most prophetic book of the year. Therefore, it's 'hats off' to Russell Chandler who has opened the drapes on the dark future and handed us a flashlight. *Racing Toward 2001* is a way of seeing around the millennial corner."

Calvin Miller, *Pastor*
Westside Church, Omaha, Nebraska

"Russ Chandler challenges Christians to stop being spectators. *Racing Toward 2001* gives us clear models of how each of us can—and must—shape the future."

Robert A. Seiple, *President*
World Vision

"Ah, at last a book even African Americans, Hispanics, and Asians should read! It's about the American future, culturally and religiously, in which all of us will be powerfully affected by what happens to each of us. If Chandler is right, we best fasten our seat belts, cause we're all in for a terrific ride."

William Pannell
Fuller Theological Seminary

"In *Racing Toward 2001* Russell Chandler has given us an insightful and well-documented analysis of futuristic issues that will provide new opportunities for us to evidence the qualities of Christian discipleship. The church for 2001 needs flexibility as well as integrity. We need to read both God's Word and God's world. Futurism is another form of the prophetic. God is not capricious; therefore, we can project from God's acts in history the manner in which God's Spirit will enable disciples of Christ to engage 2001."

Dr. Myron S. Augsburger, *President*
The Christian College Coalition

"*Racing Toward 2001* is a must for anyone concerned about the world our children and our grandchildren will inherit from us in the 21st century. In his thoroughly researched blueprint for the future, Russ not only gives a great analysis of the problem but offers concrete solutions which we should heed. We at *Urban Family* magazine want this important book to reach as wide a readership as possible."

John Perkins, *President*
Urban Family Magazine and John M. Perkins Foundation
for Reconciliation and Development

"Russ Chandler is one of the most thoughtful, discerning, and interesting writers on the political-religious scene today. Any race he's looking at is one I want to see, too."

Cal Thomas, *Syndicated Columnist*

"*Racing Toward 2001* is as exhilarating and informative as a visit to the most modern interactive museum. The reader will feel in touch with the unfolding future in a dynamic yet sure and steady way. Russ Chandler, perhaps the finest of America's religion writers, has not missed any of the significant movements or trends in the universe of believing. With economy of prose and sharpness of insight, he offers what is, in effect, a starbook and compass for those who want to understand the trans-formations taking place in institutional and personal religion. This book documents the vital, although changing, role of religion in life and, therefore, should be read by anybody who wants to understand our culture as we climb over the lip of the next century."

Eugene C. Kennedy, Ph.D., *Professor of Psychology*
Loyola University of Chicago

"Rushing backward into the future is no way to go. *Racing Toward 2001* will serve to help the church face forward, look upward, and reach outward."

Stuart and Jill Briscoe
Elmbrook Church, Brookfield, Wisconsin

"Russ Chandler uses the biblical metaphor of a race to describe how American religious leaders need to approach the future. He sets a fast pace in the fast lane. He covers a lot of territory very quickly. But *Racing Toward 2001* is far from superficial. Though it leaves me breathless, it is more than watching the scenery skim by the window of a speeding train. It provides more than the exhilaration of leaving a runway for a journey through the clouds. Basically, this book provides a sense of direction. It will help readers see where they have been and give them both courage and insight for the future."

J. Martin Bailey, *Director of Communications*
National Council of Churches

"Russell Chandler, with his years of reporting on trends and interpreting them for the church, is a perceptive and articulate guide to those who are trying to catch up with the pitfalls as he hustles us through the statistics and dire predictions of the futurologists across a vast and complex landscape. Read *Racing Toward 2001* before the future leaves you in the dust."

Stephen A. Hayner, *President*
InterVarsity Christian Fellowship

"Absolutely required reading for pastors, denominational mission strategists, and laymen seriously committed to be world changers. Perhaps the most important book written in this decade to guide us in reaching unevangelized America and refocusing the mission of Christian churches."

John N. Vaughan, *Author and Editor*
The World's 20 Largest Churches, North American Society for Church Growth, and *Church Growth Today*
Director, International Megachurch Research Center

"A prominent religion writer reflects on how current religious beliefs and practices will affect America's future, how yet coming trends may affect religion in the days ahead, and how such emerging trends are already shaping our present beliefs and practices. In journalese he projects the prospects of communications and technology, the family and society, and spirituality, with a special warning over self-indulgence and materialistic consumerism."

Carl F. H. Henry, *Theologian and Author*

"How the Holy Spirit will direct the church in 2001 and beyond we cannot say, just as we cannot say that trends will not be deflected by events yet disguised (Who could have foreseen Vatican Council II a generation ago or the 'Second Russian Revolution' just a few months ago?). Russell Chandler's book of projections based on current observable trends is thought-provoking and makes challenging reading."

Cardinal Roger Mahony, *Archbishop of Los Angeles*

"I am grateful for Russ Chandler's presence and influence in the journalistic community. He is a voice of integrity in the midst of inquiry that could easily lead to sensationalism and exaggeration."

Rich Buhler, *Author and Radio Host*
"TableTalk"

"*Racing Toward 2001* will alert Christians to paradigm shifts in society and religion. As Christians creatively interact with Chandler's insights, they will be better prepared to make the radical shifts that are necessary to engage the future for Christ."

Marlene LeFever, *Manager of Educational Services*
David C. Cook Publishing Co.

"Russell Chandler's new book is an essential resource in enabling the reader to live decisively in a rapidly changing world. A must for all those journeying toward the 21st century."

Tom Sine, *Author and Consultant in Futures Research*

"Russell Chandler, being the fine reporter he is, has a keen eye both for the big picture and for specific details producing it. In *Racing Toward 2001* he weaves together those two elements—the particulars and their cumulative consequences—to offer a perceptive look at where we're heading. While his journalistic specialty is religion, he rightly treats it not as an isolated phenomenon, but in relation to surrounding trends and conditions, recognizing that it is both affected by and affects them. He does so in a lucid, lively, and direct style that distinguishes this book from the turgid academic convolutions that usually characterize forays into the future. Chandler doesn't see himself as a prophet, but his abundant marshalling of relevant facts, both on the wider scope and in pinpointed cases, along with his clear-headed analysis, throws a reasoned, probing searchlight on the start of the next century."

George W. Cornell, *Religion Writer*
Associated Press

"Russell Chandler's long-time involvement with the Los Angeles scene has put him in a brew that has everything from curse to blessing mixed in. His ability to sift and sort is shown here—and it's a blessing."

Jack W. Hayford, D.Litt, *Senior Pastor*
The Church On The Way, Van Nuys, California

RUSSELL CHANDLER

RACING TOWARD 2001

The Forces Shaping America's Religious Future

ZondervanPublishingHouse
Grand Rapids, Michigan

HarperSanFrancisco
San Francisco, California

Divisions of HarperCollinsPublishers

ALSO BY RUSSELL CHANDLER
Understanding the New Age
The Overcomers
Budgets, Bedrooms and Boredom
The Kennedy Explosion

Racing Toward 2001
Copyright © 1992 by Russell Chandler

Copublished by Zondervan Publishing House
Grand Rapids, Michigan 49530, and HarperSanFrancisco

Library of Congress Cataloging-in-Publication Data

Chandler, Russell.
    Racing toward 2001 : the forces shaping America's religious future
    Russell Chandler.
       p. cm.
    Includes bibliographical references.
    ISBN 0-310-54130-1
    I. United States—Religion. 2. Twenty-first century—Forecasts.
  I. Title. II. Title: Racing toward two thousand one.
  III. Title: Racing toward two thousand and one.
  BL2525.C44 1992
  200'.973'01—dc20

                             91-50588
                                 CIP

Printed in the United States of America

Cover designed by Gary Gnidovic
Blue Granite Photo and Sci-Astro Photo by Westlight

92 93 94 95 / DH / 5 4 3 2 1

This edition is printed on acid-free paper and meets the American National Standards Institute Z39.48 standard.

To my grandchildren
Ryan Neil, Daniel David, Kate Lynn, Sarah Elizabeth, Melissa Marie . . .
and counting . . .
Who, I am sure, will make the race
to 2001
infinitely more exciting,
and the world of the 21st century
a much better place
to live and love.

Contents

Part 2 Changing Shapes of Churches and Religion

Acknowledgments

Most journalists are clippers and savers. I confess I'm no exception, especially when I'm hot on the trail of good material for a series of articles or a book.

So I had a little help—a lot, actually—from my "friends." In writing *Racing Toward 2001* I've quoted liberally from books, magazines, newspapers, tapes, news services, and assorted reports. These sources are acknowledged in the endnotes and often in the text itself. My thanks to all whose shoulders I'm standing upon, even though many of you have no idea you're "contributing" writers and editors.

I also want to thank the seventy-five plus individuals who graciously gave me personal and telephone interviews. About forty of you were contacted in 1989 when I prepared a series for *The Los Angeles Times* on "Churches and the '90s." This book is an outgrowth of those articles.

The next step was when David Lambert, a Zondervan editor, heard my keynote speech on "The Churches and the '90s" at the Mount Hermon Christian Writers' Conference in April 1990. Thanks, Dave, for seeing the possibilities. Luckily, your colleagues John Sloan and Scott Bolinder at Zondervan agreed that the talk could become a book.

Without you and your constant encouragement, help, and a little prodding, John and Scott, *Racing Toward 2001* wouldn't be up and running. Thanks, guys! And my appreciation also extends to the many other fine Zondervan people who assisted in the project.

When I learned that Judith Markham and Blue Water Ink in Grand

Rapids would do the editing, I knew it would be clear sailing. You did such a good job on our maiden voyage, editing my book *Understanding the New Age*. Thanks for smoothing out the choppy sentences and troubled transitions this time, too. You kept the wind in my sails without letting me become too long-winded.

Along the course I've made some new friends: George Barna, whose work in church consulting and trend forecasting has blazed a trail to the edge of the next millennium that many of us are following; Tom Sine, author and futurist, who generously let me read and quote from an early draft of his visionary *Wild Hope;* Steve Lavaggi, the Christian artist whose fresh creativity is perceived as he imagines and images what other eyes now see; and Robert Ellwood, religion professor at the University of Southern California, a brilliant sensor of the religious future. Thank you for granting permission to use the title of your book, *Alternative Altars,* as one of my own chapter titles.

Then I'm grateful to *The Times* and Metropolitan Editor Craig Turner for allowing me another leave of absence—where did those six months go so fast, Craig? To my immediate boss, Don Hunt, a big thank-you for finding different keystrokes and other folks to do my work while I was gone. I also thank *Times* editorial library researcher Janet Lundblad. You cheerfully dug out needed materials and located the obscure, often on short notice. And I thankfully acknowledge being able to quote from my articles previously published in *The Times*.

Whenever I got writer's block, I turned to my partner, wife, and writing companion, Marjorie Lee Chandler. Thank you, my dear, for your unwavering confidence, always sound advice, and sharp editing skills. You'll find some of your own words, even whole sentences, in this book. (But I'm not letting you read this page until now.) And thank you for all the great meals that stoked the inner journalist between long sessions at the computer keyboard.

Oh, yes: Mom, I love you! I could never start—much less finish—the race toward 2001 without you. Once again, my deepest affection and gratitude.

Introduction

The Starting Line

Peering into the past is more comfortable than speculating on things to come. Predicting the future may, in fact, be a fool's errand.

Still, in light of the evidence now available, a look toward the 21st century isn't as scary as it first appears. At the very least, the fuzzy outlines of megatrend landmarks are already heaving into sight, no longer remote abstractions on the distant horizon. The third millennium is, after all, scarcely 100 months away as I write this. If there's a problem, it may be that even now we're *too* close to fully understand what we're experiencing—rather like the blind men and the elephant.

Expectations about the year 2000 grow more intense with every rip of the calendar. The big two-triple-0 "bears the cumulative emotional weight of thousands of deferred hopes and unfulfilled predictions," declares Hillel Schwartz, author of the psychohistory *Century's End.*[1]

As we move up to the starting line, let's set the record straight on just when the 21st century actually begins: The 20th century ends on December 31, 2000; and the turn of the millennium happens on the stroke of midnight between December 31, 2000, and January 1, *2001!*

Never mind that the hearty party will be on New Year's Eve, 1999, rather than the following December 31. Those of us precisionists who now know the mathematical and chronological truth can smugly wait to celebrate the *real* millennium.

Meanwhile, I invite you to join me right now as we start a journey to 2001 and beyond.

Go with the Flow

As a religion writer for the nation's largest metropolitan daily newspaper, I have sensed that there is not only curiosity about, but great personal interest in, what religious belief and practice will be like in the 21st century. But I think it's also important to examine how the impending turn of the century and America's vision for the future are molding our spiritual perceptions and faith communities right now, during the 1990s.

So as you read this book, keep in mind this three-way flow: (1) how America's future will be affected by the religious beliefs and practices of *today;* (2) how future trends will affect religion *then;* and (3) how the pull of the future and its anticipated trends are shaping religious beliefs and practices *now* and through the rest of the decade.

Racing Toward 2001 takes a look through the lens of religion at the major forces shaping our future, whereby you can glimpse both the perils and the opportunities. It is a sampling, not an exhaustive treatment, that presents firsthand case studies and models—windows toward the coming millennium. As you become acquainted with some of these innovative churches and ministries, it is my hope that their influence will, in turn, inspire other works for good and for God.

In journalistic style, this book draws broadly from some of the best information, resources, and authorities available. I have sought out leaders and organizations that are creatively assessing and addressing what is happening, while keeping an eye toward the future. In all, I have personally interviewed more than seventy-five "experts," including futurists, sociologists, historians, artists, educators, journalists, theologians, ethicists, pastors, rabbis, priests, church growth specialists, and other assorted religion watchers and doers.

But I'm especially interested in the impact of coming megatrends on the ordinary person—"pew people," I call them—and I have consulted them, as well.

We humans are "incurably religious." For the vast majority of Americans, religion—and in particular, Christianity—is one of life's most powerful, pervasive, and persuasive forces. In a 1990 survey asking 113,000 American adults to identify their religion, 86 percent claimed to be Christian, and just 7.5 percent said they had no religion at all.[2]

The survey—perhaps the most detailed religious study of twentieth century Americans—revealed that, for many, religious identification is at least as important as racial and ethnic affiliation. So we will look at our common future from the angle of the diversity and pervasiveness of religion.

What It's Got and What It's Not

Racing Toward 2001 begins with an analysis of the powerful demographic forces that are reconfiguring America. These changes will affect virtually every aspect of our lives by 2001. You'll see the sweeping impact of technology and ecology, along with major shifts in education, media, the arts, politics, and economic policy. Along the way, you'll pick up information about upheavals in family and lifestyle patterns—and learn an alphabet of socio-acronyms that started with YUPPIES (young urban professionals) and escalated to BUPPIES (black urban professionals), DINKS (dual income, no kids), and SITCOMS (single income, two children, outrageous mortgages).[3]

Part 2 analyzes the shifts, dislocations, and soul-searching reappraisals that have occurred in American religion during the past several decades. It projects who the major players in the religious stadium will be after 2001 and what they'll be doing. "Alternative Altars" considers the expanding "God shelf" and the growing presence of non-traditional faiths; and you'll meet some of those many "believers but not belongers" out there. "Clashing Cosmologies" details what I see as the "mother of battles" shaping up between the worldview of New Age/Eastern mysticism versus the Judeo-Christian view of creation, humanity, and redemption.

In Part 3, we'll visit a variety of churches and ministries—promising models for the millennium that may be playing soon in your neighborhood.

And in Part 4, I weave together the multiple strands of our country's religious future to provide help to harness those forces for the journey into the Next Age. Finally, there's a list of books, organizations, and other resources.

Rather than heaping on answers or hounding you with prescriptions, I'll let you draw your own conclusions from credible choices.

Now, here are several things *Racing Toward 2001* is not:

- It's not a book about church growth, per se, or about methods of evangelism. I do give many examples of successful and growing ministries, and I do cite the leading church-growth experts. But specialty "how-to" books are already available in that category. (I list some in the Bibliography of Resources.)

- This is not a book about leadership roles and management-building. I do include a chapter on shifts in pastoral styles (20), and I give examples of effective ministry management. But, again, a number of good books are available, written specifically for professionals and those in church leadership echelons.

- Nor is this book a roundup of the latest surveys of religious trends. I do include some charts and key statistics; I quote researchers, sociologists, and pollsters. But George Gallup, Jr., George Barna, Andrew Greeley, Wade Clark Roof, and William McKinney—among others—have skillfully compiled and analyzed such data in their own writings.

- Finally, this book is not a darkly tinted look at biblical prophecy. I do acknowledge a distinct apocalyptic edge to the turning of a millenniium that can't be ignored. But I leave it to others with deeper scriptural insights—and more nerve—to delineate Armageddon and the end times.

Remember, there's no magic about a number. When the saints go marching in, whether it's 2000 or 2001 or whenever, we all want to be in *that* number.

Till then, please join me in the human race.

Part 1

Shapes and Trends of the Coming Millennium

Keeping Up with the Joneses

Shifting Faces and Places

Traffic congestion after the New Year's Day Rose Bowl game in Pasadena slowed travel to a snail's pace. So my college-age son, T. J., and his friend amused themselves by bantering back and forth with people in cars stuck in adjacent lanes. T. J. was sure to get a response—if only a bewildered look or a blank stare—for he would gaze intently at a person in a neighboring vehicle and quizzically intone, "Who *are* you?"

While it served to pass some otherwise boring time, the question is also a good one to ask ourselves as we pace toward 2001.

Who are *you*? Where are you? Where have you come from? Where are you headed? And how soon will you get there?

Who are *we*? As individuals and as family. As America—as a people and a nation and as a country of diverse races, faiths, values, and cultures.

In order to understand the forces shaping America's religious future, we need an overview; we need to grasp the big picture, and to provide a frame in which to mount the picture. Let's start by examining the root forces that have brought us to our unique position on this planet called Earth.

"Rurbanization"

America's roots are in her soil, but they have been transplanted from the farm to the city. Two hundred years ago our population was nearly 95 percent rural. By 1880, the first year the U.S. Census Bureau distinguished farmers from rural nonfarmers in its reporting, 44 percent of Americans were farmers. Today, that figure is only about 2 percent and is predicted to shrink even more. In two centuries the setting for the American family has flip-flopped, from 95 percent farm to 98 percent nonfarm.[1]

The most dramatic swing, however, has been going on since World War II. Sociologists call it the "rurbanization" of America: rural values in transition to urban values. The shift has brought not only a tremendous change in family tasks, roles, needs, and expectations, but is also producing a movement away from what church growth expert Frank Tillapaugh calls the essentially rural values of status quo, sameness, harmony, smallness, and establishment to the urban values of change, diversity, conflict management, bigness, and mobility.[2]

Seeking the Sun and the Sea and the Good Life

Mobility has indeed been a moving force behind Americans since 1950 when our nation began to follow the sun. Seeking the seacoasts and chasing "quality living," over the next four decades Americans bought 300 million automobiles and traveled along 42,798 miles of interstate highways. First, the South headed north; then the North headed south. But always, the East headed west. So, according to the 1990 census, thriving coastal metropolitan areas like Seattle and Los Angeles have gained at the expense of rural areas like the Mississippi River delta, the Appalachian Mountains of Kentucky, and the high plains of North Dakota.[3]

As a result, Gary Farley, a Southern Baptist specialist in rural and urban missions, worries about rural decay and poverty:

I see Corn Belt towns that were strong in my youth, now hard hit by family farm crises—stores closed and boarded up, few signs of economic activity, and vacant houses. I see "oil patch" towns that look much the same on the surface but whose spirits are bruised because they have known boom and bust. And I see cynical mill towns in the Southeast, the factories they stole from places like Ohio now being stolen by places like Korea. And I see coal field towns in the process of decay. And I wonder if anyone cares.[4]

About fifty miles out on the perimeter of a dozen regional cities across the nation, rural areas are becoming urban. They are a strange mix of traditional agricultural, small-town or mountain folks, and city-bred people who like the amenities—and often the lower housing costs—of rural life.

These Farley sees as signs of hope: new and revitalized communities; affluent towns being developed for retirees; old farm service towns in mountains and near lakes being revitalized for tourists and fun-seekers.

Having snoozed for decades, some of these "retirement destination" communities suddenly find themselves in the vortex of a population boom triggered by, among other things, a technological revolution that is turning country villages into fiber-optic suburbs. There a new breed of home-based workers, free to live where they choose, are linked by personal computers to city offices through "telecommuting," while fax machines and Federal Express keep them in touch with "downtown" and the rest of the world.

Disenchanted Urbanites

"The megatrend of the *next* millennium," says *Megatrends* author John Naisbitt, "is laying the groundwork for the decline of cities." The American Home Business Association predicts there will be 20.7 million full-time home-based businesses by 1995, and by 2010 one-third to one-half of the middle class will live outside metropolitan and suburban areas.[5]

Christian leaders are seizing opportunities for church planting as well as revitalizing rural and resort congregations. For example, at

Outdoor Resorts of America in Palm Springs, California, one of the nation's largest and most beautiful recreational vehicle parks, the Rev. William Gwinn directs a volunteer ministry that includes weekly worship services in the desert resort's clubhouse. He also makes hospital calls and counsels the residents, most of whom are retired and affluent and spend weekends or the entire winter in this sunny pleasure destination. The services Gwinn conducts are informal and reach folks who feel comfortable dropping in before golf but who wouldn't seek out an established church. Gwinn envisions this kind of ministry springing up in mobile home parks and RV centers across the country as more and more Americans hitch their homes to their wheels.[6]

Also, a growing flock of disenchanted urbanites is fleeing the congestion, crime, and high costs of big cities—trading proximity to work for affordable homes, fresh air, and lower taxes on the rural fringes.

For some, however, getting to work has almost become a full-time job in itself. People "want to get out of the rat race," says Ken Munsell of the Small Towns Institute. "But they're still in it if they're going to commute two to three hours each way."[7]

Consider Tom Sparandera, a thirty-three-year-old computer repairman who moved his family from Staten Island to the Pocono town of Tobyhanna in the summer of 1990. They found a three-bedroom house for less than $100,000, but the five- and one-half-hour commute has taken its toll. Sparandera sees his young daughter only on weekends.

Despite such marathon commuting, says Tom's neighbor Matanda Sabwa—who boards a bus for New York City at 6:30 every morning—the Poconos are "heaven" compared with Manhattan's "hell."

Brande Mark-Falzett, township supervisor in nearby Coolbaugh, calls the newcomers "our modern-day pioneers. Instead of Conestoga wagons, they've packed up the station wagon and set out for the woods to really change their lives."[8]

The migration is also changing their new hometowns, spreading a pall of suburban sprawl, straining services and schools, and clashing with old-time lifestyles. Local fire departments, to cite but one example, can no longer rely on an all-volunteer force. The newcomers are far away in the city during the day and often too tired when they come home to respond to anything but dinner and bed. Nor can neighborhood churches count on urban transplants to fit in with time-honored programs and customs. Meanwhile, rural old-timers resent shakeups to accommodate citified "outsiders."

At the same time, those who have migrated tend to reflect the culture of the communities to which they have moved. Indeed, as church growth expert Elmer Towns has observed, the movement of Americans—and one in five moves every year—may affect their lifestyle more than their church affects it.[9]

Where Are We Growing?

Despite the centrifugal forces spiraling the population outward as we near 2001, most big cities will keep on growing. Nearly four out of five Americans still live in metropolitan areas, including the populous suburbs. (Only one out of four would choose city life if they had a choice, however.) But since the 1980s fewer people live in each residence, reflecting the mushrooming singles population and accounting for periodic housing booms.[10]

During the last decade the nation grew by 10 percent, reaching almost 250 million. The biggest growth has been in the Sun Belt, where cities are being forced to add infrastructure. Slower gains were measured elsewhere, while Iowa, Kansas, North Dakota, West Virginia, and the District of Columbia lost population.

In the coming century, entire sections of northeastern and midwestern cities will become vacant, while southern and western cities will face chronic housing deficits.[11]

Thus, urban planners predict, a city's "quality of life" will be the best indicator of its ability to attract skilled employees.

The states expected to grow the fastest between now and the dawning of 2001 are Arizona, New Mexico, Florida, Georgia, Alaska, Hawaii, and California. Five of the ten areas expecting the most growth are in California: Anaheim, Los Angeles, Oakland, San Jose, and Sacramento. The others, with the exception of Denver, are in the southern half of the country: Atlanta, Dallas, St. Petersburg, Tampa, and Phoenix.[12]

America's West Coast states already constitute a major part of the rising Pacific Rim, where the trade cities of Los Angeles, Sydney, and

Tokyo are taking over from the old, established Atlantic trade cities of New York, Paris, and London.[13] It's not surprising, then, that California "won" the biggest numbers in the 1990 census. The state's growth surge of 6 million is nearly equal to the entire population of Oregon and Washington combined! With a current population of 30 million, the Golden State is 70 percent bigger than New York, the next largest state. And though the acceleration will ease somewhat, trend watchers predict a growth of 10 million more for California by 2010.[14]

Californians Are Different

California is, in fact, a Pacific Rim *country*, with the world's sixth largest economy, and by 2001 it will have moved into fourth place. Already California leads the United States in overall foreign investment—$100 billion annually—and one-third of the nation's high-tech and biotechnical companies are in California.[15]

California is a place unto itself, which translates into lifestyles and beliefs as well as demographics. Its population is younger than most of the nation, it has the highest birthrate, and it is divided into larger households, according to Stephen Levy, director of a private population study center.[16]

But when tall, lanky Phillip E. Hammond, professor of religious studies and sociology at the University of California, Santa Barbara, started crunching numbers from his survey data on regional differences in religion—theology by geography—his eyes popped. As expected, he found Californians and other West Coast folks "rootless" and highly mobile. But he was surprised to find that about twice as high a percentage of Californians reported having no formal religious identification as the percentage of residents in states like Massachusetts, Ohio, and North Carolina.[17]

Hammond's study also found that Californians are particularly attracted to the religiously unorthodox. A higher percentage than the rest of the population practices Eastern meditation and believes in reincarnation.

"There's a lot of loose religiosity floating around," Hammond told me in an interview as we scanned pages of computer printouts. "Like more pizza chains, winter and summer sports, athletic teams, and house styles, California will be found to be religiously more heterogeneous, more pluralistic."[18]

Strategies and models to reach these unconventional Westerners with the Christian message, then, must be tailored to address their unique beliefs, lifestyles, and preferences.

Indeed, as with California, regional differences within the United States may become as pronounced during the coming millennium as the differences between national or ethnic groups outside our borders are now. That may seem a contradiction, for in light of Americans' proclivity for mobility one might expect regional differences to disappear rather than grow. But, as I mentioned earlier, people seem to adopt the cultural patterns of the communities to which they migrate.

Wave of the Future

And what of the next ten years? Census watchers think the nation will grow another 7 percent by 2001, despite the prediction that one-fourth of our states will have fewer residents than they did in 1991. The growth will occur even though the size of the average family (3.17 people in 1990) and the average household (2.64 people) will remain constant or even decline a bit.[19]

The main engine driving the population upward is immigration, both legal and illegal. The 7 to 9 million who streamed into the United States during the 1980s—largely from Asia, Latin America, and the Caribbean—represent about 40 percent of the total increase.[20]

Larry Rose, a Southern Baptist Missions official, told a national gathering of colleagues that "churches built on homogeneous groups who lived close together, who farmed, whose children attended the same small schools, and who shopped in the same stores will [increasingly] be facing heterogeneous people of various ethnic-social backgrounds."[21]

Strong and diverse urban ministries will be required to meet the spiritual needs of this complex and dramatically different world, and it won't be easy. It will mean learning to minister in both poor and affluent areas, in many more languages, and with many worship styles.

Perhaps the greatest challenge will be mustering the resources to meet the needs of the coming minority majority. These potential "pew people" are moving into a society that is strikingly removed from the one their immigrant ancestors encountered and established.

Shifting faces in different places will erode the corporate tax base and generate what Judith Waldrop calls "service delivery nightmares." Traffic jams will take to the air as airlines double their passenger load, serving about 800 million by 2001. Unfortunately, airport expansion won't keep up, significantly increasing passenger delays at major airports.[22]

Overhead, the nation's air pollution is expected to increase, while on the ground carpooling and staggered work hours will help but not cure the increased travel time required as more and more people commute from the suburbs to the city.[23]

The future of Americans cannot be precisely deciphered by making linear projections from the present, but tracking 1990s trends and the people who influence them may help us draw a bead on what will happen after 2001. Writes Waldrop in *American Demographics* magazine:

> Their values are being shaped by mothers who work outside the home, neighbors who speak different languages, and teachers who preach about the environment. Their destinies are being determined by the amount of money we set aside for their college education and for our own retirement. They will live in a world quite different from ours.[24]

The Minority Majority

This Land Is Their Land

Walk east along First Street in downtown Los Angeles on a Sunday morning and you will find Japanese Buddhists worshiping in the ornate Nishi Hongwanji Temple, while over in the heart of Olvera Street Latin rhythms waft from La Placita, a well-known sanctuary for people from Central and South America. To the northeast, in Lincoln Heights, Primera Iglesia del Nazareno stands next to the Chinese Assembly of God; to the west, in Angelino Heights, the Bethel Temple boasts two English pastors, one Spanish, one Chinese, and one Gypsy! A block from City Hall, stately St. Vibiana Roman Catholic Cathedral rises next to rescue missions where an endless line of homeless wait for food and a place to spend the night in a "cardboard condo." These are but a few of the more than fifty places of worship I discovered within a short radius of The Los Angeles Times building.[1]

Since my wife, Marjorie, and I moved to a high-rise apartment on the edge of Chinatown in the spring of 1990, an unexpected benefit has been savoring the cultural richness and ethnic diversity of the City of the Angels. Here, thanks to immigration, the minority is the majority.

According to the U.S. Census Bureau, Latinos, Afro-Americans, and Asian Americans make up about 59 percent of the population of Los Angeles. Nearly half of the new residents are recent immigrants, which means 110,000 new immigrants are absorbed into the city each year.

And what Los Angeles is today, much of America will be by the 21st century.

"America has always been immigrant-driven," notes a ministry strategy paper published in the *United Methodist Reporter.* "Traditionally, in times past the immigrants have been European and African, but the current trend reshaping American life is the transformation of our country from a European offshoot to a multiracial 'world-nation' . . . . with ethnic ties to virtually every race and region on the planet . . . . The Holy Spirit is calling us to respond to these new groups in our midst."[2]

To be sure, the 1990 census figures showed that 77 percent of America's 250 million people were Anglo. Only 12 percent were African-American, 8 percent Latino, and other nationalities represented a scant 3 percent. But in California, where population growth has been the swiftest, census figures showed that ethnic minorities already accounted for more than 40 percent of the state's 30 million residents. By 2001, the Hispanic, Asian, and Afro-American population will swell to 17.1 million—nearly half of the state's population.[3]

This multicultural tide is rising across the nation—or will, soon after 2001.

"You'll know it's the 21st Century when everyone belongs to a minority group," proclaimed *American Demographics.*[4]

Futurist author Tom Sine predicts that young people able to converse in only one language and raised in suburbs that are still nearly all white, "will become the culturally disadvantaged of the '90s. They will be ill-equipped to participate in the increasingly cross-cultural and transnational environment of tomorrow's world."[5]

This Land Is Their Land, Too

During the 1980s, America's native-born population advanced by only about 4 percent, while the Asian population increased at twelve times that rate and the Hispanic population at five times.[6]

"This land is their land," says noted church historian Martin Marty, himself a white, Anglo Saxon Lutheran. "I can't talk demography often enough to my church and others. We may love our heritage—I do—but cannot bet on a future if the cohort on which it draws wanes and nothing replaces it."[7]

Denominational classification by ancestry will be a thing of the past in the next century. Those of Scandinavian origin will no longer be *ipso facto* Lutherans or Free Churchers; those of Dutch extraction won't necessarily be affiliated with the Reformed Church of America or the Christian Reformed Church.

Noting recent immigration statistics, Marty speculates: "Add some 'illegals' to this, multiply by 10 and 20 and 30 years, mix in the offspring, and you can see great change."[8]

In the early 1990s, however, only a relatively few white churches seemed to grasp the coming impact of ethnic pluralization upon our common future as they find themselves comprising less and less of the total U.S. church.

Consider our country's Asian population, sometimes labeled the "model minority."

- Since 1980, this group has skyrocketed by 7 million, a growth rate of 80 percent. Some census experts predict that by 2080 Asians will make up 10 percent of the nation's total population (the percentage Latinos will have reached by 2001).[9]
- By 2010, Asians will outnumber Jews by a margin of two to one.
- In the "Silicon Valley," the home of the semiconductor industry in Santa Clara County south of San Francisco Bay, 40 percent of manufacturing jobs are held by Asians. In New York City, most of the 500 clothes-making shops are operated by Chinese. Indians operate 10 percent of the nation's motels, and even in places like Tulsa and Reno, Koreans run hundreds of small stores.
- Asians are the best educated group in the United States. About 40 percent are college graduates, and nearly 20 percent of the Harvard Class of 1994 is Asian. (Less than 25 percent of whites are college graduates.)
- In the past Asian immigrants have come primarily from China and Japan, but increasingly, they are from Southeast Asia. Like

Vietnam's boat people, these newest immigrants are often peasants.

- So, while median household incomes of Asians are higher than any other group—including whites—Asians also have higher poverty rates than whites.[10]

American Income, More or Less

Income distribution among Americans is becoming more unequal, the Census Bureau found, surprising almost no one. But it is shocking to note that 1 percent of U.S. households hold one-third of all our country's personal wealth! While in 1988 almost one in three white households reported wealth of $100,000 or more, only 5 percent of black households and 12 percent of Hispanic households were in that category.[11] Thus, a more racially diverse nation may also turn out to be a more divisive one as the struggle for a piece of the American pie grows more intense.

The gap between the rich and the poor may wedge even wider, particularly if the recession of 1990–91 marked the beginning of a prolonged decline that exacerbates inter-ethnic competition for jobs and resources. Repercussions will be especially acute in the big cities: the Anglo group will be the elderly retired, while the work force will be predominantly Afro-American, Latino, and Asian.

Until the early years of the next century, at least, Latinos are apt to be on the lowest rung of the American economic ladder; many are employed at minimum wages because they have less education than the society at large. Less than two-thirds finish high school, compared with nearly 90 percent of non-Hispanics. In 1988 household net worth for Hispanic married couples was only $15,690, while that of black households was $17,640. The household net worth of white couples, meanwhile, was $62,390.[12]

Nor is the big picture optimistic for most Afro-Americans. According to a report published in 1989 by the National Urban League, Afro-American enrollment in U.S. colleges declined from 33 percent in 1976 to 28 percent in 1986. During that period, tuition costs nearly doubled while financial aid packages didn't even meet the costs of inflation.[13]

Increasing numbers, although a small percentage, of blacks will be living in affluence, while a larger chunk will be at or below the poverty level in the final years of this century. Fortunately, there are some hopeful models for black church groups wanting to help lift their people higher economically, socially, and spiritually (see chapter 16).

Unfortunately, the country's Native Americans—only a small blip on most demographic charts—not only are not growing, but are the poorest of the continent's poor, a blot the 21st century must surely reckon with.

Melting Pot or Salad Bowl?

Many observers of the racial scene believe we are losing ground gained in the civil rights era of the 1950s and 1960s.

Tom Sine sees a rampant and growing racism in America fueled by a new extremism of the right.

"Unless leadership in the church and the society takes decisive initiative," he writes in his book *Wild Hope*, "we are likely to see intensified racial polarization and violence.

"It is unusual," he continues, "to hear white Christians of any stripe speak out on the growing issue of racism that threatens the very fabric of our society. And 11 A.M. Sunday morning is still the most segregated hour in American life."[14]

Alvin Poussaint, a black associate professor of psychiatry at Harvard Medical School and author of *Why Blacks Kill Blacks*, agrees that the polarization level is rising: "Despite the success of black athletes that white kids worship, too, despite a black Miss America, despite TV shows such as Bill Cosby's, feelings of racism don't seem to be eradicated. People are segregated, so they're still basically prejudiced. That may change with the next generation, but not with these kids."[15]

Bob Fryling, director of campus student ministries for the evangelical organization InterVarsity Christian Fellowship, believes racial incidents at colleges may increase in the next several years "as Asian students become increasingly successful and black and Hispanic students feel cut out of the pie a bit."[16]

And Alvin Toffler points out in *Powershift,* the third volume of his prescient trilogy, that we must now "cope with open warfare *between* rival minority groups"—like what has happened between Cuban and Haitian immigrants in Miami and between African-Americans and Hispanics elsewhere.[17]

Resistance to the image of America as the "melting pot" is rising everywhere, a shift that will take on even larger proportions by 2001 and after. Blending, once the ideal, is passé. As society grows more ethnically and culturally diverse, say the critics, we should embrace multiculturalism.

Some have dubbed this new concept "the salad bowl," "a mosaic," or "a patchwork quilt." Toffler describes it as "a dish in which diverse ingredients keep their identity."[18]

Ethnics and Ethics

This balance is especially critical—and precarious—for the nation's schools, city governments, and churches. Coalition-building between minority groups is crucial. Religious groups must wrestle with the gospel dictum that in Christ there is "neither Jew nor Greek," while celebrating racial diversity and ethnic pride and lauding the unique contributions of a multi-hued constituency. All without being separatist.

A racially integrated, heterogeneous church model might look like this: You turn to your left in the pew and greet a young black man, a lawyer who drives to your suburban church from his downtown, luxury high-rise. His wife is Indonesian. On your right is a middle-aged Hispanic woman who, with her three sons and her husband, an auto mechanic, came to this country from Mexico ten years ago. A variety of other national origins and backgrounds are represented in this congregation where the Christian Education pastor is a converted Jew of Spanish, Portuguese, and Russian descent and is married to a Salvadoran.

Another likely model within a racially and culturally diverse neighborhood is a church with multiple congregations: The Spanish service for the Latino crowd (the largest of the weekly gatherings) is held on Saturday evenings. Cambodian, Laotian, and Vietnamese congregations meet on Sunday mornings, and a Cantonese service is held on Sunday nights. Your English service—the smallest—is held at 2:30 on Sunday afternoons, where your pewmates, with the exception of several blacks and an Oriental nightshift worker who couldn't come to earlier services, are Anglos. St. John the Baptist Roman Catholic Church in Baldwin Park, a Los Angeles suburb, already operates something like this. (We'll take a closer look in chapter 27.)

"Immigration is going to turn the churches upside down," Father Gene Hemrick, who advises the nation's Catholic bishops on trends, prophesied in 1989.[19]

He ought to know. Catholicism is the nation's most cosmopolitan religion and the only major faith whose members include Americans with roots in at least thirteen different nationalities. No ethnic group is numerically dominant,[20] although Catholic trend-watchers estimated in 1990 that one-third of their church was Hispanic—and growing.

Complicating this tug-of-war over how to define ourselves in the coming millennium will be the growing phenomenon of interracial marriage. With such marriages tripling between 1970 and 1988, babies born to interracial couples represented about 3 percent of all U.S. births in 1990.[21]

Salad bowl? Melting pot? What's a good Jewish synagogue or a Pentecostal assembly to do?

Another paradigm of a successful downtown church ministering to a difficult and turbulent population is the First Baptist Church in Los Angeles, where the pastoral staff includes a Latino woman, a Filipino, and a Korean. Senior pastor John H. Townsend tells how the congregation mirrors "God's world of magnificent differences":

> We are quite at ease with our mixture of peoples from the four points of the compass . . . . Our congregation offers a model of racial integration and harmony. Adult church school classes for Korean, Spanish, Anglo and Filipino members preserve the special interests and style of each of these groups. But we worship as one body in Christ, every Sunday, surmounting the language barrier with simultaneous translation, heard over headsets . . . . We do not sponsor separate ethnic churches within the Anglo church. Our abiding interest is fashioning ourselves into one people, one community. Personal distinctives are not forfeited in this process but shared; individual gifts are honored . . . . It is not an assimilation pro-

cess. We are working as hard as we can to preserve that ethnic and cultural mix even though we're very different in language and custom . . . . We believe this is what the church at
its best should be. And it is certainly a representation of what
our larger society needs to be.[22]

Racial diversity is not the only monumental challenge that will
test the people of God in 2001, however. Another precipitate of
demographic change is the seismic activity ahead as our culture's
center of gravity shifts from youth to age.

Gauges of Ages

Boomers and Busters, Yuppies and Buppies

Baseball pitching great Satchel Paige once asked, "How old would you be if you didn't know how old you was?" Today his pithy homespun wisdom takes on almost prophetic proportions. As Americans experience greater longevity, living *beyond* their time rather than, as in previous generations, dying *before* their time, the definition of "old" has been redefined. And as the median age of Americans reaches 41 by 2030, it will need to be redefined again.

The elderly are no longer called "senior citizens"; they are "chronologically gifted." Because of modern medical life-extension practices and the possibility of replacement body parts, the surge of seniors is sometimes referred to as "the generation of immortals."

"Our society is getting older but the old are getting younger," says Robert B. Maxwell, vice-president of the American Association of Retired Persons (AARP).[1]

This unprecedented demographic change portends more than an elderculture; a coming generational culture shock faces our nation, which has been young for most of its history. Several futurists warn that our society, as a result, may stiffen and grow less flexible.[2]

To understand this coming age wave, we need not only statistics, but an identifiable classification of the stages of ages. Following several shorthand models, we see:

- The elderly, who represent what the authors of *Lifetrends* call the "old guard," are those who had passed their seventy-fifth birthday by 1990, and the "new elders," those between the ages of fifty-five and seventy-five in 1990.[3]

- The "boosters" are those born between 1927 and 1945, so designated by Tom Sine because they "are the stabilizing edge of the generational wave of the nineties" and "tend to be the most supportive of American culture, institutions and values."[4] This category overlaps *Lifetrends'* "Eisenhower generation," born between 1935 and 1945, and the younger "new elders."

- The "baby boomers," born between 1946 and 1964, are some 76 million strong. The subject of much sociological study and media hoopla, boomers are further divided into "early" boomers (born in the first half of the "baby boom") and "late" boomers.

- The "baby busters," born after 1964, were between the ages of eighteen and "twentysomething" at the beginning of the 1990s. They fall between the illustrious baby boomers and "the boomlet of children that the baby boomers are producing."[5] Busters derive their label from being born during the period when the nation's birthrate dipped to half the level of the great baby boom following World War II.

- Finally there are today's teens and pre-teens, who by 2001 will be fashioning an identity of their own.

Is Living Longer Better?

Half of all Americans who have ever lived past the age of sixty-five are alive now! And population experts estimate that the 12 percent of our population currently aged sixty-five and older will escalate to 23 percent by the middle of the 21st century. Already the fastest-growing age segment in the country is those over eighty-five. With their numbers increasing more than three times as fast as the rest of the population, these present 3 million elders will swell to 16 million by 2050.[6] And science, meanwhile, keeps increasing the span of human life.

Is that good news or bad? At issue, of course, is more than just maintaining life at any cost.

"If we can extend life expectancy by 10 years or 20 years, we need to be assured that the additional years of life are healthy years," declares medical demographer S. Jay Olshansky of the Argonne National Laboratory in Illinois. "If we are adding 30 years of crippling disease, then I don't think we should do it."[7]

The care of the elderly is posing hard choices both at home and in government.

Elderly Americans often need help with home care or medical attention through the health-care system. This can be extremely expensive for the individual and his or her family. Substantial life savings can be wiped out in a matter of weeks.

Social Security and government medical programs are already cracking under the strain, and the scenario can only worsen when there are more recipients and fewer paying in through the work force. In 1950, the ratio of workers to retirees was 120 to 1, but if the current trend continues, the ratio will fall to a mere two workers per retiree by 2030.[8]

Former Colorado Governor Richard D. Lamm is upset about what he feels is a combination of runaway medical expenses and an excessive sense of entitlement created in the elderly.

"Poverty in America is more likely to wear diapers than a hearing aid," he complained in a *New York Times* opinion piece. Noting that the elderly have the highest disposable income and the lowest poverty rates of any group in the nation, he added that through Medicare "we are paying the health costs of hundreds of thousands of elderly millionaires, while 20 percent of America's kids don't have all their vaccinations and 600,000 American women give birth every year without adequate or any prenatal care."[9]

Meanwhile, new kinds of care for the elderly are on their way. Despite the boom of retirement-type communities, such as the Sun Cities and Leisure Worlds, they house only about 3 percent of retirement-age Americans. At present, about 90 percent of Americans over the age of fifty-five live in "regular" housing, usually in the areas where they raised their children.[10]

But this is predicted to change as more and more begin congregating into life-care facilities that provide everything from prepared communal meals to medical care. Elders who can afford it are increasingly turning to continuing-care complexes offering private rooms or suites, three restaurant-style meals a day, maid service, and a variety of activities. When health declines, nursing care is available.

In 1990, the average age of new residents in these facilities was seventy-nine. Nationwide, 700 such communities—many of them operated for profit—housed 210,000 residents at the turn of the decade; and the number and variety of continuing-care complexes is expanding rapidly.[11]

Innovative home-care services, adult day-care, and a profusion of other programs to help the disabled elderly are also proliferating, allowing the frail or chronically ill some control over their lives in familiar surroundings rather than in traditional nursing homes. These new approaches include home-repair services, day centers (there were about 2,200 such centers in 1990 compared with only a dozen twenty years earlier), foster homes for the elderly, and eldercare collectives.[12]

Foster-care networks, suggests Richard Ladd, administrator of Oregon's Senior and Disabled Services Division, can help the elderly who need long-term care but do not have complex medical needs. "Too often we put them in nursing homes where they have less control over their lives and less freedom than the average prison inmate."[13] Oregon also emphasizes assisted-living apartments in which the elderly and disabled live in a setting where meals and housekeeping are provided and additional services like nursing are added when needed.

The churches of the next millennium will need to be a part of this action.

The Parish Nurse Resource Center, based in Park Ridge, Illinois, already has nearly 100 active "parish nurses," with 400 more in training. These nurses are helping churches integrate end-of-life concerns, bioethical considerations, quality of life, and modification of worship services so all can participate.[14]

Betsy Jamerson, a former director of nursing who has been on the staff of Westminster Presbyterian Church in Lynchburg, Virginia, since 1988, has developed a church health-care ministry to old and young alike.

"Health care is part of the stewardship of our lives," says Mrs.

Jamerson. In addition to visiting and assisting the sick, she checks blood pressures every other Sunday at church, and also leads classes in subjects such as holistic health care, signs and symptoms of illness, basics of home nursing, and dealing with losses.[15]

The other side of the elder coin reflects "the new vision of retirement [which] intermingles work, play, learning and service," says Ken Dychtwald, executive of Agewave Inc., a research and consulting firm in Emeryville, California. Older people are increasingly interested in "sharing their wisdom, not retiring from life," adds Cathy Ventura-Merkel, a senior education specialist for the American Association of Retired Persons.[16]

One model of "creative retirement" for the new elders and aging boomers is the combining of volunteerism with community service. At the North Carolina Center for Creative Retirement, nestled in the furrows of the Blue Ridge Mountains, these concepts are linked with a national movement toward retirement-age learning. Here, several thousand participants annually take part in the programs, which include a College for Seniors, programs that provide mentors for young people and tutors for elementary and high school pupils, and an annual Senior Wellness Day offering everything from health screening to mall walking.[17]

Church analysts see an opportunity in the chronologically gifted. Older folks are more apt to be affiliated with a church and are, according to a recent Gallup Poll, among the most religiously active in the nation.[18] These elders, if they are in good health, will have more time than employed younger members to spend in church activities and leadership.

One Presbyterian church in Alaska started a day-care program staffed largely by senior volunteers, which keeps costs down while providing a cross-generational linkage.[19] Elsewhere, seniors are working in shelters for the homeless and tutoring in inner-city schools.

The Boomer Agequake

Baby boomers grew up in a world unlike any that previous generations had known: Dr. Spock influenced their homes with his positive-reinforcement, permissive child-rearing methods; television served as their ever-present babysitter; the atomic bomb threatened their instant annihilation; and the Pill and birth control guaranteed them the "sexual revolution."[20]

The leading edge of the boomer generation is now rounding forty and headed for fifty. When they turn sixty-five, between 2010 and 2030, boomers can expect to live an average of at least seventeen more years, with women outlasting men by about seven.[21] By 2010, a deluge of new boomer retirees will cause eldercare to eclipse child care as a national priority and potential career market.[22]

In the late 1990s, "more pioneering companies will build on the precedent of day care and begin offering partial reimbursement for eldercare costs as part of the overall trend toward cafeteria plans in which employees select from a menu of different benefits according to their needs," note Naisbitt and Aburdene.[23]

The travel industry will reap the benefits of an increased market for year-round vacationing as boomers become preoccupied with leisure time.

The impact of the boomers on the next several decades is summed up well by Paul C. Light in his book *Baby Boomers*:

> The baby boomers packed the maternity wards as infants, the classrooms as children, and the campuses and the employment lines and mortgage markets as young adults. To the extent [they] think alike, they define the contemporary culture. To the extent they buy alike, they shape the economy. To the extent they are both preceded and followed by much smaller generations, they stand out in sharp contrast to those around them.[24]

"Boomers, as a generation, differ sharply from their elders," observes James F. Engel, professor of marketing, research, and strategy at Eastern College Graduate School. "There is greater tolerance for diversity and ready acceptance of formerly taboo lifestyles. They are motivated by economic wellbeing, good personal relationships, and a comfortable family life. The international arena is not a primary part of their world view."[25]

A significant boomer legacy, declares Wade Clark Roof of the

University of California at Santa Barbara, is the lack of bearing chronological age has on specific life experiences and events.

> Baby boomers approaching 40 are not in the same life situations that their parents were at this age: they have stayed in school longer, started work later, married and had children later, and based their families on two incomes. . . . We are no longer very certain to which age group we are referring when we speak of the young, the middle-aged or the old. These are culturally created categories which are easily recast in times of demographic shifts.[26]

At this writing, close to one out of two households is headed by a person born between 1946 and 1964. He or she is media oriented and likes rock music. One-fourth have college degrees, and many are open to spiritual concerns and the church—if they are approached in the right way.

Also, within the boomer culture (and to some extent the baby busters) exists a small subculture called "yuppies"—young urban professionals—who represent perhaps 1 to 3 percent of the population. Stereotyped as the BMW-driving, affluent city-dweller, yuppies are conservative politically and economically but liberal in terms of social, sexual, and lifestyle issues. Though largely white, this subculture includes an elite class of "buppies"—black urban professionals.

Emerging out of this boomer culture is what the authors of *Lifetrends* call "the new older women," many of whom have worked outside the home and are financially independent. "They have known a diversity of family styles and are no strangers to high levels of divorce, remarriage, single parenting, and step-families. Older single women, either divorced or widowed, are the fastest-growing group in America; by 2001 half of persons over sixty-five will be single, with women in this category outnumbering men by a three-to-one margin."[27]

Single or not, boomer women will be considered "cultural transmitters" as they spend more time fulfilling a variety of overlapping family roles during their lengthened lifetime—child, spouse, parent, grandparent—than any other generation in history. *Lifetrends* authors predict that nearly one-third of boomer women in their late sixties will still have a living parent. As the mediators between, and sometimes caretakers of, several generations, they will thus find themselves at the center of family relationships.[28]

Needless to say, boomers are having and will continue to have significant impact on the face of the church.

Roof's extensive survey of baby-boom religiosity showed that roughly two-thirds brought up in a faith dropped out sometime during their teenage and early adult years, and that 40 percent have stayed out. A third never did abandon church attendance (although they may have switched churches), and at least a third of the dropouts have returned.[29]

Younger boomers are more involved in traditional organized religion. Older boomers, shaped by the civil rights and counterculture era of the 1960s, tend to be more liberal and more likely to be involved in alternative religious forms. Married boomers without children (the so-called DINKS—Double Income No Kids) are the "least religious segment" of the post-World War II birth boom.[30]

In order to plot new strategy, churches will need to examine more closely what brought the boomer returnees back to the fold. Roof thinks one magnet is that, having tried everything else, boomers are now looking for a religious heritage for their children and answers to their own spiritual questions.

In the context of family life, marriage, and careers, "my hunch is there's a lot of picking and choosing going on in this generation— one that really believes in choice," he said in an interview. "I know there is a lot of switching. There is also a searching to put it all together, to look to religion for some help on that. Churches that grow will provide new and innovative ways to deal with those concerns."[31]

In any case, the church that attracts and holds boomers in the early 2000s will have a much more hybrid, experiential style than the traditional denominational congregation of the 1970s and 1980s.

That fact, laments Rick Warren, pastor of boomer-attracting Saddleback Valley Community Church in Southern California's populous Orange County, means most churches would have to make changes that would kill their existing congregations.

"So I . . . advocate that every church should be starting new churches, and many of those should be targeted to reaching baby boomers," Warren adds.[32]

The Twentysomething "Boomerangs"

As the graying baby boomers pursue recreation, recycling, and retirement, 48 million baby busters are moving into the working world. Many in this twentysomething generation don't like what they find and would rather return to the less-demanding roles of adolescence.

American youth, observes *Newsweek* religion editor Ken Woodward,

> are taking longer to grow up. As the 20th Century winds down, more young Americans are enrolled in college, but fewer are graduating. They are taking longer to get their degrees. They take longer to establish careers, too, and longer yet to marry. Many unable or unwilling to pay for housing, return to the nest, or are slow to leave it. They postpone choices and spurn longterm commitments. Life's on hold; adulthood can wait.[33]

The baby bust generation also seems to have a hard time focusing on a cause, unless, perhaps, it is the environmental movement.

Tom Sine sees the busters strongly attracted to the acquisitive, materialistic, status-oriented values of the boosters. But they also place very high value on the autonomy of the boomers. "Busters have been seduced by the sirens of instant gratification" as no other generation.[34]

A more kindly assessment is that they are simply "open-minded samplers of an increasingly diverse cultural buffet" and that they possess "a sophistication, tolerance and candor that could help repair the excesses of rampant individualism" so characteristic of boomerism.[35]

An estimated 40 percent of young people in their twenties are children of divorce; millions more come from dysfunctional families. They are gingerly threading their way through the landmines of addictions, violence, and teen suicides. AIDS and other sexually transmitted diseases have cast a cloud over what many expected to be the sunlit age of sexual freedom. Yet those born in the late 1960s and 1970s are having sex earlier than their parents did, and fifteen- to nineteen-year-olds are having more babies than their older brothers and sisters did.[36]

Baby busters want satisfaction from their jobs—and good pay. But the crass materialism of yuppiedom is out, and public service is in. So are relationships—with caution. Many prefer living together to taking a chance on an early marriage; and more than half say they would not like a marriage like the one their parents had.[37]

Baby busters have few heroes, though they tend to romanticize a hazy past when, presumably, values were clear and people were committed.

Alert churches and youth ministries will latch onto that yearning, as well as to the teen-age generation coming after.

Although a 1989 Gallup Poll found that the lowest church attendance was among the buster ages of eighteen to twenty-nine (32 percent), teen attendance (57 percent) was the highest of any time since Gallup began collecting the data in 1980.[38]

These findings surely pinpoint the importance of youth ministry in church growth, especially since about two-thirds of all Christians make a commitment to Jesus Christ before they turn eighteen.[39]

The Information Age

Technological Takeover?

If a generational revolution lies ahead, is a technological revolution also on the horizon in 2001?

Futurists and scientists disagree at points. Some say that with the invention of the computer and the discovery of DNA, a revolution unparalleled in scientific history has already occurred. What we will see between now and the end of the century, they predict, will be a shift from innovation to application. The harnessing of existing technologies will bring new lifestyles, new ways of transmitting and assimilating information, and new ways of performing tasks at home and in the workplace.

Others believe the pace of new developments will increase exponentially this decade. They foresee revolutionary and unpredictable breakthroughs in physics, electronics, and biotechnology.

The seers are agreed, however, on one point: This is the information age, and whoever wins access to knowledge will control power.

Alvin Toffler asserts that control of knowledge "is the crux of tomorrow's worldwide struggle for power *in every human institution*."[1] And electronics expert James D. Meindl calls "the information revolution the most explosive development of our lifetime" and asserts that international competition for control of it "will take place on a scale utterly without precedent."[2] Meindl goes on to describe some of the "future marvels" that may be commonplace early in the coming century:

- Home access, via glass fiber cables, to virtually unlimited electronic libraries, commercial data, and computational capabilities.
- The introduction of artificial intelligence (AI) into many facets of daily life so that we can interact with an "expert software system" much as we would with a master auto mechanic, electrician, doctor, or tax consultant.
- Automated factories operated almost entirely by "intelligent" robots.
- Global, person-to-person communications with instantaneous language translation.

Of course in this chapter we can only sketch the barest outlines of these and a few other technological wonders, but I've tried to pick some of the most fascinating, as well as those most apt to influence how we live.

While we consider these technological wonders beckoning us to cross the threshold of 2001, it's essential that we grasp both the limitations and the potential for subversion inherent in technology. Information-hungry technology in a high-surveillance society can erode our freedoms and compromise our privacy. Already, the average American has information about his or her private life stowed away in eighteen federal computers, sixteen state and local computers, and twenty-five private-sector computers.[3]

If worshiped, technology in the end proves to be a false god, corroding human values and desensitizing the spirit. Yet few Christian authors, aside from French sociologist Jacques Ellul, have called the "technological bluff"—the title of his most recent book—in a compelling way. The siren song of "liberation technology" conceals the negative consequences of technical progress in contemporary society, Ellul says in his sweeping critique.[4]

In another probing and prophetic book, *Amusing Ourselves to Death,* Neil Postman observes:

> Public consciousness has not yet assimilated the point that technology is ideology . . . . To be unaware that technology comes equipped with a program for social change, to main-

tain that technology is neutral, to make the assumption that technology is always a friend to culture is, at this late hour, stupidity plain and simple . . . . Introduce speed-of-light transmission of images and you make a cultural revolution.[5]

Faster than a Speeding Light

Our ability to sense, manipulate, store, display, and transmit massive amounts of data is largely due to the wedding of photonics, the most recent high-tech discipline of electrical energy, and fiber optics—tiny, dense filaments of glass that are super-efficient conductors of light. A single fiber strand can transmit 16,000 telephone conversations at once, compared with 24 for the old copper wire technology. And the speed is so fast that the entire text of the *Encyclopaedia Britannica* and the Bible combined could be sent around the earth via fiber cable in less than two seconds![6]

Photonic devices convert electrons (electrical energy) into photons (light) and vice versa. The process is common to the working of television, illuminated readouts on watches, microwave and automobile instrumentation, and in photocopiers and most long-distance telephone transmissions. Although the first photonic device—the incandescent light bulb—was invented by Thomas Edison in 1879, photonics is still in its infancy as a technology, especially when it is linked with fiber optic communications.

Photonic systems, wedding high-tech electronics and the information revolution, are combining these functions with higher speed, smaller size, lower power, and less cost than ever before. In fact, photonics is thrusting us into "an Age of Light."

James S. Harris, Jr., director of Stanford University's Solid State Laboratory, helped me understand the social implications of photonics through a chapter in the nontechnical paperback, *Brief Lessons in High Technology*.[7] Here are some of the likely ways these applications will affect the way we live:

Our available knowledge base will increase dramatically.

With the capability to reproduce the equivalent of 1,000 books on just one 3.5-inch compact disk for under $10, a personal collection of 10,000 volumes will be within reach of anyone with a personal computer. And with localized fiber optic networks we could have almost instant access to current journals and magazines as well as to the entire Library of Congress.

Low-cost memories will enable us to store unlimited information.

Continuous newscasts and other information will be delivered through local fiber optic networks to our homes. Newspapers will be broadcast to a receiver and recorded on an optical disk which we may then play on our television set. News stories will likely be a mix of video and audio descriptions. With low-cost copiers, we can print selected material at home or "archive" it on optical disks for future reference.

Eventually integration may enable a single network to carry all types of information and provide all kinds of services. If that network then becomes a meta-network which sophisticated users can access to define and configure their own communications systems, there is potential for both positive and negative outcomes. On the plus side is very low cost and virtually unlimited control; on the negative side is a threat to the free flow of ideas.

Harris raises such questions as: How far do we converge toward a single world news reporting agency? How do we insure that multiple points of view are presented? Could governments restrict or control access to generally available public information by controlling the technology—prohibiting CD players and personal computers, for example? Toffler also worries about the "continuing war for the control, routing, and regulation of information."[8]

Multiple video channels provided by both long-distance and local networks offer the potential for people at widely separate locations to participate simultaneously in business meetings, large conferences, and church gatherings.

Interactive video conferences have already been used very successfully by more than a thousand national corporations and other groups, and this use will increase. Local networks link computers within a single business or complex, while worldwide networks connect workers—say for IBM or Hilton Hotels—globally.

In the field of religion, Campus Crusade for Christ put together a massive international evangelism conference with interactive video in multiple locations. And the Church of Jesus Christ of Latter-day

Saints and the United Methodist Church were among the first U.S. denominations to do teleconferencing by satellite.

Another trend likely to escalate as we race toward 2001 is church use of computers to promote dialogue between members. (Barna Research Group projects that by 2001, 83 percent of churches will be equipped with computers.)[9] In the nation's capital, the Rev. Stephen Arpee initiated "Church Without Walls," a computer "bulletin board" devoted to conversation on religious topics. Operating around the clock from his basement, the computer systems provide "log on" interaction for callers "on subjects ranging from abortion to Zoroastrianism."[10]

Meanwhile, the Christian job-matching ministry Intercristo makes worldwide job openings for Christian service in 200 occupational categories available through a new software package called "Prospectus."[11]

And in Brea, California, Norman Whan, a telemarketing specialist and creator of "The Phone's for You" evangelism technique, has helped launch several thousand congregations by dialing up prospects and inviting them to come out to an organizing worship service. Decidedly low-tech, some might say. But it works. "You can get at least 200 [out of 20,000 phone calls] to do anything," explained Whan.[12]

The extent to which electronic communication between individuals or groups can replace on-site meetings and personal one-to-one conversation remains to be seen, however; and the issue doubtless will be debated well into the next century.

Fiber optics and photonics will make it possible for people to process digital data just about anywhere.

In the next century business travel will be reduced and work forces will be less concentrated in central offices. Workers will use portable cellular phones, personal computers that handle sound and video, or high-definition TV sets that use the digital language of computers and are hooked to fiber optic networks. This high-definition TV will produce images five times sharper than those on existing sets.[13]

"For the future," notes Lanny Smoot of Bell Communications Research, "what you're looking at is telepresence—allowing me to be where you are. Not just seeing you, but seeing all of the things associated with you—all the papers on the desk, your PC, your whole environment. This is a wave that is not possible to stop."[14] For better or worse, we have "woven ourselves into a global electronic nervous system from which we will never be able to extricate ourselves."[15]

Video channels and networks may also dramatically alter the way we shop and handle personal business.

By 2001, on-line services will extend to banking, ticket and catalogue purchases, referral services, brokerage services, and social networks, according to *American Demographics* magazine. "Advertisers who know how to target market niches will profit in this new medium."[16] Christian ministries and churches will have an opportunity for expanded contacts through this medium as well.

In early 1991, the Federal Communications Commission proposed making a special broadcasting frequency available for ordering goods and services through television sets. Called Interactive Video Data Service, the technique, using digital technology and satellite transmissions, would be made available in every community.[17]

Harris wonders, however, if such electronic buying capabilities will tend to eliminate many small retail stores and shopping centers, making them "the dinosaurs of the 21st Century."[18]

A variety of new gadgets, products, and services will spring up.

Items offered for instant purchase via video will amaze and tempt us: digital audio tape recorders giving a cleaner, higher-quality sound and threatening to replace CDs; "smart" translator cards (under $100) the size of thick credit cards that can translate among five languages (more expensive versions will "speak" words or phrases for you); hand-held freeway off-ramp guides that electronically show you the nearest restaurant, gas station, motel, and other services.

Other "smart" stuff: cars with miniature offices including laptop computers, fax machines, and small microwaves to heat snacks; dashboard-mounted video displays to guide you to your destination, updating routes in light of current traffic conditions as you go; freeways with computerized traffic-flow control that will move cars automatically; shopping carts with video screens to guide customers to products and daily specials; cards with magnetic strips containing your financial and medical information; TVs that "know" what you want to watch before you turn them on; pill bottles that beep when it's time to take medication, then automatically record the time and dosage.

"Smart" automated houses will control everything centrally: turning on the lights as you enter the room; changing the room temperature depending on who's there; voice-activating the TV or stereo which has been preprogrammed to understand your viewing and listening tastes; and turning on the security system when you leave the premises. Self-diagnosing appliances and utility systems will recognize operating problems and automatically report them to repair and maintenance crews over a phone line. And your outdoor irrigation system will use built-in sensors to adjust watering in accordance with the weather.[19]

The home of the new millennium may also contain what producer Norman Lear has called "the control booth for worldwide entertainment." With high-definition TV, surround-sound systems, giant wall screens—even three-dimensional laser imaging—these technological advances may soon make home theaters a futurist's dream come true.[20]

Computerized games and gadgets will continue to fascinate children of all ages, and the younger generations—unlike many of today's older adults—will be computer literate. But a new technological phenomenon known as "virtual reality" or "cyberspace," which allows users to see and experience places and events as though they were actually present, may dominate the pastimes market.

In the future, predicts Sine, we will be able to experience both three-dimensional visual effects and other sensory experience to simulate reality through "total experience chambers . . . . We will be able to sit participants down in the middle of the Battle of the Bulge, take them into stellar space or on a guided tour inside of molecular structures."[21]

Although this technology may have beneficial educational and therapeutic uses, its frightening underside is the potential to so mesmerize futuristic voyagers that they become unable to distinguish "virtual" from "actual."

"For many," says researcher Judith Waldrop, "it will replace drugs as an escape from reality"[22]—perhaps a small comfort in an addictive society.

Technology, through robots and artificial intelligence, will revolutionize workplaces and speed up the way many tasks are performed.

Within the next decade:

> Computerized secretaries will reduce office staff by taking and editing dictation. Industrial robots will virtually take over assembly lines, and on the farm so-called agribots will rove through orchards picking fruit at harvest time. The presumed outcome will be better products and services at lower prices, but also painful pink slips for millions of low-income workers who failed to . . . train for new jobs.[23]

Furthermore, robots and artificial intelligence will be used by manufacturers to custom-design and produce goods and control inventories as well as construct the machines that make this possible!

With technology-driven, flexible design, manufacturers can offer a whole wave of variations on a new product almost immediately after they have introduced it. Using "small batch" manufacturing, for example, an Indiana casket-maker has slashed the time it takes to turn out a casket model from an array of designs.[24]

In 1985, 99 percent of robots in use in the United States were in industrial applications. Today there are an increasing number of mobile robots in the home (until recently, mostly toys), in medicine, in space, and in the military. "Entry level" military robots include "smart weapons" like the Patriot missiles. These weapons, which use electronic sensors and computer brains to destroy other sophisticated weapons, came into prominence during Desert Storm. There are also underseas robots with propellers, sonar, and electric field sensors that can search for ships, planes, submarines, and even priceless artifacts.[25]

Futurist Joseph Coates thinks that by the 21st century fire-resistant robots will rescue people from burning buildings, and robotics expert Michael Higgins predicts criminals will use personal robots to rob banks.[26]

Then there are microbots. The World Future Society predicts that these tiny "machines," after being swallowed, will perform surgery inside a patient's body. They will be "guided by a human surgeon 'seeing' the patient's internal organs through a combination of computer imaging and 3-D simulation."[27]

While robots are designed to "do the work," the technology behind Artificial Intelligence and Artificial Life will blur the line between machinery and humanity.

At the beginning of the 1990s, AI could already accurately recognize continuous speech and operate computers on voice commands.[28] Fifteen years from now, affirms communications and graphic-arts wizard Richard Saul Wurman,

> technology will be such that people can make their own artificial intelligences, so we will be able to shape semi-intelligent agents that can essentially be extensions of our own will and our own goal structure. And instead of having to go to a central database and sit there for a couple hours puzzling through it, a lot of this kind of work will be done by our agents, who will constantly be rummaging for us.[29]

The outer reaches of artificial intelligence research go beyond teaching machines to categorize and organize knowledge; AI experts like Hans Moravec of Carnegie-Mellon University have a vision of the future in which humans may achieve immortality by transferring their minds into indestructible machines.

Others, however, like Joseph Mellinchamp, director of the University of Alabama Artificial Intelligence Laboratory, have analyzed the limitations of a machine's intelligence, consciousness, belief system, intuition, and common sense and concluded that these characteristics "are qualitatively different from the same attributes in a human."[30]

Still other scientists are poking around the edges of "neural networks" that mimic the way the brain and nerves work together. Such technology can be applied to tasks related to machine vision and robotics as well as speech, text, and handwriting recognition.

Chase Manhattan Bank presently uses a neural net system to detect credit card fraud, while Japanese designers have programmed a washing machine to sample laundry water and, depending on how dirty the water is, select the optimum washing time and detergent quantity. And medical researchers have designed neural systems to detect abnormal heart sounds and interpret electrocardiograms.

Looking ahead, Peter D. Moore of Inferential Focus, a marketing-intelligence firm in New York, believes neural networks "will tend to displace white-collar workers—from middle management to top decision makers—by substituting their human-like decision-making capabilities" for those of the workers.[31] And perhaps, if these machines can think and choose with free will, they may someday acquire civil rights! And go to court!

Out on the frontier's farthest edge is the search for "artificial life," the attempt to synthesize lifelike behavior in nonliving systems. At UCLA, for example, David Jefferson and Robert Collins have created colonies of randomly generated computer "ants" that evolve, over many generations, the ability to navigate electronic mazes and search for symbols representing food.

"Can something that 'lives' inside a computer really be alive?" questions Philip Elmer-Dewitt in a *Time* magazine article about the experiment. "That is the bizarre question at the heart of artificial-life research."[32]

Artificial life scientist Christopher Langton at Los Alamos National Laboratory in New Mexico contends that "artificial life will be genuine life. It will simply be made of different stuff." He has also said that artificial life represents "life as it could be," as opposed to "life as we know it."[33] Yet Langton and other scientists in the vanguard of the artificial-life movement recognize the potential dangers of playing God with electronic creatures and the need for an ethical framework to deal with the consequences that might result from science gone berserk.

David Barnard, director of Computing Services at Queen's University in Ontario, Canada, thinks that "smart" machines will affect the way we relate to God in the next millennium, but he believes that the advancement of AI will only enhance the believer's relationship to the Lord.

"The Bible does not depict men and women as being unique because we are the most intelligent of all God's creatures," Barnard said in an interview with *Spirit!* magazine. "Instead, it teaches us that we are unique because of the personal relationship we can have with God. . . . To claim that progress beyond certain limits is impossible may only serve to invalidate our Christian faith for future generations. We simply don't know what technological advancements are possible. So we need to be careful to put limits only where the Bible puts limits and admit ignorance in areas where we really don't know."[34]

But Bill Bright, founder-president of Campus Crusade for Christ, believes the AI movement "is perhaps the most potent threat to Christianity in the immediate future." It could rival the Darwinian theory of evolution in causing problems for the faithful, he says, because AI is predicated on the assumption that man is an entirely material being and can, in principle, be duplicated and even surpassed by computer scientists.

This view "makes the concept of a soul and a Creator superfluous," Bright wrote, after participating in a symposium on "Artificial Intelligence and the Human Mind."[35]

Another technological juggernaut of the future is developing a universal language that machines can "understand" and "speak."

Although computers already can understand human speech in limited ways, Harris points out that delivering information in a single language would save up to 1,000 times the cost of delivering it in the hundreds of languages spoken worldwide or even in the 10 dominant languages.[36] Research into a universal computer language is in progress; once perfected, such a language will cause a leap forward in applications for businesses, mass communications, and education.

And finally, here's a sampling of other "mind-bogglers" scientists will seek to unravel at the century's turning:

- Information about the nature of the neuron and molecular processes involved in neurotransmission will open up a totally new view of the nature of the human mind and of psychological issues.
- In physics, the superconducting supercollider will become a major scientific instrument.[37]
- The possibility of traveling through time, of creating something out of nothing, and even spawning a new universe in a laboratory. Employing quantum theory, which describes the

behavior of atoms and subnuclear particles, theoretical physicists "have begun to take such ideas seriously."[38]

- A reassessment—and possibly a scrapping—of the long-favored Big Bang theory of how the universe was formed through an explosion of mega-proportions some 10 to 20 billion years ago. In 1991, apparent fatal flaws were detected in the Big Bang theory, and the field of cosmology was thrown into turmoil. Astronomers are beginning to search elsewhere to solve the mysteries of the birth of the galaxies.[39]

Maybe, just maybe, they'll look to God?

But while some scientists look for God in the years ahead, others will be accused of "playing God."

Bioethics

A New God?

In-vitro fertilization, organ transplants, allocation of limited medical resources (triage), surrogate parenting, do-not-resuscitate orders, withholding life support, living wills, proxy-care legislation, fetal tissue, gene surgery, and a host of other bioethical concerns will be "the major civil rights issues" of the 1990s, predicts A. James Rudin, a rabbi prominent in the field of biomedicine and public policy.[1] Few would disagree.

"We are poised on the threshold of a great era of biotechnology," says *Megatrends* author Naisbitt.[2]

"We are on the threshold of a new world as inconceivable to us as the modern world of biology and technology was at the turn of the last century," echoes psychiatrist Willard Gaylin, president of the Hastings Center, the prestigious bioethical and behavioral research organization. He continues:

> With the miracle that is modern surgery we use patches and parts, manufactured and real, borrowed from ourselves, other living human beings, or cadavers, and we stitch them together. . . . The inconceivable has become conceivable. How are we expected to make the leap into molecular biology; into DNA and recombinance; into gene splicing and the

manufacture of new species, chimera; to the potential of introducing genetic material and the traits they command from one individual to another and from one life form to another? What about this new capacity to design our descendants?[3]

Gaylin and others sense that the "new genetics" has generated more anxiety than jubilation. Some, in fact, contend that modern-day biotechnicians are "playing God."

Who will make the decisions about what Rabbi Rudin says are the "rights issues" of the 1990s? And on what basis? Economics? Need? "Advancement of science" or "the need to know"? The sacredness and dignity of life? What about the potential for abuse of autonomy and privacy? These are but a few of the prickly questions of the bioethics revolution that go to the taproot of what it means to be human—and to be created in the image of God.

But the "playing God" rap is begging the question, insists religion commentator Martin Marty: "In a way, all biology applied to humans—all medicine—is 'playing God' and 'interfering with nature,' so the question is how to do this intelligently."[4]

Anyway, the gene(ie) is already out of the bottle.

It's too late for moratoriums or cautions, declares Fay Angus, an amateur bioethics expert who lectures and writes on the subject. "The best we can do," she says, "is to exercise the depth of the wisest among us. The best we can do is to cope. There is no going back."[5]

Pull out the core of what the "pew people" want to know, Angus advocated as we talked about this chapter.

"How does that affect me—my body, my life, my death, my medical well-being, my genetic markers, family planning, and selection of children? Don't confuse me with philosophical ramifications. I'll leave theology to the theologians. My living, my aging—that's where it's at."

There may be, as my friend and writing colleague added, "a gray area of fog to wade through for a glimmer of light," but the pathway is fascinating. And, as Naisbitt notes, to be ignorant about this complex, multifaceted topic is to let other forces play God.

Reproductive Technology

Baby-making is an ancient art, usually high touch and low tech. Surrogate parenting dates back at least as far as Abraham, Sarah, and Hagar in Bible times.[6] Artificial insemination was reported in 1799, and pregnancy after insemination with frozen sperm a hundred years later.

But these days conception is becoming increasingly low touch and high tech. Hitting the headlines in the past twenty-five years have been: commercial surrogate motherhood, in-vitro fertilization (egg and sperm combined in a dish), embryo transfer, and babies born from embryos that have been frozen and thawed later. And now, as medical technology surges ahead, menopausal women can give birth to children conceived with the egg of a younger woman.

The famous Baby M case brought surrogacy to widespread public attention in 1986 when the surrogate mother, Mary Beth Whitehead, had her own egg fertilized with the sperm of the husband from the couple who hired her. Since then, more than 2,000 "traditional" surrogate births have been achieved in this manner. But an increasing number of surrogate cases have involved women who gave birth to children genetically unrelated to them. Conception, using the couple's eggs and sperm, occurs in a petri dish in a hospital lab, and one of the embryos is implanted in the surrogate mother. Perhaps eighty such births had occurred by mid-1990.[7] Soon, scientists predict, it will be possible to bring in-vitro embryos to full-term delivery in a totally artificial womb.[8]

Critics say surrogacy bears the potential for abuse. One form of abuse is by women, both married and unmarried, heterosexual and lesbian, who want to avoid the inconvenience of pregnancy. Others attack the practice as exploitative, creating a "breeder" class of women who are no more than "fetal containers."[9] Other opponents charge that hiring surrogates amounts to "baby selling."

Despite invaluable help that "assisted reproduction" has given countless childless couples, lawsuits galore have festered since biotechnology has blossomed well beyond its pioneering stages two decades ago. Indeed, while the technology is racing toward 2001, societal rules for dealing with the consequences have lagged far behind.

Shari Roan, the health writer at *The Los Angeles Times,* raises some of the problems and questions:

- How should parenthood be defined? Are the parents those who contribute genetic material to the child, bear the child, or raise the child?
- What are frozen embryos? Are they people or property? Who has the rights to the embryos in a dispute? And how should "unwanted" embryos be disposed of?
- Should the child born with the aid of an egg or sperm donor be entitled to know who the genetic parent is?
- Should egg donors, sperm donors, and surrogate mothers be paid for their services, as they often are?
- Should infertility clinics be required to reveal success rates? And should couples pay for treatment that many experts still regard as experimental?[10]

"There needs to be one person who works with the [infertility] patients who is on the patient's level," advises Andrea Shrednick, a reproductive psychologist and faculty member at the University of Southern California. "Not someone with the power to play God. Not someone with the power to make them a baby. But someone who can sit down and help them work through and understand the issues involved."[11]

Fetal Tissue and Abortion

To work through the ramifications of fetal tissue experimentation and its relationship to abortion is another difficult and sometimes daunting task.

Fetal tissue has a much higher chance of being accepted by the recipient's immune system than tissue from an "older" donor. Fetal tissue can be used by surgeons to replace worn-out parts in a diseased person, and fetal-cell implants are especially effective for adults suffering from diabetes, Parkinson's disease, and Alzheimer's. The procedure shows possible promise also for sickle-cell anemia, some forms of cancer, and even stroke.[12]

The catch, of course, is that the transplanted tissue comes from an aborted fetus. Citing ethical concerns, the National Institutes of

Health in late 1989 yanked federal funding from fetal research, thus halting such study except in privately financed work.

The ban hasn't stopped debate, however, and ethical clouds will likely brew into new storms before the century's end as conflicting attitudes concerning abortion continue to dominate and divide. The controversial legal concept of fetal rights lies close to the storm center.

Basically there are two camps regarding fetal-tissue research and use. The first is those who consider aborted fetuses cadavers and therefore appropriate material for research and tissue implants. Abortion, they reason, is a separate tissue issue.

Not so, say those who consider the aborted fetus a victim. Although some bioethicists in this camp would allow for spontaneously aborted fetuses to be used for fetal-tissue research and surgery, their real worry is that elective abortion will be used. This creates "a tragedy [abortion] for some other good," says Arthur Caplan, director of the Center for Biomedical Ethics at the University of Minnesota.[13]

Another fear expressed by opponents is that couples may conceive for the express purpose of providing—or selling—tissue from an abortion for someone else's use. (As I write this, abortions are still legal in most states, but it is illegal to buy or sell fetal tissue.)

Euthanasia

In a society that can't agree when human life begins, it's no surprise that we have trouble deciding when it should end.

"If you think the abortion issue was emotional," declares Margaret Battin, a philosophy professor and ethics expert at the University of Utah, "just wait until we get fully into euthanasia and death."[14]

In fact, a celebrated 1990 the case of a terminally ill woman focused national attention on what *Time* magazine called "an unfortunate consequence of modern medicine's ability to keep people alive in a state of semi-death."[15]

Nancy Cruzan, whose case had led to a landmark U.S. Supreme Court decision, passed away peacefully in Missouri the day after Christmas that year, "her parents by her side and euthanasia foes camped outside the hospital."[16] She was allowed to die, the plastic feeding tube that sustained her removed, after a four-year legal battle pursued by her family. In June, in a wrenching 5-4 decision, the high court for the first time established the right to die for terminally ill patients who make their wishes clear.

And in November, 1991, in the first popular vote ever held on legalized euthanasia, the voters of Washington state grappled with and then defeated—by a margin of 54 to 46 percent—a proposed "Death with Dignity" referendum that would have legalized physician-assisted suicide. If approved, the measure would have made Washington the only jurisdiction in the world where doctors could legally offer a lethal injection or drug overdose to terminally ill patients who wished to die.

Many evangelicals and Catholics condemned the measure as an attack on the sanctity of life, while others—mostly mainline Protestants and Jewish leaders—praised the initiative for its potential to ease the suffering of terminally ill patients and their families.

More carefully crafted euthanasia initiatives are sure to crop up in other states. And the complex situations of life and death created by modern technology—indeed, even definitions of life and death—are not easily settled. The issue reflects not only the ambiguity many people feel, but also the entwining of moral and civil law.

Donald C. Lamkins, administrator of the rehabilitation center where Nancy Cruzan's life was ended nearly eight years after an auto accident caused her heart to stop beating for at least fifteen minutes, tried to explain:

"There are two kinds of law here—our legal laws, those are society's laws—and moral law. Moral law is God's law; it comes from religion. Man's laws said it's all right, but that doesn't change moral law."[17]

Recent public opinion surveys show that 50–60 percent of Americans favor the legalization of euthanasia and physician-assisted suicide under certain circumstances.[18]

As life expectancy continues to advance beyond the ability of medical science to provide a comfortable existence, the medical community, lawmakers, ethicists, and religious leaders will have to fashion guidelines concerning passive—and active—euthanasia that they can live with.

The "pew people" are already doing it.

The Cruzan case prompted hundreds of thousands of requests for "living will" forms from the Society for the Right to Die.[19] And the American Hospital Association has estimated that 70 percent of the 6,000 daily deaths in the United States are "already somehow timed or negotiated with all concerned parties privately concurring on withdrawal of some death-delaying technology or not even starting it in the first place."[20]

"At the bedside level," says Marsha Fowler, who trains nurses for church-staff jobs, "the single most important bioethical issue for the 21st century is the way in which one goes about dying—withholding treatment and withdrawing treatment once it's started; and how you evaluate this in terms of the person's spiritual walk and beliefs."[21]

People deal with end-of-life issues in church, Fowler adds, and she expects more involvement on the part of churches to help people decide, for example, about such things as "durable power of attorney," a legal instrument that designates a decision-maker to determine a person's end-of-life treatment in the event the person herself or himself is unable to do so.

Genetic Engineering

In 1980, ten years before the U.S. Supreme Court ruled that life support could be terminated if there is "clear and convincing" proof that is what the patient would want, the court made another historic five-to-four decision: that new forms of life created in a laboratory could be patented.

Ever since, designer genes have been big business. Before eight years had passed, the U.S. Patent Office had been flooded with 8,000 biotech patent requests for new life forms, 21 of them for genetically engineered animals.[22]

Genetic engineering, explains scientist Ian Barbour,

> offers the prospect of the deliberate alteration of the genetic structure of organisms and even of human beings. Here again is an unprecedented power of the human future. We face promising possibilities for improving the agricultural productivity of crops in the midst of food scarcities and for lifting the burden of human suffering caused by genetically inherited

diseases. But we also face risks of unintended repercussions and controversial ethical issues, especially if human genes are altered not just to cure diseases but to achieve improvements in human characteristics.[23]

Fertilizers and pest-resistant traits are being placed in seeds, and biotech farmers say bioengineered crops and farm animals could become commercially available by 1995.

"Imagine a cow that produces skim milk, a canola seed rich in sperm-whale oil, or a naturally decaffeinated coffee bean," gushes J. Madeleine Nash in a *Time* magazine article. Changing the genetic endowments of plants and animals "could spawn a revolution in farm fields, feedlots and dairy barns."[24]

Harvard University patented the first genetically engineered mouse in 1988, the same year that seven genetically identical, purebred bull calves were produced from man-made embryos.[25]

By the 21st century, predicts Ed Cornish of the World Future Society, we will have the capacity, through DNA transfers, to create an elephant that glows in the dark. "But we might not want to bother."[26]

If revolutionary changes are already in progress in the plant and animal worlds, can genetically engineered humans be far behind?

A human's total gene composite (genome) contains up to 100,000 genes stored on twenty-four pairs of chromosomes. Genetic scientists are busy "mapping" these genes to decipher the genetic code—"with its instructions for building, running and reproducing bodies." This, Naisbitt and Aburdene affirm in *Megatrends 2000,* "may well prove to be the greatest scientific achievement in this century."[27]

Once a gene is located, it can be copied, or cloned, and cloned genes can be used to find carriers of genetic disease, diagnose genetic abnormalities—even predict a person's tendencies to develop certain defects or illnesses.

The Human Genome Initiative, a $200 million-a-year project to "list the whole encyclopedia-length recipe for making a human being," was launched through the National Institutes of Health and the Department of Energy in 1988.[28]

Gene therapy offers a host of beneficial uses just becoming

available. In 1990, in the first federally approved use of gene splicing, a team of doctors introduced some one billion cells containing a copy of a foreign gene into a four-year-old girl's bloodstream. The object: the new cells produce enzymes needed to overcome the deadly genetic disease that incapacitates her immune system; healthy replacement genes take over for defective ones. So far, the experiment has been successful.

The impact of gene therapy could be astoundingly positive, specialists say, helping to stop or even wipe out previously incurable genetic diseases such as cystic fibrosis, Down's Syndrome, and hemophilia. But altering human genes poses risks and threats as well as benefits. Some object to manipulating genes in ways that don't seem representative of the natural order; again, "playing God."

The scare word is eugenics, the attempt to make hereditary "improvements."

So far, the gene therapy being practiced affects only the patients. But it is conceivable (pun intended) that we may move in the direction of *Brave New World* with genetic engineering of sperm and egg cells that would affect the genetic inheritance of future generations.

"We may begin innocently," suggest Ann Lammers and Ted Peters in a *Christian Century* magazine article on "genethics,"

> by trying to breed out hemophilia and end up breeding in genetic traits that fit the needs of social stratification, economic productivity or nationalist interests. Might the drive for improved human beings lead finally to a drive for racial purity? Well in advance of any brave new world, we need to ask who will be making the decisions and according to what criteria. Who will be allowed to share in the benefits of genetic intervention and who will be compelled to submit to them?[29]

If it becomes possible to identify and choose genes for any inherited trait, parents could order up children customized to specification!

Such frontier biotech—so-called "enhancement" genetic engineering—gives the shudders to specialists like W. French Anderson, chief of the Laboratory of Hematology at NIH. If, for example, it extends to a normal individual the ability to acquire a memory-enhancing gene or a height-enhancing gene, what are the limits? On what basis does one individual get gene enhancement while another person is denied it?

Anderson concludes that our society "is comfortable with" genetic engineering to treat existing serious disease, but he excludes enhancement engineering "on medical and ethical grounds."[30]

In the health-care field, could this lead insurance companies to reject—or at least limit—coverage for persons whose genetic screening showed them susceptible to certain diseases like colon cancer, Alzheimer's, or a heart attack, even if they had no history of the problem? Could such individuals be required to obtain genetic surgery before they were eligible for health insurance?

Fowler, the parish-nurse and bioethics consultant, believes that access to health care and its cost will be "the Number One overwhelming bioethical concern" of the 21st century.[31]

Organ Transplants, Body Parts, and Bionics

In 1989, 13,384 organ transplants were performed, raising questions about whether a commercial market to supply this demand should be created. Enough organs might be available if donors or their heirs were paid. One ingenious proposal is for a "futures market" in which people would be given a discount on their insurance premiums if they agreed to turn in their organs to the insurer after death. But wouldn't rich patients outbid poor ones for spare body parts which, ironically, other poor would be providing out of economic need?[32]

Prohibiting the sale of the human body or its parts is "one of the ways you show special respect for the body," says Arthur Caplan, the University of Minnesota bioethicist. But other people argue that, for the common good, organ donation should be mandatory at death. The Uniform Anatomical Gift Act adopted by all the states gives patients the right to donate organs after they die and to specify the recipient (either a person or an institution).[33]

But what about forcing a child to donate an organ or bone marrow for an ailing family member? Or consider the social impact of having a recognizable limb from someone else's body?[34]

Tom Sine predicts that "a new generation of bionics promises to make us more than we can be through technology. As our bodies become a collection of implanted organs and technologies, transplanted limbs and bionic appliances, what will happen to our sense of identity?"[35]

Other medical experiments to study the power of the mind—the chemical analysis of the brain and its relationship to consciousness and thought, and the possibility of fusing the human brain with implanted microchips—are either in progress or on the drawing board.[36] And the new and controversial field of sociobiology—examining the biological basis of social behavior through its genetic roots—is absorbing the attention of molecular biologists and researchers in brain chemistry. The discipline has been called "a view from Darwin's shoulders."[37]

No Glib Answers

If reading about these innovations and conundrums of biotechnology has your mind swirling and your spirit perplexed, you are not alone. I feel the same way as I write about them. The supremacy of a sovereign God is balanced against the capability of humanity to do good—and to do evil. We're looking ahead to a world far different from any we have known, with a whole new terminology we've never even considered. "Bioethics" wasn't even a word until 1971.

Premarital counseling will take on new meaning as we advance into the next century and face the new options in reproductive techniques, while aging and life-extension will shake up all standards of health care and its attendant costs. It will be a time of tremendous challenge for Christians, "a breaking down of every biblical comfort zone we have."[38]

"Ignorant about the full range of longterm consequences," say Lammers and Peters, "we face moral choices whose resolution seems to require the benefit of a divine foreknowledge that we humans shall never—despite computer simulations—entirely possess. In short, we are by no means God's equals, even if we are in some sense co-creators."[39]

Yet all this brings tremendous opportunities for ministry—not only for clergy, but also for skilled paraprofessionals. And just plain volunteers with loving hearts who are standing by, reminds my friend Richard Spencer, a pastor who served on the ethics committees of two Southern California hospitals.[40]

The right to die, when to stop or withhold treatment for the terminally ill or the elderly, what to do for a severely handicapped newborn—these are the big issues of bioethics. But many issues, adds Katherine Bouton in an article about the painful decisions a medical ethicist faces, "involve the crucial small ones: informed consent, the right to confidentiality, the right to choose treatment, the right to know who is treating you."[41]

Although our future lies in the Information Age, in which technology married to biology will set much of the agenda for human life, the most important kinds of knowledge won't come out of the computer. To make ethical choices, set priorities, and perpetuate the dignity of the human race, we will need wisdom. And, according to the Bible, the beginning of wisdom comes only out of a reverence for and a fear of God.[42]

Earth

Dominion or Doom?

As I prepared to write this chapter, news of the largest oil spill in history came scudding across the television screen: the relentless, black wave of oil released into the Persian Gulf by Saddam Hussein's military. This foul slick of 63 to 84 million gallons elongating into a 15-mile malignancy of "environmental terrorism" threatened the wholesale death—and possible extinction—of coral reefs, Hawksbill turtles, Cormorants, and other wildlife. Who can forget the televised struggles of blackened seabirds pitifully flapping their matted wings in a vain attempt to escape the havoc of a madman's making?

This was to be the "Earth Decade," remember? When the preservation of Planet Earth would be the number one concern for the entire global community as the "green tide" gained momentum. But with the black tide rolling across the Persian Gulf, and black rain and soot falling from the burning Kuwait oil wells, a more fitting description might be "Environmental Apocalypse."

"God has given us a long rope and a big laboratory," says Rev. Glenn E. Olds, Jr., president of the Better World Society. "But the consequences of our greed, ignorance and propensity to violence and power are catching up with us very fast."[1]

The first chapter of Genesis declares that the land and its plants and animals are for human use. After God blessed Adam and Eve, he told them: "Be fruitful and multiply, and replenish the earth, and subdue it: and have dominion over the fish of the sea, and over the fowl of the air, and over every living creature that moveth upon the earth."[2]

But will it be dominion, or doom?

Beyond the concerns of suicide, homicide, infanticide, and genocide, the coming millennium will require us to turn our attention to *biocide,* the killing of the life systems of the earth, and *geocide,* the destruction of the functional integrity of the planet itself.[3]

I find it ironic that the major prize sought in the Gulf War was oil. Fueled by our addiction to its use, petroleum is the very substance that could lead to the planet's ultimate demise as a habitat for humanity.

That desecrating the environment is "a sin against nature herself" is a concept that "people across the board are beginning to realize," notes Jan Hartke, leader for the Washington-based interfaith group called the North American Conference on Religion and Ecology.[4]

There is also—underscored by Saddam Hussein's monstrous atrocity against nature—a growing sense of global interdependence. Many environmental impacts, such as the greenhouse effect, are global in cause and must be global in remedy.

"There has to be in the coming decade a major move toward restoration of the earth," urges veteran conservationist David R. Brower.

> We've got to put back together, as well as we can, the things we took apart since the Industrial Revolution. It was a big party. Now the bills are coming in: global warming, acid rain, holes in the ozone layer, loss of species and loss of hope. We've got to turn that all around. All we can do is give nature a chance . . . . We can't restore the rain forest, but we can give it our best stab. As for global warming, it's certainly going to be slowed down, and we'd better reverse it. The last moment—or the next to the last moment—has arrived. As somebody said, "The threat of being hanged gets one's attention."[5]

Environmental goals that should command our attention include sustaining natural resources, reducing pollution, and preserving species and ecosystems. And, along the way, the biblical theme of stewardship can help offset the all-too-frequent past emphasis on human dominion, often a euphemism for environmental exploitation. Rethinking our relationship to creation and the Creator will help develop goals and models for the future.

Agenda for the Atmosphere

The Worldwatch Institute's *State of the World 1989 Report* ominously asserted that for the first time human activities were changing the atmosphere itself, heightening the effect of "greenhouse" gases that are warming the earth and destroying the ozone shield that protects us from ultraviolet radiation. NASA reports confirmed that ozone depletion was no longer confined to the poles; the ozone layer was beginning to thin globally.[6]

In the longer term, climatic changes—which scientists are still trying to pinpoint as either cyclical or environmentally triggered—may cause sea levels to rise, flooding coastal settlements and islands, while ozone depletion will cause a dramatic rise in skin cancers.

Some reports indicate that the air and rivers in America are getting cleaner not dirtier, and that the pollution scare is largely a media concoction.[7] But the effects of airborne pollution seem so obvious—especially in European industrial nations, India, Mexico, and America's major urban areas—that there should be little room for complacency.

Automobiles reportedly spew their own weight in carbons back into the atmosphere every year.[8] And though the jury is still out on the precise damage that acid rain is doing to our lakes and rivers, toxic pollutants are treated with grave concern by the Environmental Protection Agency.

Who will pay for the cleanup costs for these and other environmental problems? The answer is hazy, and will remain so into the next century as long as other projects deemed vital compete for public funds. Private industry, despite platitudinous talk, will likely step in only when companies perceive that it is in their long-run economic advantage to do so. One hopeful sign is a booklet, "Shopping for a Better World," put out by the Council on Economic

Priorities, to tell people which corporations are doing well environmentally and which are not.[9]

Cleaning up smokestack industry and developing feasible non-fossil fuels appear to be at the top of near-future American priorities. Mercedes is experimenting with a car that burns hydrogen, and many experts say the outlook for automotive power sources such as methanol, natural gas, and electricity has been improving. Still, "any significant loosening of gasoline's stranglehold on the worldwide car and truck fuel market appears to be decades away."[10]

But energy conservation will likely be in vogue during the 1990s and into the next century; common sense prescribes it and tough new pollution laws will mandate it. At present, California leads the nation in developing alternative energy sources, building up a reserve supply through wind plantations, solar collectors, and geothermal energy.[11]

Meanwhile, future generations will have to deal with the legacy of the 1986 Chernobyl nuclear disaster, which could eventually result in 10,000 cancer deaths. When I attended an all-Soviet conference on evangelism in the fall of 1990 in Moscow, residents of the Chernobyl area emotionally described the continuing health problems in the region—far greater, they said, than generally known by the public.

Mismanagement and repeated safety violations have occurred at others of the 390 nuclear plants operating worldwide. Fortunately, steps are being taken to correct the problems.[12] Public pressure will have to be maintained, however, to ensure safety and proper disposal of nuclear waste.

Agenda for Freshwater, Oceans, and Coasts

Although freshwater sources in the United States appear to be adequate for human consumption for the foreseeable future, water tables are falling in many parts of the country and water for agriculture may be scarce by 2001. We are a nation of water wasters, and we are polluting our freshwater supply at a much faster rate than we are conserving it.[13]

More than 700 chemicals have been detected in U.S. drinking water; the EPA considers 129 of them "dangerous," including industrial solvents, agricultural residues, metals, and radioactive substances. Much of the contamination has seeped from underground chemical storage tanks, mines, petroleum production, and landfills.[14]

About 20 *billion* tons of waste end up in the seas each year, according to the United Nations Environmental Programme. The oceans, which have been called "the lungs of the planet," cover about 70 percent of the earth's surface. More than two-thirds of the world's population live within fifty miles of a coast. And coastal zones have the highest biological productivity for fish and other marine life—90 percent of the worldwide fish catch is taken near the shore.

The oceans, so vital to life and the beauty of the earth, are difficult to protect, and we seem to be doing a poor job. About 80 percent of the pollution that enters the oceans comes from land in the form of sewage, industrial waste, and agricultural runoff; add coastal mining, oil spills, energy production, and pollutants from ocean vessels, and it's no wonder the fragile coastal ecosystems are in jeopardy.[15]

Reform, cleanup, and conservation programs are urgently needed to preserve the waters and the teeming life within and near them.

Agenda for Land Resources

On the land, deforestation and desertification are the two prime enemies.

Forest destruction has brought on widespread flooding and loss of topsoil, contributed to global warming, and speeded the extinction of plants and animals. Every year huge expanses of tropical forests—the equivalent of one football field per second—fall to the chainsaw and the torch. In the colorful words of entomologist Edward O. Wilson, to destroy a rain forest for economic gain "is like burning a Renaissance painting to cook a meal."[16]

In a public awareness campaign in a full-page ad in *Time* magazine, the Environmental Challenge Fund pointed out that America "pays" for the Sunday newspaper by sacrificing more than a half-million trees. So, urges the ad, "If everyone in the U.S. recycled even 1/10th of their newspapers, we would save 25 million trees a year. That's a lot of forest for the trees."[17] (The ad didn't mention reusing the glossy pages of *Time* as the vehicle for the environmental message.)

Taking the admonition seriously, one large religious publishing house recycles computer paper and corrugated cardboard, saving an estimated 2,185 trees, 57,486 gallons of oil, and 1,552 cubic yards of landfill space in just five months.[18]

Ecopublishers are getting into the act, too. From a redesigned *Greenpeace* to new titles such as *Garbage, Buzzworm,* and *Design Spirit,* the ecomagazines are looking for a wider audience. Articles focus on practical subjects—from designing kitchens that make recycling easier to gardening without pesticides.[19] Nearly all the publications are printed on recycled paper, of course.

In a special twenty-eight-page section, "Forests in Distress," the Portland *Oregonian* presented a massive report on years of timber overcutting in the Pacific Northwest, examining the causes, effects, and the future consequences. Over the years, conclude the authors,

> logging practices have contributed to declining fish runs, massive landslides, severe forest fragmentation and ruined streams. Many wildlife species—not just the northern spotted owl—are losing ground. The timber industry, long the region's economic mainstay and wellspring of political power, is reaping the consequences of a history of overcutting.[20]

Tree-planting projects are a practical and effective way to stem—if not reverse—the stripping of forests. One laudable example is the partnership of Pat Robertson's Christian Broadcasting Network (CBN) and a timber company. Together they have planted more than 3 million trees in Kenya, some of which are already 12 to 20 feet high.[21]

The word "desertification" isn't in many dictionaries yet, but combating it will increasingly become a part of ecological stewardship in the coming millennium.

Desertification refers to the huge tracts of land that are becoming worthless desert through erosion, overfarming, and climactic changes. The UN's Environmental Programme estimates that 35 percent of the earth's land surface is threatened by desertification, and that three-quarters of that has *already* been moderately degraded.[22]

The vicious spiral feeds itself. Loss of cultivation increases erosion and warming, which cause worsening droughts and floods, putting more pressure on remaining arable land and ratcheting up a new round of desertification and loss of topsoil.

Surging population and diminishing productive lands are on a collision course. The result: environmental degradation, which hits the poor the hardest.

Here again, there are some positive models that need to be multiplied in the 21st century.

Christian relief and development agencies like World Vision and World Concern are zeroing in on ecological development in Third World countries. Self-help projects for the poor are geared to economic assistance while restoring the environment through reforestation and terraced farming. Here at home, World Vision has implemented FutureQuest, a program to educate children in Christian schools about their responsibility for the earth.

Another humanitarian organization with a biblical base is World Neighbors, a people-to-people, nonprofit organization working on the front lines to eliminate hunger, disease, and poverty. Efforts are concentrated in Asia, Africa, and Latin America through simple technologies, environmental conservation, and sustainable agriculture. World Neighbors' training in soil and water conservation in the Philippines and elsewhere is helping to eliminate "slash and burn" farming, which has contributed to the degradation of 77 percent of the developing world's rangelands and dry forests.[23]

Agenda for Biodiversity and Biotechnology

On this remarkably diverse planet live an incredible variety of species in an incredible variety of habitats. We have only managed to classify about 1.5 million of the world's species, and scientists aren't even sure if there are 5 million—or as many as 30 million—in all. They predict that, if the present rate of destruction of ecosystems continues, perhaps a quarter of the earth's living things risk extinction within twenty to thirty years. Up to one million species may vanish by 2001.

Thus, conservation of biodiversity should be a top international priority, with special emphasis going toward tropical forests. More than half of the known plant and animal species dwell there, but less than 5 percent of the tropical forests receive any protection.[24]

Protecting endangered species is essential, but voting legislation to prohibit fishing, hunting, or the killing of farm animals for food, or laboratory animals for vital research, is going too far. Doubtless, though, we will see increasing activism by animal rights groups in the coming years.

Also, a word needs to be added here about the potentially dangerous spread of introduced species into the environment through biotechnology in crop and animal production. New traits could be accidentally transferred to "wild relatives" of domestic species. Hardier weeds might be created, for example.

Alvin Toffler postulates that in future "eco-wars"—which he thinks will become more common and sophisticated in the decades ahead—nations "may unleash genetically altered insects against an adversary, or attempt to modify weather." There will be a need, then, for eco-intelligence to verify compliance with environmental treaties and provide Distant Early Warning systems for eco-wars.[25]

Another worry is that mass production of clonally propagated crops could seriously inhibit the natural diversity that exists, driving thousands of species to extinction.

In an effort to learn more about establishing a sustainable ecosystem, in 1991 eight "ecopioneers" were sealed into Biosphere 2, a superdome structure of steel and glass encompassing a miniature 3-acre "earth" near Tucson, Arizona. Home for thousands of carefully selected species of flora and fauna representing five ecosystems— rain forest, savanna, desert, ocean, and marsh—this $150 million private-venture experiment will last for two years. As cut off from the desert that surrounds them as if they were in a space ship, the human inhabitants will get nothing from the outside but information, electricity, and sunshine.

We can expect additional colonies of scientific and environmental pioneers to inhabit both underseas and outer space habitats in the early 2000s, if not sooner.

Agenda for Hazardous Wastes and Toxic Chemicals

In December 1984 a toxic gas leak from the Union Carbide pesticide plant in Bhopal, India, killed 2,500 people, injured 150,000 and caused the evacuation of 200,000. It was the worst industrial accident on record. But it could be matched or even surpassed in the coming decades.[26]

Every chemical is a potential hazard if used incorrectly or released by accident in large quantity. Almost nothing is known about 38,000 of the 48,000 chemicals listed by the EPA, and only about 500 have been tested for their cancer-producing, reproductive, or gene-mutation effects.[27] Heavy metals, organic pollutants, and toxins from fertilizers and pesticides daily contaminate our air, water, and soil, endangering the health of both present generations and those to follow.

Every year some 200,000 American children who drink heavily leaded water experience a loss of brain function, according to the U.S. National Academy of Sciences.

Meanwhile, we are sinking in garbage: The EPA estimates that within twenty years, 80 percent of the landfill dumps now in operation will be stuffed to capacity with the garbage of our throw-away society. Each person in the United States generates an average of almost a ton of trash each year.[28]

"We are sitting on a toxic time bomb," says Tom Sine, because until recently we have not monitored waste disposal. "Numbers of Americans have been placed at serious risk . . . and most of them don't even know it."[29]

One who thinks he recognizes the danger of burying nuclear waste is Jerry S. Szymanski, a government geologist working at Yucca Mountain, a barren ridge rising out of the Nevada desert. The government wants to dump the most highly radioactive waste in the nation inside the mountain; the project will cost up to $15 billion, and it may be completed by 2010. The government thinks Yucca Mountain—the last candidate after "a stormy, decades-long, multi-billion-dollar search . . . that eliminated dozens of other potential sites"—is the ideal place to bury the atomic debris for the next 10,000 years.[30]

Szymanski is convinced otherwise, and lately other geologists have been listening. "At the very least," one told a writer for *The New York Times Magazine,*

> the radioactive material would go into the ground water and spread to Death Valley, where there are hot springs all over the place, constantly bringing up water from great depths. It would be picked up by the birds, the animals, the plant life. It would start creeping out of Death Valley. You couldn't stop it. That's the nightmare. It could slowly spread to the whole biosphere. If you want to envision the end of the world, that's it.[31]

Dominion, or doom?

Indian reservations also seem attractive to entities that want to dispose of toxic waste. The reservations are isolated and relatively free from state and federal regulations and political pressures.

Tribes across America are grappling with some of the worst of the nation's pollution: uranium tailings, chemical lagoons, and illegal dumps. Among the most troublesome is a Mohawk reservation in Massena, New York, where a General Motors Corporation toxic waste site has fouled a river which used to provide the Indians with perch and pike. "These days, they buy their fish from New England vendors who ramble through the reservation in refrigerated trucks."[32]

Who Holds the Key?

Religion, not science, holds the key to dealing with the ecological crisis in the next millennium, says an increasing chorus of experts.

By Earth Day, 22 April 1990, organized religion had joined the front lines of the environmental movement, providing a potent army of activists among the 200 million participants in 140 countries ready for the fight to save the earth.

"Until recently," I wrote in April 1990 in a *Los Angeles Times* series about the environmental movement, "most religious groups had concentrated more on social issues such as racial discrimination and poverty than on the deteriorating environment. But that has changed with the growing realization that the environmental crisis has put human survival on the line and that ecology is a spiritual issue."[33]

One measure of that commitment was observed on Earth Day when church bells pealed for the health of the planet, sermons stressed the urgency of responsible environmental practices, and tens of thousands signed conservation declarations, pledging to recycle products, save energy, and vote for ecology-minded public officials.

But even more dramatic than the greening of religion is the way conservationists and environmentally conscious politicians have jumped on the spiritual bandwagon, embracing ecofaith. A vision of the "sacred" is critical to safeguarding the planet, many are saying now, sounding more like preachers and theologians than earth scientists or legislators.

"There's something different going on," affirms Jan Hartke, the religious liaison for Earth Day 1990, a follow-up of the first Earth Day in 1970. "Corporate, scientific and political leadership is feeling that the faith communities are needed very badly in this awakening of the spiritual and sacred dimension of environmental concern."[34]

EPA chief William K. Reilly told a gathering of Roman Catholic leaders in Washington that "natural systems have an intrinsic value— a spiritual worth—that must be respected for its own sake." A new "spiritual vision" of conservation and "an ethic of environmental stewardship grounded in religious faith . . . could be a powerful force."[35]

Meeting in January 1990 in Moscow, the Global Forum of Spiritual and Parliamentary Leaders on Human Survival issued a declaration that called for a "spiritually wise, technologically sound, ethical and farsighted stewardship of the planet." This appeal for joint efforts between religious leaders and scientists came from a group of international scientists invited by the event's organizer, U.S. astrophysicist Carl Sagan.

Even Soviet leader Mikhail Gorbachev, speaking at the Moscow forum, talked about the "ecological imperative" and noted that much of the damage already inflicted on nature "may be irreversible."

"Only recently," Gorbachev said, "has the U.S.S.R. realized the seriousness of the ecological threat. We were focused on our military and industrial growth. The country's vastness and material wealth permitted us to be insensitive. . . . Man needs to view himself as a part of nature—not above it." He went on to propose a six-point plan that included a binding global code of ethics for environmental preservation and the reduction of pollutants, and a "Green Cross," established through the United Nations, as an "International EPA."[36]

Meanwhile, the theme of environmental quality and "peace, justice and the integrity of creation" were heralded from church socials to the highest echelons of church leadership. If not eclipsed by an economic depression and/or war, ecofaith may become the "in" topic of the mainline religious chic between now and 2001.

That would be a change, for not too long ago environmentalists and religious leaders looked upon one another with antagonism, and hints of suspicion still linger.

In 1967, three years before the first Earth Day, historian Lynn White wrote a scathing article in *Science* magazine attacking the religious community for an interpretation of the Bible that seemed to give humans license to exploit nature, based on the Genesis 1:28 passage that speaks of man's superiority and gives the mandate to subdue and control nature.

But more recently, theologians as well as the people in the pew have reconsidered this "dominion theology." Now the passage emphasized is Genesis 2:15, which says God put humans in the garden to cultivate and care for it.

"While the environment is not to be worshiped, nor environmentalism to be made into a religion," says Los Angeles Episcopal Bishop Frederick Borsch, "the created world is a source of revelation to be revered, respected and fiercely protected."[37]

Although some religious activists fear that putting a major emphasis on the environment in the 1990s may dim the church's attention to social justice issues such as homelessness, health care, and racism, others reason that if people trash the planet, they also trash the food-production system, which hurts the poor. Also, as we have noted, the poor often end up living near toxic-waste dumps and working in pesticide-laden fields.

On the opposite end, some conservative Christians are afraid that the ecological movement has been co-opted by New Age environmentalists who worship the earth instead of its Creator and place concern for the environment above care of human beings.

Indeed some, like maverick religious scholar Father Thomas Berry and fellow Catholic priest Matthew Fox, speak of a "biocentric" theology and "creation spirituality." These concepts de-emphasize humanity's distinctiveness as the most important species on Earth and emphasize "the creative powers of the universe" over against redemption from sin and the need for personal salvation.[38]

Berit Kjos warned about some New Age ecologists and pantheists in *Focus on the Family* magazine, published by Christian psychologist James Dobson. They "believe in the living, evolving, self-regulating Earth. Some call her 'Gaia,' after the Greek earth goddess. Gaia can only be healed if humans will listen to her 'voice' and connect with her spirit."[39]

I agree that it's time to end the romantic nonsense about primitivism and mystic "nature people" advanced by some "eco-theologues." People who want to do something about the environment, counsels Martin Marty, "will have to do it in connection with technology, not in utopian escape from it."[40]

Personally, I go with Dean Ohlman, president of the Christian Nature Federation of Fullerton, California, who tells Christians to "be there with bells on" for ecological concerns, even if events like Earth Day do provide a platform for those who hold contrary worldviews.

> If we truly believe the God we worship was the Creator of the Earth, we need to show our concern. . . . Secular environmentalists tend to see man as the only entity that can save our planet. We believe only God can do that, but that He has chosen to use us as His servants who are expected to treat the Earth as a trust. . . . What we need to do as Christians is to clean up our stewardship act! . . . Believers need to step out of the isolation created by modern technology and begin to relate to the natural world. . . . [A]s we learn to respect it more, we will abuse it less.[41]

Designer Lifestyles

Back in the good old days if you missed the stagecoach, you'd wait around a day and catch the next one. Now, miss one place in a revolving door and you have a nervous breakdown.

"We're honking at our own taillights," says Frank Tillapaugh, with only slight exaggeration.[1]

Speed, hyper-speed, and a near-obsession with convenience, flexibility, tangibility, options, quality, short-term commitments, and individualism characterize the designer lifestyles of the fast-lane 1990s. Above all, we want to stay in control.

"What used to be called stable is now called inflexible and outdated," declares George Barna, president of the Barna Research Group in Glendale, California. "This is a video-driven generation, with a three- to four-minute attention span . . . used to short, crisp, colorful blocks" of video information.[2]

Convenience is increasingly a byword, adds Barna, who conducts marketing surveys for church leaders. "People will look for something that's ready, available and as simple as possible . . . Abstract or theoretical ideas won't interest most people. They want to be told quickly and efficiently. And they want things they can touch and feel."[3]

Individualism will be exalted, taking the place of the old allegiance to lifestyle conformity. Variety will be the rage, with experiments in new co-housing and shared community facilities. Look for novel religious philosophies as well as unusual occupations and leisure activities. But privacy, considered to be integral to individualism, will be prized.[4]

The quest for quality and competence will be critical in the competitively ruthless marketplace of 2001. The move from conspicuous consumption to critical consumption is already taking place. Satisfaction, not brand-name loyalty, will be the watchword—as true for local congregations and denominations as for consumer services.

Commitments to institutions, relationships, and products will be situational and short-term. Example: Book and record clubs found they had a hard time signing up new subscribers when multiple-year or multi-product commitments were required, so they've dropped those demands.[5]

And credibility will be hard to come by. Once lost, it will be even harder to recover. This will carry over into a "guilty until proven innocent" attitude toward alleged misdeeds of churches and their leaders.[6]

At Your Leisure

With the radical urbanization of the world's population, the radical breakdown of natural units like the family, and the radical reshaping of the way the mind processes information, many of our "traditional" values are on the way out.

In the next ten years, routine schedules will be rare. Vacations will be shorter and more frequent. We'll spend shorter and shorter blocks of time on more and more things. And the wristwatch will be more important than the wallet in determining priorities for most Americans, according to Barna and other trend-watchers.

Americans spend less time working now than they did twenty-five years ago—gaining about five hours of leisure a week. We may have a bit more nonworking time by 2001,[7] but what are we doing with all that "extra" time now?

Experts say that, regardless of the hours supposedly available, we generally *feel* as if we have *less* free time. This is attributed to such things as intensified job pressures, the dizzying explosion in leisure options (even for couch potatoes, there's more on television to choose from), and the fact that many members of the vocal baby boom generation only recently got around to having children of their own.

For many, the list of scheduled activities steadily lengthens. To accommodate people who complained they didn't have enough room on their calendars to fill in their daily plans, Hallmark Cards is now making ones with bigger day boxes.[8]

What we do with discretionary time is now the single most important thing to Americans, says Barna. And our concept of "discretionary time" is changing. If we've made a choice about how to use that time, then it's something we have to do and is no longer "free."

Take exercise. For many of us it's a "must," so it doesn't count in the leisure docket. But a growing focus on "active, productive leisure" rather than "mindless activities" is shaping the kind of activities that go in those calendar boxes. "It's purposeful things" for the boomers: seminars, health, therapy groups, cultural activities; the elders, in contrast, prefer travel, games, TV, dancing, and other pleasing pursuits they don't have to "work" at.[9]

All the while, television is barging ever more aggressively into the lives of our children: "Except for school and the family, no institution plays a bigger role in shaping American children," profoundly influencing the way they learn—and don't learn.[10]

Look also for this video/music generation to continue its fascination with heavy metal, rap, and themes that fixate on violence and sex and sneer at traditional religion. Increasingly, it would seem, schools and churches will need to use video and rap to communicate with this generation.

On another level, psychologists and counselors contend that many people are "overwhelmed and anxiety-ridden" because fast isn't fast enough anymore in a modern world paced by time-saving products and services. In fact, in an expected backlash from high-speed living, the later 1990s may well be a period of "cocooning," with many people spending more time at home.[11]

"What with VCRs, microwaves and the knowledge that the sexual revolution is over, it's easier than ever to stay home," maintains Ash DeLorenzo, trend director of BrainReserve Inc., a New York marketing firm. "People are also feeling that life has gotten too complicated and the excessiveness must be simplified."[12]

Couple this with the vague guilt experienced by many men who feel they aren't giving enough time and energy to their families, and you have the makings of a home-again trend. And, hey, with home-delivered videos and Domino guaranteeing a piping-hot pizza at the doorstep within thirty minutes, what's to go out for?

As for the current health kick, DeLorenzo and others think the freneticism will slow, while staying healthy will remain a priority well into the new century. People are bored with "tiny vegetables" and want real "mom food" like lots and lots of baked potatoes, meat loaf, and ice cream, he adds.[13] And menu maven Julia Child says we're going to "have more sense, go back to the pleasures of the table in a reasonable way. I think we'll go back to the simple foods—baked potatoes."[14] Joining potatoes will be a yen for international foods, particularly Asian cuisine, according to both Child and Naisbitt.

In fact, American decisions about food, clothing, and entertainment are fast blending with those from a potpourri of foreign cultures. "The merging global lifestyle," observe Naisbitt and Aburdene, "walks a thin line between greater options and greater homogenization, which decreases options."[15]

In fashion, global is in. For women it's going to be away from the "power dressing" and "aggressive look" of the 1980s. Soft, feminine, prettier; less uniform and more personal, predicts *Vogue* editor Anna Wintour. "At the same time, the athletic, more relaxed approach is going to be very important."[16]

Burgundy, pinks, variations of apple red, and earth tones will be popular colors in bedrooms and living rooms, predict designers. Furnishings of the mid-1990s and beyond? Bringing indoors anything previously used only outdoors.[17]

Bringing in the Values

But a far more serious consideration than what we eat or what we wear will be how we should live the next years—indoors and out.

"The great public battle is over culture—how we ought to live," says Richard Neuhaus, director of the Institute on Religion and Public Life in New York. "At least in America, for the overwhelming number of people, the moral questions are inseparable from the religious questions."[18] At the same time, more and more people are pointing to their lifestyle as the best definer of who they are and what they stand for.[19]

As Christian believers are barraged by secular influences which, in subtle and not-so-subtle ways, threaten to drain the credibility of their witness, many are uncritical or unaware of the distinction between culture-based values and values that derive from the Gospel of Jesus Christ. And 21st-century lifestyles will coalesce with moral and ethical issues radically different from anything known in biblical times.

"There is a growing distinctiveness in being a follower of Jesus," says lay Presbyterian Mark Cutshall of Seattle. "This is a time when there is greater tolerance of diverse beliefs and an unwillingness to challenge non-orthodox beliefs."[20]

Cutshall and others interviewed for this chapter were in strong agreement that sexual issues, particularly homosexuality and the devastating effects of AIDS, will be at the top of the moral challenges facing religious believers and organizations in the years ahead.

Bob Fryling, director of campus ministries for InterVarsity Christian Fellowship in Madison, Wisconsin, adds that dysfunctional families; alcohol, drug, and sexual addictions; pornography; and physical abuse and violence in childhood will also continue to grow at alarming rates in the next decade. (Sexual abuse of children has tripled since 1980.)[21] "We haven't seen the bottom of the iceberg on this one," Fryling told me with a sigh.[22]

"There's no question about it," nods George Gallup, Jr., the famous pollster. "The sex-related issues are going to be the most important issues facing all churches in the foreseeable future. Abortion, AIDS, premarital sex, homosexuality, all those are going to be at the vortex."[23]

Controversy over abortion and forms of contraception such as Norplant, a new female arm implant that lasts for up to five years, and RU 486, an "abortion pill" made in France, will continue to be a combat zone for ambivalent Americans as we cross into the next millennium.

But without doubt, both conservatives and liberals agree, homosexuality is "The Issue" for the church. The "Gay Nineties" surely have a different connotation than they did a hundred years ago!

Liberal minister William Sloan Coffin has said that homosexuality is probably the most divisive issue since slavery split the church.[24]

Meanwhile, conservatives in mainline churches are watching to see whether their denominations will go on record approving ordination for homosexual persons. Some regional bodies are already ordaining homosexuals and installing them as pastors; others are blessing the "marriage" covenants of same-sex couples. To many conservatives, The Issue is a kind of litmus test for whether they will stay in or leave their denomination.

Virtually all conservative denominations and evangelical colleges officially oppose homosexual behavior as unbiblical. But the number of homosexually inclined persons within conservative church circles may be no different from the percentage in liberal denominations or society at large. Commonly cited figures are 4 to 10 percent of men and 3 to 4 percent of women.[25]

The pressure to accept active homosexuality as an appropriate— even normal—lifestyle will only increase as the 1990s fade into the next century. By 1990, gay travelers were finding more places where they could openly travel and vacation.[26] Lesbian college students were "coming out," taking a higher profile and even founding lesbian social sororities.[27]

And while individuals and church committees struggle to interpret recent research about gay men and lesbians, the AIDS epidemic looms, an overshadowing specter.

Coming to the AIDS of the Afflicted

In January 1991 the number of known deaths in the United States attributed to AIDS passed the 100,000 mark—more than died in the Vietnam War.[28] Experts predict that New York City alone will eventually tally more AIDS-related deaths than America suffered in its last *four* wars.[29]

AIDS, caused by the Human Immunodeficiency Virus (HIV), is shaking the very foundations of America's future and threatens to change our culture for decades to come. Alarmingly, the epidemic is spreading most rapidly in the nation's inner cities.[30]

Because the infection rate is probably twelve to fifteen times greater among blacks than among whites, says Shepherd Smith, who with his wife, Anita, heads Americans for a Sound AIDS/HIV Policy (ASAP), a national Christian organization, "by 2000 we will consider AIDS to be a 'minority disease.'" And because the messages about the danger of AIDS have not had an impact on teens, "after the turn of the century, it will become a disease of *adolescents* of all races."[31]

Sexual activity among teens climbed in the 1980s; the proportion of girls aged fifteen to nineteen who had sexual intercourse rose from 47 percent in 1982 to 53 percent in 1988, with the increase being greatest among whites and in higher-income families.[32]

Today's 1.5 million to 2 million HIV-infected individuals will become ill and die in the decades ahead. This, the Smiths say, will present "one of the biggest ministry challenges ever to confront the church in America." Through education in churches and schools, they emphasize,

> Our strategy is to send a strong message regarding sexual integrity. The risks must be shown, but we don't want to overreact out of unreasonable fear.
>
> The optimal message is abstinence [before marriage]. If not, you must know the HIV status of your partner. Next, is condoms, but in the context that condoms have a failure rate of 10-15 percent.
>
> What will end this epidemic is interrupting its transmission, through knowledge.[33]

"By 1993," says Smith, "AIDS/HIV will affect us all. Experts tell us every person will know at least one individual infected by HIV. That means every church in the United States will ultimately have to address the issue."[34]

The Smiths' ASAP organization is one of several Christian models for ministry that can play a decisive role, emphasizing redemptive compassion for those infected and presenting a clear message of prevention for those not infected. Part of ASAP's work is to help churches develop AIDS policy statements so that when the question of AIDS ministry arises—as it will sooner rather than later—a congregation is ready.

Archbold Evangelical Mennonite Church in Archbold, Ohio, for example, adopted a written statement that supports, through foster care and adoption, children infected or affected by AIDS. And the congregation has faced the sticky wicket of what to do when HIV-infected children appear at church: "Should a parent or guardian of an HIV-infected child desire fellowship at Archbold EMC, we shall seek to support them by providing nursery care that is age-appropriate."[35]

Another ecumenical AIDS work is Beyond Rejection Ministries, based in Long Beach, California. It is directed by James Johnson, a lay Catholic, who became involved in AIDS work through counseling homosexuals. Beyond Rejection Ministries operates two shelters for persons with AIDS and an AIDS "hotel" for homeless persons with the disease.[36]

Another group, the AIDS Interfaith Council, an association of clergy and laity, provides educational and service programs as well as "congregation-based care to people with AIDS and their loved ones."[37]

"It is time," writes Dr. Robert R. Redfield, Jr., of the Walter Reed Army Institute of Research,

> to reject the temptation of denial of the AIDS/HIV crisis; to reject false prophets who preach the quick-fix strategies of condoms and free needles; to reject those who preach prejudice; and to reject those who try to replace God as judge. The time has come for the Christian community—members and leaders alike—to confront the epidemic with the commitment that comes from Christ's example.[38]

For Christians, the question will persist: how to respond in the midst of the crises of values and designer lifestyles that will stretch, bend—and perhaps break apart—the society of 2001.

Nuclear Family Fission

Arriving home from work, the harried husband, hand on his forehead, has just realized his ghastly goof. His wife—I'm assuming they're married, although that's a bit risky these days—opens the front door to let him in. "Great!" she says. "You remembered to pick up dinner, but where are the kids?"

This was a promo for a fall 1990 television special, "You've Come the Wrong Way, Maybe" about the "modern American maze."

"Too often," said the ad copy, "dual careers lead to dueling priorities. We're eager to balance fulfilling lives at home and the office—but can we really 'have it all?' From careers to companionship to children, today's women and men are facing tougher choices than ever before."[1]

And we ain't seen nothin' yet!

Family experts warn that value conflicts may be the fastest-growing area of family concern. Still, our churches seem to offer little help.

"Many churches emphasize the importance of traditional family life, and although many people claim to believe in this traditional approach, they do not act on these beliefs," declares researcher George Barna. "Because of this, they are uncomfortable with what the church is preaching."[2]

What is this "traditional" American family that so many idealize?

A Family Is . . . a Family

The so-called nuclear family was based on the model of an intact marriage with the husband as breadwinner and the wife at home caring for two or more children. Forty years ago more than half of all American families fit that pattern; now, about 10 percent do. In the typical family today both husband and wife work. Another 6 million households are headed by single parents (one in four families); and some 8 million seniors live alone.

In 1960, married couples (with and without children) made up three-fourths of U.S. households. Twenty years later that had dropped to 60 percent—and by the turn of the millennium it is projected to decline to 53 percent. The other side of the coin is that while "nonfamily" households accounted for 15 percent of all households in 1960, they will reach almost 30 percent by 2001. Today, more than 2.9 million households are composed of unmarried couples,[3] an increase of 80 percent over that of 1980.[4]

In 1990, however, homemaking mothers married to breadwinning fathers still comprised the largest category of families with young children: one-third of the nation's 14.8 million families with preschool children. The DIWK (double income with kids) households (about 30 percent) are catching up fast, though. And the single-parent family is also gaining because of divorce and the birth explosion among unwed mothers: up from 5 percent of all births in 1960 (and 22 percent of all black births) to 22 percent in 1985 (60 percent of blacks).[5] Also, the trend is growing for partners living together to have children without being married: by 1990 about one of every 15 children was born to partners out of wedlock.[6]

It isn't just the traditional family people—like James Dobson and his Family Research Council or Christian broadcaster Pat Robertson—who are worried about nuclear family fission and the effects of married women working outside the home.[7] In a *Time* magazine article on the dilemmas of child rearing, Philip Elmer-DeWitt points to some probing questions:

> Parents today, primed by racks of best-selling child-care manuals, are haunted by questions about their changing roles. What kind of bonding takes place when a child is passed

from one paid caretaker to another? What are the risks of growing up without a stable nuclear family or any real community support? How do values get passed from one generation to the next when the dominant cultural influences on children are television, pop music and Nintendo?[8]

After culling a wide variety of sources, here's how Judith Waldrop and several other experts think home life will be redefined in the 21st century:

- By 2000, more than half of all children will spend part of their lives in single-parent homes.
- By 2010, about one in three married couples with children will have a stepchild or an adopted child.
- Interracial marriage and adoption, spurred by immigration and growing social acceptance, will "darken the face" of the average American family.
- Most children will never know a time when their mothers did not work outside the home.[9]
- The fastest-growing segment of homemakers in the 21st century will be unmarried men who live alone or head families.
- Alternatives to marriage will be sought by older people as well as young singles.
- Households now defined by the U.S. Census Bureau as "non-families" will eventually receive legal recognition as "families" in every state. Such arrangements will include unmarried heterosexual couples, homosexual couples, and friends who "intentionally" live together.[10] (The current standard definition of what constitutes a family is a group of two or more persons related by birth, marriage, or adoption and residing together.)[11]
- There will be increasing pressure to redefine "family" as "a group of people who love and care for each other."[12]

Two-Career Families

Usually impelled by the need for money, the two-career family faces the dilemma of balancing work and home. Unless there is a dramatic shift away from the kind of economy that we have become accustomed to, this dollar factor isn't going to leave us anytime soon.

In many households two incomes are essential to pay for the necessities. Still, many are plagued by anxiety, fearing that they are spending too little time with their children. Nearly 40 percent of fathers and 80 percent of mothers in Los Angeles and Orange Counties said they would quit their jobs, if they could, to rear their children at home, according to a survey commissioned by *The Los Angeles Times* in 1990. The poll found that with 65 percent of couples with children, both husband and wife were employed. The good news in the survey was that a large majority of parents "care profoundly about family life."[13]

Commenting on the survey, Dr. Joyce Brothers, psychologist and syndicated columnist, said it was important that "men on all economic levels are worrying about the family and putting it and children's welfare front and center in their lives. For 80 percent of men, family and children were the most important things in life, beyond even work, career and leisure time."[14]

This squares with a survey conducted at 521 of the nation's largest companies among employees who work at home: 40 percent who work from home are men, and 88 percent of these are managers. "More and more executives are making career decisions based solely on what kind of home life they can have with a particular job," said Kathleen Christensen, who conducted the study.[15]

The bad news is that there is little evidence that parents—especially men—actually spend as much time with their children as they say they would like to. "Many cannot live up to their ideals of even the most mundane family traditions, such as eating dinner together," the Southern California survey revealed. The largest gap, interestingly, was between those parents who felt it was important to attend church services (65 percent) and those who actually attended (48 percent).

Some statistics indicate that many teenagers spend an average of less than thirty minutes a week in a "meaningful relationship" with their mothers and fifteen minutes a week with their fathers.[16]

Apparently young adults now in their twenties experienced that when they were growing up. This group

> wants to spend more time with their kids, not because they think they can handle the balance of work and child rearing any better than their parents did but because they see them-

selves as having been neglected. "My generation will be the family generation," says Mara Brock, 20, of Kansas City. "I don't want my kids to go through what my parents put me through." . . . Says Kip Banks, 24, a graduate student in public policy at the University of Michigan: "When I raise my children, my approach will be my grandparents', much more serious and conservative. I would never give my children the freedoms I had."[17]

Nine out of ten evangelical Christians accept the changing gender roles that accompany the two-career pattern, saying that spouses should equally shoulder parenting and household tasks. But again, in practice, a 1990 study by *Christianity Today* magazine found that only moderate shifting of household responsibilities occurs when the wife works full-time. Working wives must frequently do double duty, or at least the lion's share of the denkeeping. Apparently husbands think they do more at home than their wives do! And the breakdown of traditional sex roles has blurred responsibilities.

The *Christianity Today* study also found that evangelicals (both men and women) are evenly divided between those who approve and those who disapprove of women who work outside the home while their children are young.[18]

The child-care issue is at the heart of the controversy. Only the next generation will tell us for sure whether day care and substitute parenting provide the same support and psychological nurturing that parents can give.

A 1990 Census Bureau report showed that 30 percent of preschoolers are cared for in their own homes by someone other than their mother—about half by their fathers, slightly more than a quarter by other relatives, and about one-fifth by babysitters, nannies, or other professional caretakers. Another fourth of preschoolers were in day-care centers or nursery schools.

As the 1990s tick by, American families will be using child-care facilities in increasing numbers. And they will be paying more for the services, which by 1987 already cost the nation a whopping $15.5 billion annually. Day-care centers doubled during the 1980s and home-care services increased at an even faster rate.[19]

Child care is still in short supply, so expect more private business firms to fill the gap as employee pressure mounts for the service to be provided as part of their compensation. Campbell Soup Company, for instance, has an exemplary on-site day-care center that draws inquiries about the program from five or six major companies every week.[20] More churches and other religious groups will have to organize to provide quality day care to fill the swelling need of the 1990s and beyond. And underline the word *quality.*

Meanwhile, as the government continues to hash over ways to target child-care aid to needy families through vouchers or tax credits, some voices are suggesting that tax credits be given to reward women who stay home and care for their children.[21]

Single-parent Families and Unmarried Couples

And what about children in single-parent homes, which represent about one out of four family groups at present and are expected to grow to 13 million households by the end of the century?[22] For such households, a mother or father who can stay home rather than work is a rarity if not an impossibility.

Single-parent families occur through divorce, the death of a spouse, and unwed parenting. According to the March 1988 report of the Census Bureau, a third of single-parent families were headed by a divorced mother, 28 percent by a never-married mother, 22 percent by a separated mother, and 6 percent by a widow. Divorced fathers, meanwhile, headed 6 percent of single-parent homes; separated fathers, 3 percent; never-married fathers, 2 percent; and widowers, 1 percent.[23]

Some single-parent families are outstanding successes, and experts caution against generalizations. But a study by the American Academy of Pediatrics describes the risks, ranging from "mild cognitive delays in preschoolers to withdrawal and depression in older kids. Children pressured by aggressive scheduling often show signs of chronic stress."[24]

Single-parent poverty is another major problem, exacerbated by the rising number of black, female-led families (now more than half of all black families). These mothers tend to be on the lowest rungs of the wage ladder.

Each year more than one million teens will become pregnant.

Four out of five will be unmarried, and 30,000 under the age of fifteen.[25] Ninety percent of the babies born to blacks between the ages of fifteen and nineteen are born out of wedlock. And as teen mothers of all races are less and less inclined to marry or put their children up for adoption, most of their infants will be reared in fatherless homes.[26]

Another "permutation of the American family" is the small but increasing number of unmarried women who have made "a calculated and intentional decision to raise a child single-handedly, despite a tangle of cultural, biological and sometimes legal complications."[27] When the desire to reproduce overtakes the desire to be married, these women may opt for intercourse with a selected partner, or artificial insemination from a known or unknown donor.

"I could imagine going through life without a man," explains Paula Van Ness, 39, executive director of the National Community AIDS Partnership in Washington, "but I couldn't imagine going through life without a child. My biological clock started sounding like a time bomb."[28]

Sociologists are astounded by another social change: the swift rise in unmarried cohabitation, official-speak for couples living together.

Half of all adults under age thirty will live with someone before they get married. Sixty percent of recently marrieds acknowledge they lived with their new spouse before getting married.

But the LTA (Living Together Arrangement) hasn't improved marital stability. Census Bureau statistics cited by Barna indicate that people who cohabit before marriage are even more likely than others to divorce.[29] Nevertheless, families will surely be in conflict over these premarital living situations well into the next century despite what seems to be a gradual, and perhaps resigned, acceptance of the practice even in conservative church circles. Whether such couples will generally be welcome as active members or leaders remains to be seen.

Solo Singles and Childless Couples

By 2001, more than half of all American adults will be single. Older single women, either divorced or widowed, are the fastest-growing household group in the nation.[30]

Because of this growing number of singles, vital congregations will need strong singles ministries that provide a sense of family and a network of support.

One that already does is Second Baptist Church in Houston, a city where 53 percent of the population is single. The congregation, pastored by H. Edwin Young, boasts the nation's largest church program for singles. It has an enrollment of 3,600 in just its singles ministries and twenty-two age-graded singles classes![31]

But while a number of churches have effective singles programs, few are doing much, if anything, for another increasing segment of the population: the many couples who are choosing not to have children.

Recently a young Catholic couple without children, friends of ours, lamented that their church has nothing designed for them. In fact, they say, they feel an inhospitable environment there.

Perhaps what they sensed was a reflection of the view prevalent in Catholicism, Judaism, Mormonism, and Protestant fundamentalism: that bearing children is "essential and central to marriage."[32] If that attitude persists through the decade, don't be surprised to find few childless couples coming to church.

Divorce, Remarriage, and Blending

Pennsylvania lawmaker George Saurman introduced a bill on the last day of the 1990 legislative session that would give the clergy power to divorce couples. Although he admitted his measure had little chance of passing—at least not very soon—he reasoned that if clergy are entrusted to create legal marriages, "we could entrust them to dissolve them legally."[33]

That's going too far, in my opinion, even in a country where divorce and remarriage are accepted by seven out of ten people.[34] Better would be the proliferation of clergy-led services where couples recommit to their wedding vows on important anniversary dates—say at ten, twenty, or twenty-five years and in five-year increments beyond that. It would be a celebration that "we've made it" in a divorce-prone era and at a time when typical longevity means that couples have the potential for a longer married life than ever before.

Divorce rates in the United States doubled between the 1950s and the 1980s, from 2.5 per thousand to 5.2.[35] Then in the late 1980s and early 1990s there was disagreement over whether the divorce rate had leveled off or was even dipping slightly. Optimists cited the availability of many more materials to help hurting families and the accessibility to more and better-trained counselors. They saw these as signs that the incidence of splitting up was slimming down.

But two University of Wisconsin researchers claimed that the government was "seriously underreporting" divorce and separation and predicted that two out of every three currently married couples would break up.[36]

Whether the Wisconsin researchers are right or wrong—hopefully wrong—many family analysts say the biggest marital change of the 1990s will not be fewer married people. Rather, it will be acceptance of "serial monogamy"—people consciously planning to have different mates for each stage of life. "Term" marriage options will be a reality, predicts Fay Angus.[37]

"By 2000," says George Barna, "Americans will generally believe that a life spent with the same partner is both unusual and unnecessary. We will continue our current moral transition by accepting sexual relationships with one person at a time . . . to be the civilized and moral way to behave. But we will not consider it at all unusual to be married two or three times during the course of life."[38]

Since these predictions already appear to be materializing, we can expect the number of remarriages and "blended" families to sky-rocket.

The authors of *Lifetrends* suggest, not facetiously, that a child of divorced parents whose grandparents have also separated may need a computer program to tell which relatives are where in his or her family. "In fact," they write, "making family trees may take on a much greater—and more practical—importance for this generation of grandchildren. It would not be surprising to see a standardized form, not to mention computer software, readily available for families that want to teach their grandchildren how they are related to everyone else in their family."[39]

The Stepfamily Association of America estimates that in 1990 there were 35 million stepparents and that 1,300 new stepfamilies are formed each day, with 10 percent of all children under the age of eighteen living in stepfamilies.[40]

The question for the church is: While still championing the nuclear family as the ideal, are they offering effective curriculum, counseling, and family services to help those—both children and adults—dealing with divorce, single-parenting, remarriage, and blended family situations?

Adoption and Foster Parents

Although the adoption option is nothing new, in recent decades it has undergone major changes that will persist into the next century if other lifestyle trends discussed here remain in place. Because more young mothers with unplanned pregnancies either abort or keep their babies, adoptive parents often wait years, hassle with incredible paperwork, and spend thousands of dollars before they succeed in securing a child. And the children who can be adopted tend to be "older children, handicapped children, sibling groups, or international children."[41]

Foster parenting bears similarities to adoption, but the care is usually temporary (eighteen months is the median length of time a child remains in continuous substitute care). Also, foster families, who must be legally certified, receive modest compensation.

The possibilities for short-term investment in a child's life through foster parenting can be rich and rewarding. I'll never forget the six months I was a foster father to a high school senior when I was in my early thirties and my wife and I also had two toddlers of our own. Penny won a permanent place in our hearts and stayed on until she turned eighteen and was married.

Don and Helen Gibbs, both in their fifties with three grown children and three grandchildren, cared for more than ten youngsters in their Southern California home over a three-year period. They were enticed to try foster parenting by a program at their neighborhood church.

"We wanted to do what we could for children who are often abused, nearly starved, molested and hungry for love," said Helen.[42]

More foster parents like the Gibbses will be needed as court-ordered care increases during this decade. Nationwide about 300,000 children under eighteen were in substitute care in 1988; more than half were teenagers.[43]

One innovative Christian group doing something about abandoned children is Child S.H.A.R.E. (Shelter Homes: A Rescue Effort). Child S.H.A.R.E. draws together foster-parent "shareholders," volunteers, consultants, and financial partners and networks with about fifty Los Angeles-area churches.

Foster care for babies born with AIDS is another crying need. Health officials estimate that one-fourth of such infants will not be cared for by their biological parents.[44]

Joyce Pilotti is a mother of three whose husband died from AIDS. She says God led her to found Arise and Shine Ministries to assist special-needs children by identifying Christian families to serve as transitional homes for children who are in the foster-care system. These "branch homes"—named for the scriptural metaphor of the vine and the branches—"provide Christian care for children whose mothers may be hospitalized or in drug rehabilitation programs, or who have been orphaned and will go on to be adopted."[45]

"Intentional" or Extended Families

Another family type that will blossom in a variety of shapes and hues as we approach 2001 is the so-called "intentional" family—a grouping of persons with or without children who share a common residence. There is nothing new about this style, of course; cooperatives, communes, and enclaves of various sorts have flowered for years across social, racial, and economic lines. Many have also faded.

Some of the more promising models for the 21st century will involve intentional families clustered around religious commitments, pooling resources and housing for ecological as well as financial benefit. Other extended families will evoke multigenerational models and cross-cultural units. Insights from Asian or African family patterns, for example, may be incorporated.

Ken Dychtwald, a well-known consultant on issues of aging, thinks the "child-focused nuclear family" will increasingly be replaced by the "matrix family, an adult-centered, transgenerational unit bound together by friendship and choice as well as by blood and obligation."[46]

Family experts Richard P. Olson and Joe H. Leonard suggest that church leaders attempt to raise the consciousness of their congregation regarding intentional families. If this happens, they aver, folks can be found who would benefit from new alliances:

> For example, a lonely older person needing attention but living in a spacious home might be teamed with a young family needing a place to live. Churches may be led to understand clearly that they are actually a larger intentional family (filled with adoptees), an extended family that includes all family units, including those units with one member.[47]

Chapter **9**

Educating Dick and Jane.
And Ramon and Natasha.

If your forecast for American education is "overcast," join the consensus:

- Quality education in the nation's public schools is in serious danger as language and discipline problems mount. Mass education, if not obsolete, needs a major overhaul—and quickly.
- While formal educational methods are on a slow trip to oblivion, information technologies—well advanced in the scientific and business worlds—won't make it inside most classrooms in the 1990s.
- Educators are split over the positive and negative aspects of using television and computers to educate Dick and Jane, Ramon and Natasha in the coming millennium.
- Education will—and does—compete with television, radio, and other forms of high-tech visual and electronic entertainment.

Media theorist Marshall McLuhan was right: the medium has become the message.

Amusing but Confusing

Specifically, educators and communications experts like Neil
Postman say that "television's principal contribution to educational
philosophy is the idea that teaching and entertainment are inseparable."[1]

What's so bad about that?

Plenty, says Postman in *Amusing Ourselves to Death*. In the closely
reasoned pages of his chapter on "Teaching as an Amusing Activity,"
Postman builds his case that the "Sesame Street" style of learning
has undermined the traditional notion of schooling.[2]

"'Sesame Street' appeared to be an imaginative aid in solving the
growing problem of teaching Americans how to read, while, at the
same time, encouraging children to love school," Postman writes.
"We now know that 'Sesame Street' encourages children to love
school only if school is like 'Sesame Street'. . . . It encourages them
to love television."

Not that television cannot be educational; it can. But, argues
Postman, it has usurped the classroom and the printed page as the
chief means of education "by its power to control the time, attention
and cognitive habits of our youth."

"One is entirely justified," he concludes, "in saying that the major
educational enterprise now being undertaken in the United States is
not happening in its classrooms but in the home, in front of the
television set, and under the jurisdiction not of school administrators
and teachers but of network executives and entertainers."[3]

TV's "anti-family" sitcoms like "The Simpsons" and "Married . . .
With Children" play up the cynical and the negative. Purporting
"realism," these anti-family storylines mock the traditional family and
its stabilities while causing viewers to passively accept the dysfunctional family as the "norm." Ozersky shows how the TV screen

> is an implicit invitation to participate in a vision of "society"
> largely designed to flatter us in sinister ways, manipulate our
> attention, and commit us to the status quo. In discrediting
> "yesterday's" family values in its various "breakthrough"
> shows (ostensibly defining "A Different World" for us, as the
> title of one series has it), TV seeks only to impose its own

values—which is to say, the values of the marketplace. Bart Simpson, master sneerer, is the prototype of the modern series character who—by the social scripts of TV—reflects us.[4]

Whether or not you agree with Postman and Ozersky, it seems incontrovertible that the audience shaped by "Sesame Street" has now reshaped all of television, as Jeffrey Moritz, president of National College Television, points out.[5]

Techno-Education

The answer, however, is not to spurn electronic education. Today's students are video-sophisticated and used to interactive screens—"screenies," Moritz calls them. They understand "video-logic" and are accustomed to making screens "do things." So, to be effective, tomorrow's educational systems will need to stay in sync with tomorrow's media systems. As we saw earlier, tomorrow's media will be complex, interactive, global, mobile, and virtually instant. And that is why savvy corporate sponsors are now nudging their noses into the education tent.

As we approach 2001, more and more corporations will be spending billions of dollars to provide employee-training programs that teach the basics—like reading and writing and arithmetic—missed the first time around by many students. They'll also teach technical, job-related skills indigenous to the information age. The firms hope the payoff will be brighter and more efficient workers who will improve the company's bottom line. The emphasis will be less on accumulating knowledge and more on knowing where to find information, which, say Toffler and others, is the key to power.

"We can cut schooling and teach people what they need to know when they need to know it, rather than laying up a store of knowledge," advocates Robert Theobald, chairman of Knowledge Systems, Inc.[6]

Although futurists generally agree that communications and computers will be at the core of future education, consensus is lacking regarding the degree and the rapidity that this will happen at the elementary-school level. So far, educational technology is underused. The typical school in 1990–91 spent just $35 per student—less than 1 percent of its budget—on all information-age technology.[7]

James A. Mecklenburger, director of the Institute for the Transfer of Technology to Education, touts the opportunities that modern tech presents: eliminating barriers that prevent disabled students from participating in schools; facilitating students' collection of original, local information to create their own "real-world" databases, and "distance learning." As examples of the latter, Mecklenburger lists "German by satellite," in which a native-born German professor teaches German to students in remote sites; and students in Virginia experience "electronic field trips" via satellite to mainland China or hold discussions with students in Wales.

"Information technology . . . is the most powerful educational force since chalk," enthuses Mecklenburger.[8]

Not everyone agrees. A top-heavy emphasis on techno-education overlooks the larger question of the decade—and no doubt the coming century: What is education for, and what are the common values we want to share with the next generation? Nor does it address the flaws of a nation with a growing population of the *morally* illiterate, not to mention the literally illiterate and the culturally illiterate.[9]

"Values clarification" will rage into the third millennium for sure. And educational issues will continue to be compounded by social issues such as poverty, the breakdown of families, and the ravages of crime, drugs, and AIDS.

"Unless we're able to solve the economic and social issues simultaneously, we will have an underclass that will drag America down economically," warns Vartan Gregorian, president of Brown University. "As Europe and Asia become strong, we will no longer be able to draw skilled immigrants—only the unskilled, compounding the problem of educating the waves of them coming in."[10]

Also compounding the problem will be the expanding need for multicultural curricula: Race and ethnicity have become an increasing source of both inspiration and friction for the country's frayed public education system.[11]

How should minority ideals—and whose—be portrayed in our

classrooms? We're not educating just Dick and Jane anymore; there's Ramon and Kae and Natasha and . . .

Failure of Public Education

By most indications, public education is failing. Massive funds, new leadership, and a change of heart regarding educational philosophy are needed to "fix" it. Some say it's broke, all right, but "it ain't worth fixing."

Analysts head their "problem lists" with these items:

- The huge high school dropout rate—at least one in four, with Hispanic students more than twice as likely as whites not to graduate.[12]
- More college dropouts as education costs skyrocket and degrees don't necessarily produce well-paying jobs. In 1990, four years at a private college or university cost an average of $56,000 (tuition, room and board, books, and fees); expect twice that by 2001, when the average costs for four years at state schools will have risen to $57,000.[13] (Figures in 1990 for four years at Christian colleges—tuition only—were in the $16,000 to $25,000 range.)[14]
- The high degree of functional illiteracy—estimated to be somewhere between 23 million and 60 million U.S. adults. One study indicated that 61 percent of all seventeen-year-olds can't read their high school textbooks.[15] Churches will need to be at the forefront of the literacy movement as well as teaching simple math and household finances.
- A shrinking faculty and lack of strong leadership. Projections show a shortage of 1.1 million elementary and high school teachers and a half-million professors in this decade. About half of the nation's tenured professors will retire, and up to 75 percent of the current chief administrators in the big-city school districts will step down before the turn of the century.[16] "So where is our seed corn? And who will educate the educators?" ponders Brown President Gregorian.
- Huge and wasteful expenditures. Most informed people believe there is a poor return on the taxpayer's education dollar. Through polls, referenda, and frequent defeat of school-tax

increases, the public is turning thumbs-down on a system that "appears costly, ineffective and inefficient."[17]

Bright Patches on Campus

Despite the dark skies, there are signs that, at the college level at least, immigration and innovation may lift the clouds as we move into the next century.

Asian-Americans, whose numbers are increasing rapidly in the United States, tend to be well educated: 44 percent hold college degrees compared to about 25 percent of the U.S. population as a whole.[18] Meanwhile, there will be no letup in the rush by tens of thousands of foreign students to enroll in U.S. universities, especially the research and graduate programs. In 1989 foreign students earned more than a quarter of the doctoral degrees awarded in the nation.[19]

Then there are the baby boomers and the elders mentioned earlier: they will be increasingly attracted back to schools and campuses during the decades of the 1990s and beyond.

The retirement destination of many elder boomers will be the outskirts of college towns, the atmosphere in which many of them matured, where they will take advantage of visiting lecturers, creative artists, music events, and physical recreation facilities. Universities will become centers for lifelong study and enjoyment of the arts and will offer training and noncredit classes in many art forms.[20]

"With a smaller generation of college students due in coming decades," suggest the *Lifetrends* book authors, "the schools will need boomer elders and will make class auditing and recreational facility privileges part of their housing packages. These arrangements will encourage developers to endow cultural activities at nearby schools, with the proviso that residents of the projects receive reduced rates on tickets."[21]

Elderhostel, a prominent adult education program, will become "a major institution in our country." It offers study opportunities on more than a thousand U.S. campuses and in thirty-seven other countries for seniors over sixty. Participants spend a week in college dorms attending campus cultural events, auditing a wide variety of classes, and using school recreational facilities. Growing at a rate of about 20 percent a year, Elderhostel often enables seniors to combine travel and study at reasonable rates.[22]

Have churches thought about devising special programs to link up with these folks when they're in town?

Expect education programs in shopping malls and public libraries to be popular for older adults in the decades ahead.

Career changes, commonly four to six in a lifetime during the coming decades, will necessitate a back-to-the-classroom move by many young and middle-aged adults. And, because lower-level jobs will be plentiful, many young people will work for awhile before they go to college. When they do matriculate, they'll mix school with part-time work. By 2001, half of all college students will be aged 25 and up.[23]

The nation's 1,200 community and junior colleges will help fill the gap between the cost crunch and the need for job-related training, serving as a more useful model for many students than the four-year college.

Alternatives to Public Education

The weather picture for Christian higher education is variable patterns with storms and intermittent sun. A layer of thin endowments and high costs will prevail across the entire horizon.

Colleges and universities affiliated with mainline denominations are in for a hard time, with both the budget blues and an erosion into secularization. The secular slide is already well under way and destined to be virtually complete by 2001.

"The modern university has forgotten its spiritual foundations," observes Mark R. Schwehn of Christ College at Valparaiso University.[24] Dorothy Bass, a professor at the University of Chicago Divinity School, agrees. Most church-affiliated colleges and universities have become so totally "missions for secularization [that] it's hard to know a church-affiliated college when you see one," she said, adding that the drift is the reason why many people drop out of mainline churches.[25]

If, then, distinctively Protestant higher education has been left by default to the evangelicals, what's the weather report in this quarter?

Trend-watcher Sine thinks that "in spite of many of the fine things they are doing and all the publicity about the 'integration of faith and learning,' they tend to be profoundly coopted by the values of the dominant culture . . . . I believe they are doing more to prepare the Christian young to fit into upscale lifestyles and professional occupations of modern society instead of learning to be a counter-cultural agenda working for the kingdom."[26]

Others, like University of Virginia sociologist James Davison Hunter, conclude that the coming generation of evangelicals may be moving away from the key beliefs that once defined evangelicals.[27]

Church growth analyst Elmer Towns foresees the collapse of the old-line Bible colleges, but thinks emerging "denominations" like the Vineyard Fellowship and Calvary Chapels, as well as some of the megachurch congregations, will form new Bible schools. These new institutions will usually center on methodology: They will have a statement of purpose and mission, he says, but will be "functional, not doctrinal," in orientation.[28]

Scholars like Carl Lundquist of the Christian College Consortium are anxious to have the academic environment remain open so students can grapple with contending ideas in order to strengthen their own beliefs. "We need to find room between rigid indoctrination and a wholly open campus atmosphere."[29]

Private, Parochial, and Home Schools

If money were not a factor, according to about half of the parents of public school students, they would send at least one of their children to a private or parochial school.[30] Indeed, the demand for both has increased as quality public education has spiraled downward, and these trends are likely to continue.

While parochial schools have declined in number and enrollments during the past decade, the Catholic church is committed to holding the line wherever possible, producing quality education with religious and moral values. These schools provide a bright patch of light in contrast to the dismal public-school scene, especially in the inner cities.

Meanwhile, between 1965 and 1988, enrollment in non-Catholic religiously affiliated schools grew by 150 percent to 2.5 million students.[31] Evangelical schools now compromise about 6 percent of America's elementary and secondary school population.

"The evangelical Protestant community is increasingly disenchanted with the non-Christian schools of the country," says Paul Kienel, executive director of the Association of Christian Schools International, which represents about a half-million students in 2,750 schools. "They feel alienated; their views are not listened to in the public school system."

But despite a steady growth of about 5 percent a year, conservative Christian schools enrolled children from only one in five evangelical families in 1991.[32]

The explosive growth is in the mushrooming home-school movement—parents teaching children privately at home. The phenomenon is gaining support from more educators as well as enthusiastic parents who like the individual attention, lower costs ($500 to $600 a year for the best materials), and hands-on control. Home schooling was the choice for parents of somewhere between 500,000 and 1 million children in early 1991, ten times the number just a decade earlier.[33]

I foresee the numbers multiplying at a dizzying pace well past 2001, forcing state authorities to further ease existing regulations; in turn, parents will feel more confident about overcoming the remaining legal ramifications of home schooling. (Laws in some states were being challenged in 1991, such as requiring teacher competence tests or college degrees for parents.)[34]

The home-school movement is neither exclusively religion-oriented nor a backwoods alternative to liberal education, but the conservatives and fundamentalists do make up its backbone.

"The school system and the National Education Association are so out of step with the average American family," declares Pat Sikora, a Redwood City, California, parent who home-schools Joshua, 6. "What American families want is a good education for their children in a values-oriented, violence-free atmosphere."

Joshua's schooling at home is augmented by activities with a group of about thirty Christian families who have formed a local home-school support group.

"Home schooling allows tailoring each subject to a child's

developmental and intellectual level," adds Pat. "Nobody is going to love my child like I do or take care of him the way I will or pay the price to make sure he's learning and enjoying learning the way I will. I will go that extra mile for him. I want him to love learning and to retain it."[35]

Apparently Joshua and many others like him do: he was in "first grade" in 1991 but reading at a fourth- to fifth-grade level. Home-schooled children seem to do better than "school-schooled" kids on standardized tests, and concerns about "socialization" have faded "as more Americans have realized that the environments provided by strongly committed parents compare favorably with the value-free, peer-dominated culture of many public schools."[36]

A study in 1986 showed, in fact, that (1) children taught at home appeared not to be socially deprived; (2) the longer children were taught at home, the higher their self-concept; and (3) self-concept was unrelated to the parents' educational levels.[37]

Look for new models of education as 2001 nears, with churches providing increasing numbers of "home-school co-ops." Here's how the Sikoras's group works:

> We have seven families and thirteen kids who gather at our church each Tuesday morning for three hours. Having the larger group encourages us to do more time- and energy-consuming projects. So far this year we've studied kings, knights, and the medieval period (complete with a medieval feast and costumes); horses (with a Western day and costumes); Thanksgiving (with an almost authentic Pilgrim and Indian feast); and a nativity play for the dads and grandparents. Clearly, this is the high point of the week for all of the children.[38]

Next thing you know, they'll have more group meetings and a few more children and then more parents will volunteer as teachers and then they'll pay them a little and. . . .

Another model involving parental choice is in place in Milwaukee. There, parents of 1,000 low-income public-school children receive a $2,500 voucher from the city for tuition at the private school of their choosing. If successful, the Milwaukee plan is to spread throughout Wisconsin.

Similar and modified plans will spring up all over America by 2001, Pat Robertson expects: "a free-market educational system well on the way to returning quality to our classrooms. If 40 percent of our school systems move into the free market, I predict that the remainder will follow quickly . . . . There would be no more education monopoly where parents had one choice: the gray mediocrity of present-day public schools."[39]

Sunday School on the Rocks

While home-schooling is growing, church school is not. Sunday-school attendance is on the skids.

In the major old-guard Protestant churches, Sunday school enrollments are plummeting even faster than overall membership (we'll look at the causes for that in chapter 13). Between 1970 and 1990, church-school participation in the mainline denominations decreased an average of 55 percent.

Dorothy Bass, a Chicago Theological Seminary professor, blames the mainline decline on failure "to transmit the meaning and excitement of Christianity from one generation to another, one person to another."[40]

Comments Martin Marty wryly: "The populace complains that 'they took God out of the schools' and has shown how little the complaint means by doing nothing about locating the kids where God-talk is encouraged."[41]

Well, almost nothing. Some "boomer churches" are booming with the boomers' kids, but not enough to reverse the overall downturn.

"The Sunday school," says Robert Lynn of the Lilly Endowment in Indianapolis, "while never as dismal and enfeebled as detractors say, is increasingly archaic in a time when family patterns have changed."[42]

And yet, as Harvard professor and psychiatrist Robert Coles discovered in his extensive exploration of children's minds and souls, youngsters grapple with profound questions about spiritual things.

"I've been stunned by what they told me about God," he says. "In trying to figure out how the planet came into being, how man as a species came into being, how long all this will last, they call upon God for an answer."[43]

But what's happening in children's lives in hidden, inner reflection doesn't easily translate to exterior action and participation.

Is there an answer?

Studies seem to show that there is hope in revitalizing the *adult* Sunday school, which, in turn, may carry on down the line, as Bass says, to transmit excitement about the faith from one generation to the next. The churches of the 1990s and beyond could begin by looking to the model of Jesus' Sermon on the Mount where the crowd is described as being "astonished at his teaching, for he taught them as one who had authority, and not as their scribes."[44]

Also, a congregation doesn't have to be large to educate well, according to Peter L. Benson, director of the Search Institute in Minneapolis. "Smaller congregations often excel at providing one or two outstanding ways to learn."[45]

He also recommends:

- That the elderly be connected in a meaningful, relational way to children, adolescents, and younger adults.
- That more emphasis be placed on teaching parents faith-development skills.
- That service be made a cornerstone of educational programming, since some of the best religious education occurs in moments of giving, of connection, of bonding to others.[46]

The Search Institute conducted an extensive study of six major Protestant denominations involving 11,000 people in 561 randomly chosen congregations. The conclusion was that, of all aspects of church life, "an effective Christian education program has the strongest tie to a person's growth in faith and to loyalty to one's congregation and denomination." Yet only three out of ten Protestant high schoolers and adults devote as much as one hour a week to study, reflection, and conversation at church (beyond worship).

Nothing matters more than quality Christian education, the study concluded.[47]

Phantoms of Stage, Screen, and Canvas

As I headed north on Robertson Boulevard toward the Makk Gallery in Beverly Hills, I was eager to meet artist Steven Lavaggi. Having heard him described as a "modern-day Michelangelo" and "a positive, spiritual Salvador Dali," I was curious about his style of "visionary painting."

I was not disappointed. The curly-haired artist, displaying a perpetually sunny smile, showed off his "glimpse of glory" cloud series; the "jungle journey" series of man's physical pilgrimage through life; the "beside still waters" series inspired by the Twenty-third Psalm, and the sleek, streamlined images of his "in the light" series, emerging from darkness into eternal light.

"There is a need for newness all the time," explained Lavaggi, who describes himself as a Spirit-filled Christian. "Younger people are tired of the old 'praying hands' kind of traditional art. They want to look forward, not back. Yet they need to be lifted up to the greater, unseen, kingdom-reality that lies beyond their next paycheck."[1]

Lavaggi collectors range from a Motley Crue music producer and the Scorpions' lead guitarist to movie-makers and entertainment luminaries. "Rock stars and movie celebrities need peace, too," states Lavaggi, adding that he often gives a verbal Christian witness to such notables.

The new dimension in *spiritual* art (Lavaggi eschews the term *religious* art) is a subtle witness, "an intelligent, loving sharing of Christ."

Spiritual Dimensions

The risen Christ is also the theme of much of the forward-looking art of Isabel and Edith Piczek. Their large mural paintings, mosaic and ceramic tile murals, and stained-glass windows grace more than 400 buildings in seven countries.

At the age of fourteen, Isabel won the International Grand Award for painting and was soon commissioned to paint a 400-square-foot fresco mural at the famed Pontifical Biblical Institute in Rome.

The Piczek sisters share with Lavaggi the belief that people are turning toward the "spiritual" in painting as they seek reason and reassurance in a world of confusion.

"While abstract art is dying, secular art is turning to 'realism' and photographic art—like a huge glossy photo with gigantic faces," said Edith.[2]

The theme of "ultimate spiritual art," interjected Isabel, "is God's intention in putting the universe together—what is the divine blueprint?" Isabel, who is also an adept amateur scientist, believes that art and science will draw ever closer in an attempt to answer that question. "The two will come so close they will almost dissolve into each other.

"More and more artists are involved in science. Scientists are also interested in art. They need art for a greater freedom of mind. And art can help all of us grasp the theoretical [side] of physics and mathematics."

In the coming century, the formidable task of art will be to change the "ordinary person into an extraordinary person who can understand beyond the 'usual,'" say the Piczeks. And church art "will do things with light and lines to match the reality of the times."

Thomas Kinkade, a young painter from the Mother Lode town of Placerville, California, uses light to translate his luminous faith into an artistic technique that makes parts of his paintings appear to glow. As the exterior light shining upon his landscapes, street scenes, and nostalgic works is dimmed, the illuminated portions of the paintings grow brighter: headlights, street lights, candles, and moonlight on the snow, for example.

Realism in art still attracts a following, Kinkade says, adding that he is "a minister with a paintbrush," using pigment and canvas "to create images that are uplifting and representative of the One who lives inside of me. My goal is to be a strong force in the secular art world—to help reclaim that territory for the gospel."[3] Kinkade made his mark early in life, winning recognition in the marketplace as co-author of the *Artist's Guide to Sketching,* and background artist for the Hollywood fantasy film, *Fire and Ice.* His works have spiraled in popularity during the early 1990s.

This fresh kind of art should turn on the visually sophisticated, media-savvy twentysomething generation that has seen and heard it all.

Arts Alive

The Old Masters aren't exactly old hat, however. Van Gogh's "Sunflowers" brought in $39.9 million at a recent auction, and his "Irises" later sold for $53.9 million. "These icons of today's renaissance are only one facet of an art boom that bolsters a burgeoning market for quality prints and lesser-known artists," say Naisbitt and Aburdene in *Megatrends 2000.* They go on to quote economist and art historian Leslie Singer, who says that more people are "collecting art today as a percentage of the population than ever before, even during the Renaissance."[4]

In fact, Naisbitt and Aburdene confidently predict that the visual and performing arts will enjoy an extraordinary boom in the 1990s. The arts, they say, will "gradually replace sports as society's primary leisure activity."

To back up their argument, the authors cite the following statistics:[5]

- The arts have already pulled ahead of sporting events in attendance and spending.
- Since 1965, American museum attendance has increased from

200 million to 500 million annually. And new and expanded museums are popping up like dandelions.

- The 1988–89 Broadway season broke every record in history. And big British musicals like *Phantom of the Opera, Les Miserables,* and *Cats* are still packing in audiences across the country. *Phantom* pulled in $19 million in ticket sales before it even opened. Meanwhile, local theaters are prospering in more than 150 towns and cities.

- Membership in the leading chamber music association grew from twenty ensembles in 1979 to 578 in 1989. Regional and local symphony groups are thriving, especially those that feature outdoor summer programs and special festivals highlighting one composer.

- Since 1970, U.S. opera audiences have nearly tripled as opera sheds its "for-highbrows-only" image.

- Professional dance has grown 700 percent in the United States since 1972, and cities that can't afford a full-time ballet or dance company are cosponsoring them with sister cities.

Too Rosy a Portrait?

But not all analysts are as sanguine as Naisbitt and Aburdene about the arts. There may be some phantoms on the stage, screen, and canvas.

Naisbitt and Aburdene say that lovers of the arts tend to be affluent and well-educated. Although their assertion is no doubt correct, only a minority of our population fits that description. Tax reforms have reduced incentives for making donations to nonprofit organizations—only about 8 percent of which are designated for "arts, culture, and humanities." And the growing populations of black, Asian, and Hispanic Americans will not necessarily perpetuate artistic traditions deeply rooted in Western European culture.

John K. Urice, dean of the College of Fine Arts at Ball State University, is not optimistic about the future role of the arts in education. He sees four trends down the pike:

(1) There will be a blurring between popular culture (entertainment) and high, or fine, art. As a result of communications technology, "culture, art and entertainment will all overlap and be so

accessible that they will be demystified to the point that education will not be needed."

(2) Economic forces will push schools to "revert to their basic role . . . preparing future employees for the workplace. . . . [T]he arts will be integrated into educational curricula only to the degree they can contribute to a future worker's understanding of another culture and thus make him or her more economically efficient."

(3) Taxpayer pressure will force schools to drop the "frills" to become "even more like educational factories. . . . There will be less time for bands, art classes, choirs" and other activities. Social agencies and parent groups will have to pick up the slack. So will churches.

(4) "There will be fewer role models for youth who might want to become dancers, musicians, actors, sculptors, or other artists in the traditional sense. Ironically, [with the new technology] almost anyone will be able to make music, . . . and computer graphics will stimulate visual art in unprecedented ways."[6]

The bright spot Urice sees, however, will come from universities. Only universities will have the resources, although limited, to "preserve culture, maintain the arts, and continue the creative traditions through education."[7]

Urice is speaking primarily about the not-for-profit arts. The picture will be further darkened by more cuts in federal funding for the arts. During the Reagan Administration, the arts budget was reduced by 40 percent.[8]

Future cutbacks will be triggered by the backlash over 1990 grants by the National Endowment for the Arts for works such as the now infamous photo of a urine-submerged crucifix. Although government funding for religious displays is prohibited, tax dollars can be used, under the guise of art, to denigrate symbols of religious faith.[9]

While radical artists are painting themselves into a corner, other artists and innovative new forms of commercial art may surge ahead.

"The 'starving artist' is going out of fashion," said Isabel Piczek. "Art is very much wanted. Artists of the future will not be 'glorified clowns.' They will be serious, moral persons."[10]

Artists, concerned about originality, will team up with museums, mass communications companies, architects, and urban planners.

The wedding of art with technology will produce more unusual artists like Bran Ferrens. He "designs things so new that names have to be invented for them, at the place where architecture, cybernetics and video come improbably together," writes Jerry Adler in *Newsweek*. Ferrens's latest challenge is in "virtual architecture"—creating spaces defined by lights, video images, and sound as much as by ordinary walls and ceilings.[11] Likely customers for this concept are shopping malls and museums, and perhaps church and parachurch organizations.

Art as Transformation

If you consider art mainly a viewing or delivery system—such as a gallery or museum, an orchestra, or a dance or theater group—be prepared for a new form of do-it-yourself art called transformative art.

In the spring of 1991, the UCLA Extension program presented a six-month "Art as Transformation" course taught by a team of visionary painters, sculptors, musicians, playwrights, psychotherapists, art historians, and assorted spiritual practitioners.

A flyer advertising the two-weekends-a-month program called it "a supportive, nonjudgmental environment" providing "guidance in tapping the wellspring of . . . imagination and creativity." Techniques included guided visualization, active imagination, dreamwork, spontaneous drawing, and ritual.[12]

Art increasingly will be a spiritual quest, but with an economic foundation securely in place.

Ties between the arts and the media will increase in the 1990s. Not only will major corporations use the sights and sounds of the arts to promote products over the airwaves, but the media will become a prime-time vehicle for delivering blockbuster arts events to your home. The Arts & Entertainment (A&E) network already offers drama, live performances, and documentaries to thirty-eight million households through some 3,000 cable systems.[13]

TV Land—Soon We'll All Be Wired

Television is the clear leader in the media field. More than 90 percent of Americans own TV sets, and VCRs will be in 80 percent of households by 2001. By 1993 more than 60 percent of our homes will be wired with cable TV.[14]

"Television has radically changed the public discourse," observes church growth expert Lyle Schaller. "In western Kansas, you're not in rural America. In northern Mississippi, you're not in rural America. Regardless of where you are, you're not in rural America; you're in television land."[15]

Television journalist Bill Moyers asks whether TV can be "a force in the central issue of our time, the search to signify and affirm meaning, open our souls to others" and be a channel for the "biggest story of the century, the struggle to define what it means to be spiritual." That "little screen . . . [is] the largest classroom, perhaps the largest chapel, God has given us in a long, long time."[16]

Television is also changing the way we perceive, assimilate, and interpret news. The 1991 Middle East conflict appeared on the screen as it unfolded—a "real-time war"—and world leaders bypassed established diplomatic channels and "talked" to each other on CNN. Only seven or eight correspondents covered the Vietnam War on location, but in the Persian Gulf the press was 700 strong. The "fourth estate" poked for angles, speculated on endless "what-ifs," and occasionally published "at rumor's early light."

Ever-improving state-of-the-art visuals, re-creations, and special effects will be used more and more by news producers struggling to get top ratings for their programs. And newspapers and magazines will respond by trying to make their pages look like TV screens, "with more color, better graphics, flashy layouts and simulated pictures through digitalized alteration of photos."[17] Other pressures, however, cautions attorney-ethicist Michael Josephson, "will cause stories to be shorter, lighter, geared more to gaining and holding the interest of readers rather than enlightening them."[18]

Meantime, companies are pioneering in the field of interactive TV. Le Groupe Videotron's TVI service comes equipped with a special "zapper" that lets viewers choose what aspects of an event they want to watch. The interactive news program shows twelve headlines and viewers "zap" whichever segment turns them on.[19]

And in media arts, "interactive" is also on the leading edge. A Los Angeles firm makes a video disc that plays on home TV screens and "takes you on a tour of the Smithsonian and lets you manipulate the exhibits as you stroll through."[20]

Music, Movies, and More

A revolution in the music and movie industries is inevitable as well.

Before long, record and disc buyers will be able to manipulate sounds or mix them with other electronic media. An experimental Warner Brothers disc released in 1989 called "Fleetwood Macro" lets fans of the rock group Fleetwood Mac "select songs and videos from a menu and delete instruments so they can play along at home."

Wall Street Journal reporter Michael W. Miller says that someday "even movies may be computerized, and that could transform the way people watch and make entertainment. . . . Viewers will load up a movie and have their choice of languages, ratings (a G version for kids, an R version for adults), and maybe even story lines."[21] Talk about transformative art!

Donald Kurt, supervising producer for Warner Brothers studios, believes that as home entertainment centers and screening rooms become ever more popular during the 1990s, creative television producers will vie for a larger slice of the shrinking financial pie.

"TV networks are a dinosaur," he said, and syndication of films for later television programming "has dried up." Although in his opinion the extravagances of the 1970s and 1980s are over, screenwriting "can still be great. The guy who can deliver a good, creative show for less money will be working all the time."

Kurt likes to emphasize values such as "commitment, family, friendship and education"—values he says came through in his movies *House Party II, Homocide* and *The Flash*. And he hasn't given up on Hollywood. Religious values can—and will—be instilled, he said in an interview, if the writers convey the message subliminally and subtly, rather than frontally. Comedy and uplifting family films like *Driving Miss Daisy* will always be in demand, he added, although sex and violence will be there, too, "because the public demands it."

Blockbusters similar to the 1992 hits *Hook* and *Beauty and the Beast* will be around in 2002, Kurt thinks, guaranteed by hype and presales promotion. Most of the blockbusters have been rated PG, incidentally. But the trick will be "to make a film economically without losing quality. It's a matter of choices, planning, and an experienced crew," says Kurt.[22]

Predominantly young people in the twelve- to twenty-four-year-old range and persons of retirement age will be the most likely audiences at movie houses during the late 1990s. According to Kurt, the young like to get out of the house and go to premieres of highly touted pictures—but only in theaters with high-quality sound and projection. And the older set will attend because, presumably, they have more leisure time and spare cash than parents in the forty- to sixty-year-old category.

Fiction writer Bret Easton Ellis's description of the climate at the end of 1990 may give us a clue to what we can expect in future films. At least for those in their twenties, writes Ellis, who at age twenty-six had written three popular novels,

> the comedy that audiences respond to wholeheartedly is in blockbuster crash-and-burn epics and horror films, usually after a body has been bloodily dispatched and the hero or villain (twentysomething audiences often root for both) gives us a knowing wink by capping off the slaughter with an ironic fillip. Media-savvy, we are pessimistic yet prone toward fantasy, but it's often a mean-spirited horror-show fantasy: a comic-book version of urban squalor (*Batman*) or gooey pop-mysticism (*Ghost*). Since we're so visually sophisticated, these fantasies, though obvious, are densely layered. Fleeting pleasure is found in junk culture. . . .
>
> If violence in films, literature and in some heavy-metal and rap music is so extreme that it verges on the baroque, it may reflect the need to be terrified in a time when the sharpness of horror-film tricks seems blunted by repetition on the nightly news.[23]

Ted Baehr, founder and chairman of the Christian Film and Television Commission, wants Christians to choose the films they see with great care—not only "to avoid filling their minds with cinematic garbage, but also to send a message to Hollywood." If decent movies make money and indecent ones don't, then Holly-wood will make wholesome films, he reasons.[24]

And because of tougher competition and the probability that not all three of the major TV networks will survive to the year 2000, the survivors will be searching for wider audiences. This gives the church a major opportunity, Baehr believes, to exert leverage at the box office and influence the industry. He predicts that Hollywood will undergo "an ethical revival" and that the Motion Picture Code may be reinstated in some form by the end of the decade.[25]

On the music front, rap, MTV, and repackaged versions of works by the "classic" artists of the 1960s and 1970s like Bob Dylan and Cat Stevens will probably hang around for the first half of the 1990s.

The only militant messages that appear headed for the top of the pop charts in the near future are from the new contingent of self-described "radical rappers." Hearing the raps of groups like Laquan, Movement Ex, or Paris is a foretaste of urban debates on race, education, drugs, and crime, suggests Jon Pareles. Radical rap is evolving fast, and "its vision of America as a racial and economic battleground is apocalyptic," he says.

> Despite the dogma and occasional wrong-headedness, it re-mains one of the most promising zones of popular music. It confronts problems with commitment rather than apathy or nihilism or escapism, and where most popular music pro-motes pleasure, radical rap urges listeners to seek knowledge before titillation. . . . Radical rappers aspire to be teachers, not gangsters. The question is whether they are building a movement, or simply a market.[26]

Perhaps commercialism has already bummed out many younger music fans. "Kids aren't stupid," says Mike O'Connell, 23, leader of his own band, Rights of the Accused. "The [Rolling] Stones aren't playing rock 'n' roll anymore. They're playing for Budweiser."[27]

Reading, Writing, and Researching

Even with all the competition from electronic media, reading for pleasure will remain a favorite pastime at the turn of the century.

Boomer spending, especially, will keep the market for books and magazines healthy.[28] And the book and periodical market will increase internationally with more simultaneous printings in multiple languages.

Although the appetite for Christian reading may slacken a bit, romance novels, how-to, self-help, and Bible study materials will sell well, in my opinion. And there's no end in sight for the sale of—you guessed it—end times and prophecy books.

On the other end of the publishing process, authors will see vast changes in the ways they research and write. We'll access "hyper-media" databases that store graphics, music, speech, and other sounds, as well as text, that can be quickly (but not cheaply) retrieved from a vast, flexible, interactive, web-like reservoir of almost limitless resources.[29] And with up to thirty-five times as much information available in 2001 as in 1990, we will switch from getting information to analyzing and using it.[30]

If our brains aren't on information overload.

Apparently that's already happened for the under-thirty generation when it comes to the news.

A study by Times Mirror, publisher of *The Los Angeles Times,* found that people aged eighteen to thirty know less, care less, and read newspapers less than any generation in the previous five decades. Andrew Kohut, who conducted the survey, says that young people are not so much disillusioned as indifferent, displaying "a failure to find public events compelling." They bore more easily; their eyes glaze quicker.

"Catering to this new generation has spawned a new kind of news media," commented *L.A. Times* media writer Thomas Rosenstiel, "offering a lighter fare and 'infotainment,' a hybrid of information and entertainment."[31]

Perhaps it's time to exorcise a few media phantoms.

"'Mindless' entertainment is a misnomer," says Elizabeth Thoman, whose *Media and Values* newsletter is a leading resource for examining media issues. "Even the most ephemeral sitcom or video movie has an impact on our hearts and minds." She believes we need to develop "a values-based media awareness movement that will educate individuals to become critically aware of the pervasive influence of media—not just the content of programs but the role of media in driving our consumer economy."[32]

Unfortunately, unrelenting demands for profit and advertising revenue will color media standards well into the next millennium.

"Because media is so expensive and such a team effort," says film producer/writer Mel White, "we could lose a marvelous learning tool if it doesn't make a profit or if it isn't underwritten by some massive government grant. The loss of artistic creativity and talent is what I'm most afraid of. But if we hold together financially, there can be a great and exciting future for educational media, with interactive video."[33]

The most likely future scenario, according to White, is a mixed bag, with a few major studios making a few big pictures, and "many little filmmakers and noble little video houses making wonderful films."

White predicts that because of the double effect of spiraling production costs and shrinking budgets, much of media will be "pirate and underground, with handmade super-8 video film that people pass around." He anticipates a continuing demand for video in the church market. But religious films are "dead." Nor, in his opinion, is there a market for creative, thought-provoking or controversial subjects that would help the church grow.

"As the need for income becomes more acute, more and more stuff verging on hysteria will come out, pushing people to give money to support ministries," said White. "The thoughtful and the ideas of the thoughtful" will be lost in the process.[34]

Market-dictated strategies and uncritical consumerism will in fact drive much of the future American economy.

Cash Flows
and Flaws

Peter Jennings of ABC News played the role of Peter Prometheus, a fast-track corporate engineer, inventor, and entrepreneur. Valery Giscard d'Estaing, France's former president, was the CEO of a French company. Japan's vice minister of foreign affairs played a Japanese middle manager, and U.S. civil rights activist and 1988 presidential candidate Jesse Jackson took the part of a worker complaining of racial discrimination.

They were participants in a panel of fifteen business, economic, and political leaders from nine nations called together for the *Wall Street Journal*'s Future Forum. For two and a half hours they gazed into the 21st century—wrestling with problems of loyalty between employers and workers, creating new businesses and technologies, and investing and selling across international boundaries.

As the panelists acted out hypothetical business situations, they projected a world of intensifying global business opportunity and competition that could eventually blur national loyalties and boundaries. Twenty-first-century businessmen could be saluting company flags instead of national flags, suggested Kenichi Ohmae, a Tokyo-based international management consultant. And when Mr. Prometheus announced he had invented a fantastic new battery and was leaving the mythical Creative Motors Corp. to found his own company, Ohmae urged him to start the new business in Japan.

If your business grows in the United States, he warned in the simulation, "You will be raided, restructured, and taken over." Japan "will protect you from all of that," he said.[1]

The "real" business and economic worlds of the approaching millennium could be far different, of course, but all of us will be deeply affected by government economic policies and private economic decisions. We will be better able to cope if we first scope out these forces that will shape the future.[2]

Trouble is, economics is not an exact science—economists can't conduct experiments with carefully monitored control groups of people or rats. And economists have a rather poor track record in predicting such things as household savings rates and what the stock market will do. The league of the winning Superbowl team is as good an index as any for predicting a bull or bear market. (The market goes up if the National Football Conference team wins, so the theory goes.)

The experts are divided over the likely scenarios for economics in the decades ahead—more divided, in fact, than the experts on any other topic in this book.

Nevertheless, let's sample some informed economic thought about jobs, pay, and the workforce; let's peek at possible corporate structures, banks, and the government; and let's assess how cash flows and flaws may affect the health of the U.S. economy at the dawn of the new century.

Working It Out

The best one-word description for the U.S. labor force in the 21st century is *diversity*. And demographic change will be at the heart of the issue. Women, minorities, and immigrants will account for 90 percent of the labor force expansion of the 1990s.[3] "Cultural diversity" is a desirable goal, companies are discovering.

Yet workforce growth will slump to 1 percent this decade, well below the 2.9 percent growth of the 1970s, predicts the Hudson

Institute. Nearly two-thirds of the new entrants into the job ranks will be women; an additional 20 percent will be nonwhite or immigrant men.[4] But white, non-Hispanic, native-born males will comprise a mere 9.3 percent of the new workers by 2001.[5]

Women still lag behind men in pay. For example, in their first year after receiving an MBA degree, women take home an average of 12 percent less than men in annual salary.[6] And women still face the now-familiar "glass ceiling" that often bars their access to top management positions.

Nevertheless, they have been making dramatic progress in occupations previously considered to be largely male preserves. About 18 percent of doctors are now women, as are 22 percent of lawyers, 32 percent of computer systems analysts, and nearly half of accountants and auditors. Before the decade is over, women will hold down the majority of new positions for skilled and educated workers. And they are starting their own businesses at twice the rate of men; in 1987 women owned twice as many companies as they did a decade earlier.[7]

Despite the clear barrier, the breakthrough of women managers will continue as more and more firms set quotas for female workers. The glass ceiling won't be shatterproof after all, and the "feminine style of management" will become more prevalent "not only because more women will achieve positions of power but also because a flexible, mediating approach will be vital in dealing with America's ever more heterogeneous workers."[8]

The baby boomers who swelled the labor force for the past two decades are being replaced by the less-plentiful baby busters. So companies that once rejected applicants without necessary skills are scratching around to find out what prospective employees can do—or be trained to do.

Where the Jobs Will Be

Meanwhile, workers in large plants will play a larger role in designing and refining production processes. And unions, no longer the powerful negotiating force they once were, will recognize that "their prosperity rests on the success of the company, not on the extraction of high wages without concomitant increases in produc-tivity."[9]

Eight of the twenty-five fastest-growing jobs in the next decade will be health related, says *U.S. News & World Report.* In addition,

> Lawyers specializing in toxic-waste regulations and accoun-tants familiar with European trade standards will gain an edge over their colleagues. In the automobile industry, technicians who can keep robots running will be worth more on the fac-tory floor than assembly-line workers. While industry contin-ues to replace workers through automation, many corporations will continue to trim middle managers. The 1990s will offer you less job security, but they will distinctly enrich your job possibilities.[10]

Yet many new workers lack even the rudimentary skills. The dividing line for working America will be between those who have learned how to learn and those who have not.[11]

Most low-skill jobs will be in retail trade and services—segments that don't pay enough to make rent affordable, much less home ownership. The Bureau of Labor Statistics projects that about 70 percent of the new jobs expected between now and the end of the decade will be in those sectors. Thus, by 2001 nearly *half* the jobs in the country may not pay what's needed to rent decent housing.[12]

The decade ahead will see increasing numbers of unemployed Americans. Joblessness of youths among minority groups and in large cities will continue to be a particular problem. Many Americans will be able to hold only low-paying, unskilled jobs which will keep them at or below the poverty line. This class will clash with workers whose highly marketable skills make them candidates for brighter economic futures.

Hope in Detroit

In an effort to help the poor through job training and technology, a tough-talking Roman Catholic priest has set up a nonprofit civic organization on Detroit's northwest side. Father William Cunningham's organization, Focus: Hope, is part charity, part business, and part job-training program. It has grown from a grass-roots group that began preaching racial harmony after riots swept the city in the mid-1960s. Focus: Hope operates food banks that distribute groceries to 80,000 people a month, and it employs about 180 inner-city workers in its homegrown manufacturing enterprises. It also provides math, computer, and machinist's training "to scores of willing but poorly educated Detroit residents."[13]

At the end of 1990, Focus: Hope added its most ambitious project yet: its Center for Advanced Technology. Funded by $15 million in Defense Department grants, the center explores ways to improve the production and technical skills of inner-city workers.

Government and industry experts say the program could be a model for training young people and could help alleviate a critical shortage of highly trained machinists.

But to Cunningham, who preaches economic salvation through hard work and high tech, it's "more than a jobs program, more than just helping blacks keep up. The issue here is to provide the tools and discipline and very best of training and equipment to bring minorities and poor whites into real positions of control, at the very center of the technological revolution."[14]

Several hundred miles away, Eastern College, an evangelical Protestant school in Philadelphia, has become the nation's first college to offer the MBA degree to students who then become entrepreneurs among the "marginalized." Graduates help the disadvantaged, both overseas and in this country, achieve economic independence.[15]

Yet despite these and other efforts, the richest one-fifth of the U.S. population is getting richer while the poorest one-fifth either holds steady or grows poorer. White households typically have ten times as much wealth as black households, and the disparity is likely to continue even if the income of blacks catches up with that of whites.[16]

Adjusted for inflation, "the purchasing power of working people has retrogressed," said former United Auto Workers president Douglas Fraser. And if the national debt continues to surge, the next generation will be saddled with interest payments on our huge obligation, further threatening economic growth and standards of living.[17]

In fact, the budget deficit may pose the greatest single threat to standards of living in the 21st century.

"Heavy borrowing by consumers and by the federal government has turned the United States, once the world's largest creditor, into the world's largest international debtor. And the burden of paying interest on that debt will drain American incomes well into the next century, particularly if productivity growth remains slow," said Alan Murray in the *Wall Street Journal*.[18]

Savings, Social Security, and Retirement

Americans must learn how to live within our means instead of borrowing from our future, says Tom Sine.[19] And that must be accompanied by an increase in personal savings.

One reason saving is difficult is the mounting Social Security withholding tax; more is taken out of the typical American worker's paycheck for Social Security than for income taxes.[20]

This may be necessary to keep the Social Security system solvent, but unfortunately Congress for many years has used Social Security Administration funds "like a checking account. No capital has ever been accumulated and no interest or other benefits . . . allowed to accrue" to these accounts.[21]

Lifetrends authors predict that by 2020 full Social Security benefits won't start until age 70 and that

> To save Medicare from bankruptcy, some costly medical procedures, such as bypass surgery, will be curtailed. Money will be funneled away from heroic measures and into preventive medicine; funding for nursing homes will be minimized, expenditures on home care substantially increased.[22]

Early retirement may tempt executives, but many 21st-century employers will have eliminated retirement incentives as they try to retain—and sometimes retrain—their best workers. And both the high costs of retirement plus longer life expectancies will mean that many workers may stay on the job longer; 70 may replace 65 as the "normal" retirement age.[23]

By 2000, predicts Judith Waldrop, one retiree in three will return to work within two years. "To retire in 2030 on today's equivalent of $1,000 a month, workers will have to save $4,800 a year starting now."[24]

Corporate Cooperation and Competition

As the era of domestic-only competition fades, the one-industry, one-company chief executive is also on the way out. By the dawning of 2001, a company's selection for top honcho will be governed by international competition, globalization of companies, spreading technology, and speed of overall change. Ohmae, the Tokyo-based international management consultant, wasn't just role-playing when he said employees may be saluting company flags instead of national.

The corporate chief of the next century, says Ed Dunn, corporate vice president of Whirlpool Corp., "must have a multienvironment, multicountry, multifunctional, maybe even multicompany, multi-industry experience."[25]

Expect to see growing numbers of foreign-owned plants in the United States as the next century rolls into sight. Nearly every business will have to compete globally, and joint-venturing will become more common.

In 1990, Japan seemed to be buying everything in sight, taking over more and more U.S. companies. Although the prospect of more Japanese megadeals raises corporate eyebrows—even hackles—not all economists think that would spell sayonara for U.S. interests. "Given the fact that they've got all those U.S. dollars, I'd much rather have them turn around and be invested back in the U.S. than in Germany or Japan itself," says Murray Weidenbaum, former chairman of the Council of Economic Advisers.[26]

The acquisition of U.S. businesses and real estate by the Japanese and other foreign investors "should lead to greater productivity here, greater taxable income, a higher standard of living, more jobs and yet greater investment," says John F. Welch, Jr., CEO of General Electric.[27]

Furthermore, the British—not the Japanese—hold the largest share of direct foreign investment in the United States. All told, foreigners own less than 5 percent of the assets of the U.S. economy. Anyway, what's foreign? What's domestic anymore? More than

300,000 Americans work for Japanese companies while 100,000 Japanese work for American ventures in Japan.[28]

And there will be plenty of room for the little guy too. Experts predict that businesses employing fewer than 100 workers will spawn as many as half of all new jobs this decade. While Fortune 500 companies have slashed 3.5 million jobs since 1980, small businesses generated 20 million new ones.[29]

"In place of an economy dominated by a handful of giant monoliths," observes Alvin Toffler, "we are creating a super-symbolic economy made up of smaller operating units, some of which may, for accounting and financial reasons, be encapsuled inside large businesses."[30]

Because smokestack industries are declining in favor of service jobs and microelectronics, not only will the size of the average workplace shrink, but so will the number of employees who work there. And because of better control, customizing and specialization, and quicker turnaround time most businesses won't have to stock large inventories. But as specialization increases and mass manufacturing and mass marketing recede, competition will intensify.[31]

We already see some of that happening as private businesses give the government a run for our money by providing services historically furnished only by the government. Services such as education, transportation, and mail and package delivery come to mind as examples.[32]

Toffler colorfully describes "a tsunami of business restructuring that will make the recent wave of corporate shake-ups look like a placid ripple. Specialists and managers alike will see their entrenched power threatened as they lose control of their cubbyholes and channels. Power shifts will reverberate throughout companies and whole industries."[33]

Diversity is indeed the new ideal in the corporation boardroom and the family-owned workplace. Diversity is a "way of encouraging workers to contribute their best ideas and efforts in an intensely competitive international arena."[34]

Banking on It

No less than a tsunami swept through the savings and loan industry and the junk bond market in 1990–91. The collapse of junk-bond firm Drexel Burnham Lambert "epitomizes this paradigm shift away from paper shuffling and the creation of artificial wealth. . . . Real capitalism will replace paper capitalism, the latter having to do with all of the foolishness engulfing Wall Street today."[35]

Is this really a paradigm for prosperity at the new millennium's early dawning? And was it foolishness or moral failure on the part of business moguls like convicted felon Michael Milken, the junk-bond "king" of fraud?

Corporate leaders have become increasingly worried about the erosion of moral and ethical values in their companies, according to a study of thirty-three business, banking, government, and academic officials.

"Self-indulgent permissiveness . . . has become so pervasive and corrosive that . . . executives have lost confidence that their employees and colleagues will act in ethically responsible ways," their report said. As a result, they are "worried more than ever about law suits, institutional instability and the erosion of respect for business as a profession. . . ."[36]

This comes as no surprise to Christians who have been sending warning signals about our nation's loss of moral structure. As *Christian Century* editor James Wall points out, if the religious worldview is left out, Milken's illegal manipulating of the U.S. financial system is "merely a miscalculation, a failure to be prudent in one's drive to maximize profits . . . [W]ithout input from our religious traditions we have no moral language to refute St. Milken's secular religion of greed."[37]

Partly as a result of the junk-bond fiasco (which may have lost $50 billion in investors' money) and the savings and loan debacle and subsequent bailout (which may require $1 trillion in government dollars),[38] an enormous credit crunch looms.

The nation's weakened financial structure might buckle if the economy nosedives for any lengthy period and sets off a huge wave of defaults, warns James J. O'Leary, economic consultant to the United States Trust Company of New York.[39]

Ron Blue, the author of several books on personal finances and a partner in a financial planning and management firm, also sees more blue than rose in the economic future. There are flaws in the cash flows, he says, and during the 1990s we will see taxes go up, inflation extend, and interest rates continue to reflect inflation. Our economy will become even more global, and over-consumerism will persist.

But based on his counseling experience with Christians nationwide, Blue believes Christians during the 1990s will "give more, save more and spend more wisely . . . because with continuing and increasing economic uncertainty" they will turn to the Bible. The Scripture, Blue believes, "is very clear about how to experience continued financial success" in changing and uncertain times.[40]

Rosy Boom or Gloomy Bust?

Toffler remains an optimist. Downplaying America's "relative economic decline," he says that the United States still represents "about the same share of Gross World Production that it did 15 years ago."[41] In all fairness, it should be noted that his book *Powershift* was completed before Iraq's invasion of Kuwait and the subsequent Gulf War.

But if Toffler is Mr. Positive, John Naisbitt is a mega-optimist, the ultimate bull on America's future. As does Toffler, Naisbitt minimizes the "supposed twin deficits" of U.S. domestic and trade debt.

> In reality the domestic deficit is not out of line with what it had been for the past 40 years, is declining, and as a percentage is not much greater than other Western countries. . . . In constant dollars, the total U.S. government deficit has fallen by 57 percent since 1986. As a share of the GNP, it is one of the lowest in the world.[42]

And they say it isn't clear that the United States actually *has* a trade deficit with any nation.

"Sadly, Naisbitt is wrong," counters Pat Robertson, the one-time presidential candidate. Though not an economist, Robertson has marshaled an array of figures to show that the key indicator to look at is the federal debt in relation to our national output—the debt/GNP ratio. In 1990, that ratio was 60 percent—twice the 1980 level.[43] Direct national debt, Robertson says, now exceeds $3 trillion, in addition to government-guaranteed loans amounting to $2.8 trillion. Total U.S. debt now outstanding tops $12.5 trillion. It was just $2 trillion fifteen years ago, according to economics columnist Leonard Silk.[44]

"However one counts the numbers, it is clear that America is in hock up to its eyeballs," says Robertson, and we "will see a debt blow-out which could trigger a serious worldwide depression."[45]

A panel of seventeen prominent futurists tends to agree: A global economic collapse is possible, they say, and some debts will have to be written off in order to keep some nations from going broke.[46]

Despite its sometimes exorbitant cash outflows and flaws of excessive consumerism, the United States of America is still the world's preeminent power and the best working model of free enterprise. That is likely to remain true as we approach the threshold of the next century.

"Can this country still lead?" asks Henry Grunwald, onetime U.S. ambassador to Austria and former editor in chief of Time Inc. "Can it impart its ideals of freedom and justice, its formula for creating wealth, its generosity? . . . Must America lead?" he continues, answering, "Yes, because the world is now too interdependent for the United States to create a prosperous enclave."[47]

But the larger question is not whether America has the *ability* to lead, but whether she has the *will* to lead, if she is again stirred by what Henry Luce called "the blood of purpose and enterprise and high resolve."[48]

May God mend our every flaw. And may he give us the political and spiritual leadership to accomplish it.

Political Spears?
Or Plowshares?

January, 1990. We were just beginning to talk seriously about the so-called "peace dividend" of domestic economic development and programs for the poor. Expensive military defense projects were being scaled back. The arms race was winding down. U.S.-Soviet relations were basking in long-awaited warmth following the cold war thaw. Political swords were being beaten into economic plowshares.

January, 1991. The War in the Gulf exploded. All thinking about the political and economic future was exchanged for military strategy. Plowshares were fashioned into Patriot missiles.

Suddenly the peace dividend seemed a lot farther down the road than we had hoped, and when we weren't thinking about the horrors of war we were pondering the economics of war. Who would pay for our high-tech, multi-million dollar display of military might?

One thing was sure when the smoke started clearing over Iraq: the battle for political ascendancy and world influence would be closely tied to economic well-being.

And private initiative will have to carry a larger share of responsibility for global well-being. This will need to happen "in combination with more intelligent, imaginative and flexible government policies that tie social services to incentives for self-help," suggests Henry Grunwald.

The United States may need to take the lead, he continues, to "partially reinvent capitalism—and do a more imaginative job of it than the heavily welfare-statist economies of Europe."[1]

Futurists agree that to manage emerging global issues, corporations must play a larger role. They will take over governing functions and provide more services in a society that is growing ever more privatized and individualized. The basic shift will be away from central government to individual and local empowerment.[2]

"Democracy is entering its decisive decades," writes Alvin Toffler. "For we are at the end of the age of mass-democracy—and that is the only kind the industrial world has ever known. . . . In any system, democratic or not, there needs to be some congruence between the way a people make wealth and the way they govern themselves. If the political and economic systems are widely dissimilar, one will eventually destroy the other."[3]

In light of the new "knowledge-based economy," Toffler reasons, we should brace for a "historic struggle to remake our political institutions, bringing them into congruence with the revolutionary post-mass-production economy."[4]

This "historic struggle" doesn't at all sound like the "End of History" essay written by Francis Fukuyama, deputy director of the U.S. State Department policy planning staff. His provocative article argued that with the collapse of Marxism we have come to the end of history. Democratic free enterprise is catching on world-wide, the ultimate goal of both industrial and semi-industrial nations.

Evangelist and church statesman Leighton Ford summarized Fukuyama's treatise: "The battle over ideology has ended. The idea of liberal democracy has won. It's only a matter of time until democracy extends to every part of the world. In that sense history is over."[5]

Ford noted that Fukuyama, almost off-handedly, admitted that two other forces "might possibly still compete for the hearts and minds of the world: nationalism and fundamentalist religion."

Only a few months after publication of Fukuyama's essay, the two forces he all but dismissed came together, igniting a major war in the Middle East.

Beyond the conflict over oil and the global economy, Ford observed, "Religion and nationalism become the vehicles: the pride, passion and fears of the human spirit."[6]

But just where are these vehicles likely to take us?

Nationalism, Regionalism, and Religion

The struggle between Jews and Arabs has roots in nationalism and stems from the ancient rivalry between Abraham's two sons: Ishmael, born to his servant woman, Hagar; and Isaac, born to his wife, Sarah.

In Israel, national identity is an explosive issue, intensified by large-scale immigration. In a post-Communist Soviet Union, statism in the Baltics and ethnic regionalism elsewhere have sprouted as dangerous political scions. Nationalist uprisings have emerged in other Eastern European countries as well. And ultra-nationalism is spreading in Japan.[7]

Toffler sees a "resurgence of flag-waving xenophobia"—a hatred of foreigners—in the United States. A growing nationalist backlash is being fed by, among other things, fears that America is in economic and military decline.[8] Anti-immigration sentiment simmers, particularly against Mexicans and Central Americans. Japan-bashing is popular. And religious zealots, breathing fire and theocracy, are committed to taking over America's institutions and levers of political control.

"Governments controlled or heavily influenced by extremists who put their particular brand of religion, ecology, or nationalism ahead of democratic values do not stay democratic long," Toffler warns.[9]

As the decade wears on, we will see in this country less nationalism and a growing emphasis on state, regional, and local politics. Analysts say that growing urban problems and the need for greater regional planning will start the shift away from federal efforts. In his 1991 State of the Union address, President Bush spoke about a shift of responsibility—and financial burden—to the states.

Oliver S. Thomas, general counsel for the Baptist Joint Committee on Public Affairs, urges the churches to improve local promotion of moral and social views in the 1990s. The shift needs to be toward city councils, school boards, and state legislatures. The reason for that strategy, Thomas says, is that the arena for church-state issues is moving out of the federal courts.

"Churches are going to have to become more intentional about state and local organizing. We can't just have an office here in Washington, D.C., and be a key player in church-state issues," said Thomas, an expert on church participation in the political arena.

According to Thomas, religion in the schools—including textbooks, the evolution-creation debate, school prayer, values and sex education, and contraceptives and family planning—will all be at the heart of the 1990's dialogue on how churches should minister. Other agenda items include counseling, screening child-care workers, and providing social services.[10]

Church, State, and the Kingdom and the Power

Although the U.S. government shunts responsibility to local jurisdiction, that will not stop legislators from becoming increasingly regulation-minded. This will apply not only to business and industry, but to religious organizations as well.

A key factor for all religious groups will be accountability, especially as it relates to income gathering and reporting and to licensing and operation of child-care facilities and church-related schools. Medical treatment will be mandatory even for seriously ill or injured members of groups that reject traditional medical care on religious grounds.

Government surveillance activities may be legally executed within churches—reminiscent of monitoring congregations that harbored Central American refugees during the 1980's church sanctuary movement. The rationale for snooping could be that it is in the best interest of national security to tighten immigration policy and squelch political dissent.

Furthermore, the control of intangibles—"ideas, culture, images, theories, scientific formulae, computer software—will assume greater and greater political attention in all countries as piracy, counterfeiting, theft, and technological espionage threaten increasingly vital private and nat.onal interests," Toffler forecasts.[11]

Christian organizations will likely be under more pressure to comply with laws against gender and racial-discrimination practices, particularly regarding employment.[12] Church organizations may even have difficulty maintaining the requirement of like faith for hiring anyone except ordained personnel. And legally enforcing church discipline may prove problematic.

Other signs indicate Christianity is moving toward a minority status in the United States and other First-World countries. By 2001, predicts religion futurist Sam Dunn of Seattle Pacific University, there will be no preferential tax treatment for churches; religious chaplaincies will be eliminated; religious grounds for conscientious objections will not be recognized by law; and advocacy of religion in publicly funded institutions will not be allowed.

"In short," Dunn lamented in *The Futurist* magazine, "the special status of the church in the eyes of the government will be all but eliminated."[13]

"Intolerance" is not too strong a word to describe what is already happening in some court cases against the free expression or exercise of religion.

George Barna thinks vast sums will be spent lobbying legislators on Capitol Hill to make churches accountable to the government. He suggests that churches "band together" to respond to these likely attacks and inform their legislators about their concerns.

The Supreme Court will be backlogged with "a prolific caseload of constitutional challenges," and "thousands of lawsuits" will be lodged in the 1990s against clergy, church staff (especially family and psychological counselors), and even lay leaders, Barna fears.

How can we stay on guard? Barna suggests lots of liability insurance; maybe even an attorney on the church staff to offer preventive counsel![14]

At the same time, analysts see a moderate-to-conservative U.S. Supreme Court prevailing into at least the early years of the coming century—perhaps in tension with a more liberal Congress, statehouse leaders, and civil-rights activists.

The separation of church and state has traditionally been considered a bar to the government's directly paying churches to do such things as feed the hungry, house the homeless, counsel substance abusers, conduct sex education classes, and the like. But because of a lack of government resources, the religious community will be pressed to move into a three-way partnership with government and private enterprise to provide needed services.

As an example, in 1992 a public school opened in the facilities of Central Lutheran Church in Minneapolis—a three-way partnership of the Minneapolis public school system, several corporations, and the congregation.

Oliver Thomas expressed "grave concerns about the possible impact of close partnerships where money from the state is flowing into the church.

"This is a major issue of social welfare and religious education, and the degree to which the government can support it will be in the forefront," Thomas said.[15]

The potential conflicts are numerous. For example, can the government work in partnership with the church to fund religious day care without the church having to remove all religious content and symbols?

Rabbi Yechiel Eckstein, head of the Holyland Fellowship of Christians and Jews in Chicago, predicts that "There are going to be all kinds of strange bedfellows who differ on a host of issues [but they will be] coming together" on issues such as violence, abortion, and school prayer. Eckstein also foresees evangelical Christians uniting in "a call for a more moral and sacred society that is not naked in the public square"—a reference to Richard John Neuhaus's book *The Naked Public Square*, which speaks about the absence of moral leadership in civic life.[16]

One group that wants to mobilize conservative religious groups into a united army during the closing years of this century is the Coalition on Revival. Founded by Jay Grimstead in 1982, its chief theoretician is Reconstructionist theologian R. J. Rushdoony of Vallecito, California.

Fred Clarkson describes the group as "a secretive, theo-political movement that seeks to bridge theological gaps among conservative Christians and foster religious and political unity." The coalition's goal is to establish its vision of the kingdom of God in America.[17]

Some consider COR the standard-bearer for Reconstruction (or Kingdom or Dominion) theology, which sees Old Testament law as pertaining to correct governing of modern society. COR is also perceived as the refocused successor to the "failed" Christian right of the 1980s, the political movement frequently associated with Jerry Falwell's Moral Majority and Pat Robertson's run for the presidency.

Some supporters have backed away because of its radicalism, but COR and its National Coordinating Council (NCC), the political and action arm formed in 1990, could be a force to reckon with in the next few years. The NCC advocates the abolition of public schools, the Internal Revenue Service, and the Federal Reserve by 2000. It also seeks to "Christianize all aspects of life from the arts and sciences to banking and the news media," according to its twenty-four-point platform. And it proposes setting up a "kingdom" counterculture that includes a "Christian" court system.

According to *Church & State* magazine, the NCC plan also calls for a grassroots effort to elect "their kind" of Christians to county boards of supervisors and sheriffs' offices, who, once in power, will establish county militias.[18]

In the years ahead "a significant minority of Christians will attempt to impose religious and/or moral ideas on society, and . . . a few Christian Reconstructionists will attempt to gain converts to Christian theocracy," says Samuel Dunn. But these efforts, he adds, "will not bear fruit."[19]

Polls About the Polls

In November of 1990 the religious right had virtually no impact on major elections and no new clergy were elected. In addition, on five referenda where religion was considered to be a key factor, voting results were seen as a defeat for the religious groups and considered a victory for proponents of church-state separation.[20]

According to Dunn, most citizens believe the state shouldn't prefer one religion over another. But the religious affiliation of voters has been—and will continue to be—one of the most accurate, and underrated, political thermometers and indicators of how people vote.

As examples, black Protestants, white Catholics, and Jews are more likely than white Protestants to support increased federal spending on domestic social problems. Catholics and black Protestants are the strongest supporters of unions. White evangelical

Protestants are the most conservative group in the country on social issues. Except on abortion, Catholics are more liberal than white Protestants on almost every public issue.[21]

The pressure for social change in a liberal, or "progressive," direction, concluded George Gallup Jr. and Jim Castelli in *The People's Religion,* "comes primarily from those who are *not* white Protestants; pressure for social change in a conservative direction comes from white evangelical Protestants. White non-evangelical Protestants are often pulled between the two; when it comes to specific issues, they most often seem to be influenced in the liberal direction."[22]

Yet mainline Protestant and Catholic leaders at the highest levels tend to be far to the left on economic issues. Leaders of mainline Protestantism, which has historically set the tone for American society, were "liberal on every dimension," said social scientist S. Robert Lichter.[23]

This has serious implications for the future of these denominations because, as Gallup and other surveys show, white Protestant "pew people" are fairly conservative—much more so than their denominational bigwigs.

When it comes to denominational political affiliations—which appear to have been relatively stable since 1984—Catholics, Jews, and Baptists are the most Democratic, while mainline Protestant denominations are the most Republican. In 1988, Baptists comprised the most Democratic Protestant group, while American Jews topped *all* religious groups in the Democratic category. Presbyterians were the most heavily Republican denomination.[24] Mormons are also strongly Republican, with about 50 percent claiming allegiance to that party.[25]

American Jews are considerably more liberal and politically active than the rest of the population. A Gallup survey for The Times Mirror Corporation also found that the most politically active Americans— both Republicans and Democrats—are more likely than other Americans to be highly religious.[26]

In the decade ahead this activism will be tapped by astute religious leaders who have the ability to effectively marshal causes and campaigns.

According to an *Associated Press* poll in November of 1990, three-quarters of Americans believe that the clergy should speak out on social issues and public policy. But 58 percent said clergy shouldn't endorse political candidates. And they overwhelmingly reject ministers as presidential candidates; in fact, in another poll they rejected all direct clergy involvement in politics by a 3-to-2 margin.[27]

But the chances are good that Americans will vote for a strongly committed, openly Christian (but nonclergy) candidate for president.

The religious representation of Congress, meanwhile, appears to be shifting, with a growth in "nontraditional" Protestant groups. This reflects a corresponding increase among the electorate. A total of thirty members in the House and Senate in 1990 said they were "Protestant," but did not identify with a particular denomination.[28]

Relatively more Roman Catholics, Jews, and Mormons were elected to Congress in 1990, and fewer Methodists, Presbyterians, and United Church of Christ members. Baptists gained and Episcopalians declined. The forty-one Jewish members and thirteen Mormons were record highs. Only about 60 percent of members newly elected to Congress were "traditional" Protestants, broadly defined—a significant change from 77 percent in 1960.[29]

Voter Constituency

What else can we learn about voters who will put presidents, governors, mayors, and legislators into office as we cross into the third millennium?

As every politician knows, the most powerful voting bloc is persons age fifty-five to seventy-four because they are more likely to go to the polls than any other age group.

Elders and boomers will comprise an increasing share of the electorate in the next decades, so politicians will be listening to the needs of these folks. And to the voice of the Gray Panthers (founded by the Presbyterian Church) and the American Association of Retired Persons (AARP). With nearly 30 million members, the AARP is twice as large as the AFL-CIO and has signed up about 25 percent of all U.S. registered voters. Most AARP members are white and middle-class—the very constituency whose allegiance will be fiercely fought for in the coming bid for political primacy.[30]

The authors of *Lifetrends* expect more intergenerational political coalitions to form in the next fifteen to twenty years, as well as coalitions speaking up for the great numbers of disabled Americans.[31]

Well-educated and well-off boomers and seniors are likely to spend more of their free time in social and political activism. Barna lists issues such as abortion, AIDS discrimination, racial injustice, gay rights, environmental abuse, nuclear power, pornography, drug abuse, and drunk driving. Product boycotting, letters to television producers and network executives, stockholder protests, and stock divestments from companies perceived to have objectionable racial, environmental, or military-defense policies are also apt to escalate in the approaching century.[32]

"Whereas one out of three adults had participated in some protest in 1990, more than half of all adults will have done so by 2000," Barna estimates. He adds that referenda will be more common as "boomers seek to take control over more of the public decision-making apparatus" in order to effect laws and policies they favor.[33]

Since boomers lean toward a "progressive" stance on many political issues, this may tilt in favor of what has traditionally been a Democratic vote.

Minority Power in the Precincts

And don't forget the minority segments of our population: Hispanic numbers are growing five times as fast as the rest of America and will carry increasing clout at the ballot box. An ethnically mixed society is likely to favor the Democrats, if present alignments persist.

Blacks, Latinos, and Asians will capture more seats and political offices in the 1990s and beyond. That will be especially true in the largest cities, where a majority of minority mayors will be in office by 2001. Racial crossover voting will be more common.[34]

This is also the decade of women in politics, says pollster Mervin Field. They got a fast start out of the gate. In 1990, record numbers of women entered political races, topping the rush in 1972 when trying to pass the Equal Rights Amendment gave women the incentive to run.[35] And by the first presidential election of the next century, 53 percent of voters will be women.[36]

Therefore, women may again find themselves at home in the House—and the Senate. Maybe even as Chief at the White House on Pennsylvania Avenue.

"Cleaning up messes has long been relegated to women's work," says *Time* writer Margaret Carlson. So have other issues now at the top of the political agenda, "like worrying over the young, the aged, the sick and the environment. Surveys show that women are perceived to be better than men on these issues, as well as to have higher ethical standards and greater honesty." Says Colorado's Democratic Congresswoman Pat Schroeder: "Our stereotype is finally in."[37]

Yet, figuring out what the electorate wants is getting tougher all the time. Political reporter David Yepsen says that 30 to 40 percent of the voters don't decide how they'll vote until the last few days before an election.[38]

Political analyst George Grant, who is considered a Reconstructionist, thinks the views of many voters aren't adequately expressed by the two major parties. "A plethora" of small new parties is likely in the near future, Grant told *World* magazine. "Historically, in the American political experience third parties—new parties—are very real options. And they can suddenly take on national proportions."[39]

Spiritual Politics: an Oxymoron?

In this changing milieu, the church of Jesus Christ—which is truly transnational, multiracial, intergenerational, and cross-cultural—will have a decisive role to play. Its task is to make "world Christians," helping them to understand the complex, interrelating forces of economics, politics, culture, and religion.

It would be tragic if bitter political divisions between liberal and conservative people of God were to undermine religion's essential role in laying a moral foundation for society. If religious values are relegated to the sidelines, power struggles of special interest groups will prevail over a common morality. And the church's prophetic voice will be lost.

But, conversely, if spirituality is properly political, says Glenn Tinder, politics will be properly spiritual. If politics is seen as entirely secular, it "loses its moral structure and purpose and turns into an affair of group interest and personal ambition . . . carried out purely for the sake of power and privilege," Tinder says.[40] He then points out that in the Christian view,

> while every individual is exalted, society is not. On the contrary, every society is placed in question, for a society is a mere worldly order and a mere human creation and can never do justice to the glory of the human beings within it. The exaltation of the individual reveals the baseness of society. It follows that our political obligations are indeterminate and equivocal.[41]

But while Christianity "implies skepticism concerning political ideals and plans" it also has faith "that the universe under the impetus of grace is moving toward radical re-creation." And this, Tinder affirms, "gives a distinctive cast to the Christian conception of political action and social progress. . . . If we turn away from transcendence, from God, what will deliver us from a politically fatal fear and faintheartedness?" he asks.[42]

If we divide the spiritual from the political, all that remains for us to do is fashion swords, spears, missiles, and finally destroy ourselves.

But according to the Old Testament prophet Micah, God will someday judge between the peoples and "they will beat their swords into plowshares and their spears into pruning hooks. Nation will not take up sword against nation, nor will they train for war anymore."[43]

Part 2

Changing Shapes of Churches and Religion

Chapter 13

Mainliners and Sideliners

William McKinney, dean of Hartford Seminary and a first-rate sociologist, uses sports images to describe how the privileged mainstream Protestant churches have moved from the mainline to the sideline.

The early Protestant groups built the stadium, supplied the teams, and defined the rules of the American religious game, says McKinney. In the late eighteenth century, the Protestants were forced to admit other teams. By the 1920s, other teams had their own stadiums, but mainline Protestant churches still supplied the umpires.

"What's happened in the last 30 years is the umpires are gone and nobody knows what the rules are," McKinney says.[1]

In the new ball game, liberal Protestantism is only one player among many.

In *American Mainline Religion: Its Changing Shape and Future*, McKinney and co-author Wade Clark Roof describe the startling, continuing decline in America's mainline churches. They note that the Protestant majority slipped from 67 percent in 1952 to 57 percent in 1987.[2]

Hardest hit are the liberal churches that have been the core of American religious life and are today the mainstays of the National Council of Churches. In the mid-1960s, many well-established Protestant churches not only stopped growing, they began an exodus to the sidelines or clear out of the stadium.

Roof and McKinney define mainline, or mainstream, churches as "the dominant, culturally established faiths held by the majority of Americans."[3] These include the Episcopalians, Methodists, Presbyterians, United Church of Christ, the major Lutheran bodies, and the Christian Church (Disciples of Christ).

"For all these churches," Roof and McKinney write, "those losses represented an abrupt and dramatic turnaround in their privileged status and respectability: churches seemingly as American as apple pie and the Fourth of July suddenly fell upon hard times. As many as 10 of the largest Protestant denominations were in the throes of what can only be described as a serious religious depression."[4]

In 1965, when eight of the largest mainline Protestant denominations were close to the zenith of their growth, they had a combined membership of 30.8 million. But in 1988, the total was 25 million, a decline of 18.8 percent. During this period the Episcopal Church lost 28.4 percent of its 1965 membership total, and the Christian Church (Disciples) lost a staggering 44 percent after a de facto schism.[5] (See chart on following page.)

Between 1987 and 1988, these six families of faith (three major Lutheran bodies had merged into one) counted a net loss of 194,000 members. That's the equivalent of closing down a 530-member church every day of the year![6]

Rodney Stark, professor of sociology and comparative religion at the University of Washington, says the history of organizations shows that whenever a denomination gets liberal, it declines. So mainliners like the Methodists are in trouble, while sects that broke off from Methodism are "still growing like gangbusters. . . . The splits grow until they, too, become liberal." Stark adds that

> In the 1990s we will see the evangelicals growing and the oldline mainliners declining. They're already old and not virile. The church bureaucrats have seen it [the writing] on the

wall, but they always say that religion itself is going out of business. They don't have money and staff; they must know that something is wrong. But there is immense duplicity [on their part]. The problems aren't going to go away.[7]

Meanwhile, the existing mainline members are graying. Fast. The average age of members of American Baptist Churches was sixty-one in 1991; 38 percent of United Methodists in 1990 were over fifty, compared with 26 percent of the U.S. population at large; and a 1988 study of Presbyterians showed that because nearly half the active lay members were headed for retirement, money problems will be "almost beyond belief." Other mainline agencies face a similar pocketbook crunch.[8]

According to the 1990 *Yearbook of Churches,* giving in nine U.S. denominations was 3.5 percent higher in 1988 than in 1987—from $331.35 to $344.97 per member. When the increase is adjusted for

DECLINING MEMBERSHIP IN MAINLINE DENOMINATIONS (In Millions)							
	1965	1970	1975	1980	1985	1987	1988
American Lutheran Church	2.54	2.54	2.42	2.35	2.33	*	*
Lutheran Church in America	3.14	3.11	2.99	2.92	2.90	*	*
Evang. Luth. Church America					*	5.29	5.25
Lutheran Church–Mo. Synod	2.69	2.79	2.76	2.63	2.63	2.61	2.60
Christian Church (Disciples)	1.92	1.42	1.30	1.18	1.12	1.09	1.07
Episcopal Church	3.43	3.29	2.86	2.79	2.74	2.46	2.45
Presbyterian Church (USA)	3.98	4.04	3.54	3.36	3.05	2.97	2.93
United Church of Christ	2.07	1.96	1.82	1.74	1.68	1.66	1.64
United Methodist Church	11.1	10.5	9.86	9.52	9.19	9.12	9.05

* The Evangelical Lutheran Church in America was organized in 1987, merging the American Lutheran Church, the Lutheran Church in America, and the Association of Evangelical Lutheran Churches.

SOURCE: Yearbook of American & Canadian Churches, 1989, 1990.

the 4.4 percent inflation rate, however, the denominations actually received less real income.[9] And there is "a quiet, building crisis" over decaying church facilities; the cost of maintaining aging churches grows steadily, especially in urban areas.[10]

McKinney agrees that the oldline denominations are "in a deep funk. . . . These are tough times for the groups that once dominated religious life."[11]

And it's likely to get worse before it gets better.

Why the Deep Funk?

What has happened? And why? Can anything be done about it?

While the churches historically identified as the most ecumenical have been losing ground, gains in Protestant evangelical and fundamentalist churches—mostly in freestanding, interdenominational or nondenominational congregations—have been flourishing. So have the neo- Pentecostals and Roman Catholics.

In other words, the "market" for religion hasn't shrunk, but "market share" has shifted drastically.[12]

At the center of the Roof-McKinney analysis is the belief that the cultural upheavals of the 1960s and 1970s demolished a "bridge" between religion and culture that was highly traveled in the 1950s— the heyday of the National Council of Churches. When the bridge was in place, "a vital synthesis of beliefs, values and national ideals existed, sustained by a cold war ideology and close links between civic society, national visions and self-understanding." The churches most clearly aligned with those dominant cultural values, the authors say, were the liberal mainliners. Their beliefs, values, and behavior "were virtually indistinguishable from the culture."

Along came the assassination of President Kennedy, the civil-rights struggle, an unpopular war in Vietnam, and the generational conflict, all of which "contributed to a sense of despair and disillusionment," say Roof and McKinney. These events weakened the sense of shared cultural values like patriotism, hard work, success, and family and no longer inspired a common religious solidarity or nurtured the faiths most closely associated with those values.

Conclude Roof and McKinney: "The bridge between public and

private faith collapsed, and liberal optimism and belief in utilitarian progress and rationality faltered."[13]

At the same time, the distinctive identities of mainline denominations faded and "brand loyalty" weakened. Children no longer remained in the church in which they were reared. And many never bothered to find a church to replace the one they left.

"In today's secular, individualistic culture," Roof writes, "religious belonging is often not viewed as a presumed outgrowth of belief. It's a matter of taste and preference." His research shows that the "big story in religious switching" is the young adults who, rather than changing churches, have simply "drifted out of the established churches without fanfare or bridge-burning experiences."[14]

Elizabeth Nordbeck, a United Church of Christ clergywoman, agrees. Mainline worshipers "don't storm out of their fellowships in righteous anger and into the waiting pews of the independent conservative Christian congregation across the street. Instead, they simply drift away in apathy," she says.[15]

Cultural and sociological factors have played a part in this massive shift, but so have increasing mobility of the American people, competition from the constant planting of new churches across the nation, a decline in the birth rate, and an anti-institutionalism that some say is a holdover from the 1960s.[16] Organizational reshuffles, headquarters-relocation, and denomination-merging also have played their part. But none of these reasons adequately explains why *some* religious groups—notably the conservatives—are thriving.

One oft-quoted explanation for the mainline malaise is that church leaders have been preoccupied with political and social issues, having mistaken priorities and neglected the fundamentals of biblical faith. That critique comes not just from conservative churches.

"Not only are the traditional denominations failing to get their message across," asserts *Time* religion editor Richard Ostling, "they are increasingly unsure just what that message is."[17]

The mainline Protestant denominations that are losing members share the same patterns. The proportion of their members under thirty is well below the national average "and they are virtually invisible when it comes to evangelism."[18]

A study conducted for the Episcopal Church Center revealed that

Episcopal church members fall "considerably short in terms of regular and consistent . . . study of Scriptures, evangelism and invitation, financial giving, churchgoing, prayer habits, and small-group participation."[19]

Can the Sidetracked Get Back on the Main Line?

"Recovering the Gospel seems a better bet for reversing membership decline than does recovering liberalism," advises Alan Wisdom in *Religion and Democracy.* "Unfortunately, it is not clear that oldline agencies have put aside their political enthusiasms. . . . We must learn to distinguish our political judgments, which we make tentatively, from the eternal Gospel of Christ, which we receive by faith."[20]

Sounds a bit like Glenn Tinder's question about politics: "Can we be good without God?"

Officially, at least, many oldline churches are declaring evangelism to be a ministry priority.

The Episcopal Church is calling the 1990s the "Decade of Evangelism."[21] In its General Assembly in 1989, the Presbyterian Church (U.S.A.) adopted evangelism and church development as twin priority goals.[22] The United Methodist Council of Bishops, acknowledging that the denomination faces a "critical turning point" and that many Methodists "have no vital relationship with God," resolved that they "must choose to be faithful to Jesus Christ in our time." And the bishops asked church members to join them in plans to "fast and pray" for new congregational vitality.[23]

At the National Council of Churches, a new working group was formed in 1990 to explore better relations among mainline Protestants, evangelical Protestants, Pentecostal Christians, and Roman Catholics.[24]

And within most of the mainline denominations there are committed—sometimes militant—conservatives who would rather stay in and fight than switch churches. They are at work through a variety of renewal groups whose goals range from "promoting a more biblical, orthodox theology to steering denominational leadership away from preoccupation with a liberal political agenda."[25]

The Rev. John Mulder, president of the Louisville Presbyterian Seminary, believes the 1990s will be a kind of "mobilization of the moderate middle." Toward the middle or late 1990s the Presbyterian Church will begin to reverse some of its losses, or at least stabilize. He argues that evangelical Protestantism is becoming more mainline while the mainline is becoming more evangelical.[26]

Mulder also sees "a lot of ecumenical activity at the local level; a banding together for common purposes in practically every urban area of the United States."

To him, "the megaquestion" is whether a kind of secularization is developing in the U.S. similar to that prevalent in many European nations. "The challenge is from the direction of secularity rather than conservative forms of Protestantism," he said.[27]

That's a concern shared by Roof and McKinney: In the 1990s, liberal Protestantism's major "competition" will not be from "the conservatives it has spurned but the secularists it has spawned," they say.[28]

And like most researchers—including Marty, Barna, and Gallup—they are not sanguine about any quick turnaround to the mainline churches' slide in numbers or social influence. It's unlikely the mainline "A Team" will ever again own the stadium. But then, neither will any other "established" faith.

The next millennium may be a good time for renewal, but not for restoration. In McKinney's words,

> The oldline denominations have no hope of reaching out to the new populations of America—to people of color, to those drawn to the TV preachers, to those who struggle to make ends meet—if they remain bound to the notion that it is either possible or desirable to restore our churches to their earlier position of dominance. It is only when we accept the fact of our own new off-centeredness that we will have a chance of partnership with peoples whose current experience is also not of the center but of the margins.[29]

The Rev. Dorothy Bass, a professor at Chicago Theological Seminary, offered similar counsel to a gathering of theological educators, saying that the margins of society may be a good place from which to minister. After all, "the most lively and faithful periods of the church's history have not been periods of establishment and ease,"[30] she reminded them.

On the other hand, Hartford Seminary sociologist Jackson Carroll comes at the dilemma from a wholly different perspective. He says that the new contours of Protestantism will materialize "in special interest-oriented groups that cut across denominational lines, and that reflect social, political or theological agendas on either conservative or liberal tracks."[31]

It looks like "pew people" of 2001 will want to be in on the action once again—not sitting on the sidelines.

Chapter 14

Frontliners and Headliners

If the mainline Protestant denominations have moved to the sideline of American religion, the evangelicals have moved to the front lines and grabbed the headlines. In a 1990 survey of the nation's 500 fastest-growing Protestant churches, 89 percent were evangelical, non-mainline congregations.[1]

The broad umbrella group known as evangelicals includes fundamentalists as well as charismatics and Pentecostals, who believe in faith healing and speaking in tongues.

The Assemblies of God—the largest Pentecostal group in the United States, with 2.1 million members—has quadrupled in size since 1965. The Missouri-based church suffered a slight downturn in the late 1980s after Assemblies' TV preachers Jimmy Bakker and Jimmy Swaggart, who have since been expelled from the denomination, attracted worldwide press and fell from grace over sex and money scandals. But, with more than 11,300 congregations and a billion-dollar-plus annual budget, the Assemblies were on the grow again by the early 1990s.[2]

Meanwhile, the nation's largest Protestant denomination, the theologically conservative Southern Baptist Convention—despite more than ten years of acerbic internal wrangling between fundamentalists and "moderates"—has sustained a slow but steady and unbroken membership climb. Under 11 million in 1965, the Southern Baptists numbered nearly 15 million twenty years later.[3]

In general, as mainline losses have slowed, so have evangelical gains. But predominantly black and other ethnic evangelical and Pentecostal churches are expected to display significant growth throughout the decade. No one I interviewed for this book challenged the assumption that evangelical churches will continue their upswing.

The "higher octane religions . . . the more sect-like," will be the growth leaders, according to religion-watcher Rod Stark. "As long as churches are relatively more evangelical or orthodox, ask a little more of members, prohibit a little more of members, they grow. . . . If it doesn't cost something, it isn't worth much."[4]

Who's Hot and Who's Not

A good clue about frontline action can be gleaned from John Vaughan's 1990 list of 512 churches that reported at least 100 more people at weekend worship services than were attending the previous year: Southern Baptist, 117; Assemblies of God, 79; independent charismatic, 37; United Methodist, 36; independent non-charismatic, 29; independent Baptist, 29; Lutheran Church-Missouri Synod, 19; Evangelical Free, 18; Churches of Christ, 14; Presbyterian (USA), 14; Presbyterian Church in America, 14; and Foursquare Gospel, 10.

Atlanta, Los Angeles, Houston, Dallas-Fort Worth, Denver, Nashville, and Seattle topped the cities with the most rapid-growth churches. Heading the states' list are California, 84; Texas, 54; Florida, 42; Georgia, 37; Tennessee, 27; Illinois, 21, and Washington, 20.[5]

A number of smaller, evangelical denominations also posted large membership gains between 1987 and 1988: Presbyterian Church in America, 9.1 percent; Christian and Missionary Alliance, 6.3 percent; International Church of the Foursquare Gospel, 3.3 percent. Others with net gains were the Church of God (Anderson, Indiana), Church of the Nazarene, General Association of General Baptists, the Free Methodist Church of North America, and the Seventh-day Adventist Church.[6]

Smaller denominations that are willing to take risks and focus on church growth are likely to stay on the fast track as the clock ticks into the next century.

So Who Are the Evangelicals?

It's probably fair to say that no religious group has attracted more publicity—much of it unfavorable—in the past decade and a half than evangelicals, or born-again Christians.

In 1976 reporters and editors in the newsroom of *The Los Angeles Times* often asked me to interpret what Jimmy Carter meant when he talked about his evangelical Southern Baptist faith. "What is all this 'born-again' stuff?" my colleagues wanted to know.

About the same time, evangelicals—especially the fundamentalists and charismatics among them—were increasingly audible and visible on radio and television. And the media, which for the most part had ignored this segment of American Christianity, poised its pen and perked its antenna when evangelicals emerged in the arena of social activism, particularly against abortion and for school prayer.

Found in varying numbers in virtually every denomination, evangelicals are somewhat difficult to define, as Gallup and other pollsters have discovered. Since 1986, his poll has settled on accepting self-identification, asking: "Would you describe yourself as a born-again Christian?"

Gallup and Castelli concur that "it seems safe to say that the percentage of Americans who are born-again Christians has remained fairly stable since 1976." Thus, 31 percent of Americans are evangelicals, they concluded in 1989. Among Protestants, 44 percent say they are born-again. And 13 percent of Roman Catholics and 20 percent of Mormons so identify themselves in Gallup surveys.[7]

Estimates from other sources have placed the nation's total number of evangelical Christian adults in the 40- to 50-million range.

Evangelicals tend to be a tad older and slightly less educated than Americans as a whole, and a disproportionate share live in the South.

There are signs this is changing in the 1990s, however, as evangelicals achieve upward social, educational, and economic mobility.

Evangelicals are decidedly more conservative about matters of sexual morality and lifestyle than non-evangelicals. But, refuting a popular stereotype, they are no more conservative on many domestic and foreign policy issues. In fact, they are slightly more liberal on some economic issues, according to Gallup findings.[8]

The fundamentalists among them get the most media attention. Fundamentalism's most visible strength, say Naisbitt and Aburdene, is its effective use of the media, "an outlandish, incongruous, perfect balance: the hard edge of technology in service to the high touch of religion."[9]

Because of this prominent profile, the so-called "religious right" organizations are thought to represent all evangelicals and fundamentalists. Of course this is far from the truth. The National Association of Evangelicals, with forty-eight member denominations, loosely represents a constituency of about 5 million members and has a theological and political diversity that makes it difficult to reach a consensus on many issues. Therefore, they seek agreement only on questions perceived to have a clear biblical mandate.[10]

Martin Marty, for one, thinks the "fundevangecostalists" will remain an important political caucus during the 1990s and that their tribe is not endangered.

"I say unto you," he wrote in his newsletter, "there are not fewer fundamentalists than there were before the Pentecostal scandals, the folding of Moral Majority tents, and the signs of corruption that came with power. They believe roughly what they always did but have slunk away from some of the frontal attacks."

This decade, he continued, look for organizations such as James Dobson's Focus on the Family, Donald Wildmon's Clear-TV, Operation Rescue, "and many sometimes durable and often ephemeral efforts" to drive the wedge into the frontline issues of the 1990s. The venues will be school, library, zoning and hospital boards, and church councils. The action will be "diffuse, widespread, protean, blurry."[11]

But amid the social activism of some, many evangelical congregations are quietly staying out of political involvement and simply adding members.

In sync with marketing surveys showing that upscale congregants spurn denominational tags, many denominationally affiliated churches are dropping the labels. For instance, Community Church of Joy in Phoenix is the fastest-growing congregation in the Evangelical Lutheran Church in America, but you wouldn't know it from its name. Nor would you associate newly named Shepherd of the Hills Church in Chatsworth, California, with the Southern Baptists. Pastor Jess Moody decided to change the old name, Van Nuys First Baptist Church, after surveying people in movie lines, ball parks, and shopping malls. Shepherd of the Hills, like other churches not wanting to limit their drawing power to one community, has omitted any geographical reference in its new name.

Also, more groups in the coming years may shun even the word *church* in their title. Capital Christian Center (in Sacramento) and Crossroads Cathedral (Oklahoma City), for example, are both large Assemblies of God churches.

The name "New Life Christian Fellowship" says "it's not some place where you'll be bored out of your gourd," explains the Rev. Scott Linscott, associate pastor of the nondenominational church, er, *fellowship*, by that name in Biddeford, Maine.[12]

Marty, parish consultant Lyle Schaller, and church-growth specialist Vaughan caution, however, that what's in a name can either help or hinder would-be-attenders in deciding whether it's "their kind of place."

Downright Humongous Churches

On the 1990's inside track to fast growth are the megachurches and "metachurches." Vaughan defines megachurches as those with membership above 2,000 and metachurches as those with 10,000 or more. About thirty Protestant churches move into the megachurch ranks each year.[13]

Vaughan, who is also director of the International Megachurch Research Center in Bolivar, Missouri, has these tips for a church that wants supergrowth: (1) a new location, (2) a new auditorium, (3) a new pastor, (4) more services, and (5) a growing community.[14] In other words, just jack up the windshield wipers and slip a new car underneath!

Many growing churches are mainly taking in members who transfer from existing smaller congregations. But some, like Willow Creek Community Church in suburban Chicago (see chapter 25), are reaching hundreds each year who make first-time professions of faith. And more than a few megachurches are spinning off "daughter" churches and "satellite" congregations.

Fred Smith of the Leadership Network, a resource group for large churches, says only 100 U.S. congregations were at the megachurch status in 1984, but by the beginning of the 1990s there were twice as many.[15] Schaller estimates that well over 1,000 churches draw an average weekly worship attendance of at least 1,000—and counting.[16]

Jim Dethmer, one of the teacher-pastors at Willow Creek Church, even predicts that by 2001 many major U.S. cities will support evangelical metachurches with 100,000 to 300,000 members! But, he says, "they will be incredibly personal [with] deep, personal connectedness at the small-group level."[17]

Leadership Network's Robert Buford believes the superchurch is the coming successor to both the neighborhood church and the parachurch organization. The large church, he told *Fortune* magazine reporter Thomas Stewart, is "like a shopping mall. It contains all the specialized ministries of parachurch groups under one roof."[18]

Already, Schaller noted in 1989, a "slew" of downtown churches, especially on the West Coast, were moving out to much larger sites to build one-stop complexes with bigger buildings and more parking. "Not just to follow their members but to be able to become regional or metropolitan churches," he added.[19]

The emergence of the megachurch, he proclaims, "is one of the four or five most significant developments in contemporary American church history."

Schaller says the central secrets of success are relevance, motivational preaching, and quality and multifaceted programming.[20] Yet he, among others, has some misgivings about humongous churches. The children of today's megachurch members may want something "new and different," he suggests: small, intimate congregations that average between 150 and 700 at worship.

He predicts that sometime during the 1990s the U.S. Supreme Court will be asked to rule on the constitutionality of restrictions that an increasing number of municipal officials are now adopting and enforcing. These pertain to land-use, parking, zoning, size, noise, and other criteria for places of public worship and assembly. "That decision, rather than the marketplace, may decide the fate of future megachurches," he attests.[21]

Evangelicals in the Pre- and Post-Millennium

For all the hype and stereotype, the evangelicals have "produced a great yield out of those committed from childhood to what they stand for. They devised institutions that attract loyalties. They have overcome negative imagery (such as 'redneck,' 'hillbilly,' and 'fundie') and become respectable from the White House to the Miss America Pageant to the National Football League to good graduate schools,"[22] says Martin Marty.

Evangelical groups are generally savvy in marketing and communications skills, which are, at their best, turned into instruments for evangelism. At their worst, they become the tools for consumer-oriented superchurches that twist the faith into a gospel of individual acquisitiveness.

Quips Tom Sine: "The Evangelical church is being co-opted slowly by the American dream—do it all and have it all—with a little Jesus overlay."[23]

Sociologist James D. Hunter, author of *Evangelicalism, the Coming Generation,* warns that the next generation of evangelicals may be moving toward accommodating "the world" while edging away from the key beliefs that once defined the "historic faith" of evangelicalism.[24]

A disconcerting study by the Roper Organization lends credence to Hunter's fears. Conducted in 1990, it tested the behavior of born-again Christians before and after their conversion experiences. The shocking result: conversion made little difference. In fact, the use of illegal drugs, driving while intoxicated, and marital infidelity all *increased* after the born-again experience!

The study was made "because we believed the results would show that born-again Christians are significantly different and pose fewer problems in these crucial moral and societal issues," commented Don Otis, vice-president of High Adventure Ministries, the organization that commissioned the survey. But the findings revealed the opposite.

We've reached a point, Otis lamented, where there is little correlation between what evangelicals say and do. "Accountability is lacking, confrontation is lacking, and we are 'marketing' salvation in such a way that discipleship is simply not occurring."[25]

During a roundtable discussion about strategies for evangelicals in the 1990s, Eddie Gibbs, president of the American Society for Church Growth, ventured the opinion that secularization "in a virulent form" was sapping America's spiritual vitality. "We are seeing a polarization" and the evangelical growth is "not sufficient to turn the tide," he said.

Another panelist, Joe Webb of Global Village Communications, a Southern California organization emphasizing evangelical values among baby boomers, sees evangelicals carrying their "image problem" of the late 1980s well into the 1990s. The legacy of the sex and money scandals that tarnished the televangelism superstars will remain a credibility blot, hardest to erase with the present under-forty-five crowd, he declared.

Recalling the climactic scene in the motion picture "High Noon," Webb commented, "It's high noon for evangelicals. Right now, we control the stage. But there's going to be a gunfight."[26]

When the smoke clears, we will see what kind of faith this generation of evangelicals handed off to the next.

Chapter 15

Roamin' Catholics

When six-week-old Joseph Garcia Soares, Jr., resplendent in his embroidered white gown, was baptized at St. Anthony's Roman Catholic Church in Wendell, Idaho, Sister Mary Louise Deroin played a key role. And earlier that morning the Holy Cross nun had led an entire Communion service by herself. As "pastoral administrator" at St. Anthony's and St. Catherine's—her other rural parish twelve miles away in Hagerman—Sister Mary Louise knows parishioners intimately and is in charge of the churches' daily activities.[1]

If you thought Roman Catholicism was a fortress of unbending tradition where only "Father knows best," you've come to the wrong decade.

As the clergy shortage within the U.S. Catholic Church grows ever more acute, more and more nuns, deacons, and lay men and women will be appointed to fulfill roles and duties traditionally carried out only by priests. The practice, hailed by some and criticized by others, is shaping the way Catholic churches will be run in the future.

Some church leaders fear parishioners will find the arrangement so satisfactory that they will feel less need for priests—downgrading the sacramental nature of the church and the importance of the all-male priesthood. Others worry that just the opposite will happen: Parishioners will shun non-ordained leaders who aren't able to perform the sacraments—thus increasing pressure to ordain women and married men.

Despite objections, the 1989 authorization allows bishops to designate a deacon, non-ordained sister, brother, or lay member to lead prayers, read Scripture, preach, and perform a Communion service if bread and wine consecrated by a priest is available. Following this guideline, Sister Mary Louise is one of the hundreds of nonclergy now being empowered to perform pastoral duties.[2]

The phenomenon of "priestless parishes" isn't confined to the wide-open spaces of places like Idaho, where more than a third of the 110 parishes in the Diocese of Boise are without resident priests. It's also affecting big-city archdioceses. In Richmond, Virginia, for instance, Father Tom Caroluzza says that by 1996, twenty of its 131 parishes will need to be served by either a nun or a lay person.[3]

One out of ten U.S. parishes had no regular priest in 1990, according to a survey by the Institute for Pastoral Life in Kansas City, Missouri. At least 1,000 of the nation's 22,733 Catholic parishes have no *resident* clergy, and almost a third of the dioceses have parishes that occasionally hold Sunday services without a priest. Before 2001, that figure will jump to 85 percent, the institute forecasts.[4]

Fewer Priests, More Parishioners

Between 1970 and 1990, the number of American priests dropped from 59,000 to 53,500. But the U.S. Catholic population increased by more than 7 million. Now 57 million strong, the church is adding 2 million new members each year. Since 1965 it has gained more than 20 percent—almost as much as Protestantism declined during the same period.[5] Perhaps as many as one in five Roman Catholics call themselves charismatic, or Pentecostal,[6] and somewhere between 13 and 21 percent say they are born-again Christians.[7]

In the wake of the Second Vatican Council "reformation" of the mid-1960s, Catholic leadership has assumed a new "center" position on the American religious landscape, presenting a social vision to its members as well as to the larger society.

"The Catholics," says Richard Mouw of Fuller Theological Seminary, "are the calm, dignified, authoritative voices, insofar as there are any at all."[8] And church researchers Roof and McKinney believe the Catholic Church appears to be "in the best position ever to assume a custodial role for American culture at large."[9]

Despite absolutist theological stands on many issues, the Catholic Church has become an effective player in national politics. The bishops' high-profile pastoral letters on disarmament and the economy, for example, grabbed the ears of government officials. Martin Marty, among others, thinks the U.S. bishops will continue to be important power brokers—even though they're divided.[10]

Catholics now account for about 28 percent of the nation's population—a jump of 40 percent since 1947.[11] And the number of Latino Catholics, enlarged by immigration and prolific birth rates, comprises the church's most rapidly growing segment. Nearly a third of the country's Catholics are Hispanic; before the turn of the century, half of them will be.[12]

But Hispanic Catholics are often "roamin'" Catholics. Using information gathered by the National Opinion Research Center in Chicago, sociologist-priest Andrew Greeley concluded that about 23 percent of all Hispanic Americans—despite most of them coming from a Catholic background—are Protestants and that some 60,000 Hispanics join Protestant denominations each year.[13] In a 1990 survey by the City University of New York, one third of all Hispanics said they adhere to non-Catholic faiths.[14]

Father Allan Figueroa Deck, a Catholic theologian who specializes in Hispanic studies, thinks Hispanics often struggle to be noticed in Catholic churches, while evangelicals offer a simplicity and emotional power that is appealing. Evangelical and Pentecostal groups often provide Spanish-speaking ministers and small churches "especially appropriate for immigrants who need all the personal communal support they can get," he told a national meeting of the Catholic bishops in 1989.[15]

The sprawling, three-county Archdiocese of Los Angeles, the nation's most populous, illustrates Deck's point. In 1990, about 70 percent of the 3.5 million Latinos who lived within the archdiocese were Catholic. But in the early 1970s, that figure was about 85 percent. Many have converted to "the aggressive fundamentalist and Pentecostal churches," said Louis Velasquez, associate director of Hispanic Ministry for the archdiocese. Worse, he added in an interview, probably no more than 20 percent of

Southern California Latinos who consider themselves Catholic attend Mass regularly.[16]

That squares with national figures showing a general decline in worship attendance by Catholics over the past thirty years or so. Gallup noted a "dramatic" skid at weekly Mass between 1958 and 1988—attendance fell from 74 percent to 48 percent.[17]

The church is losing black Catholics as well. The desire for African-style liturgy and concerns about alleged "institutional racism" have leaped to center stage. These issues will probably continue to be prominent on the agenda of many of the nation's 1.3 million black Catholics, who are served by only about 300 black priests (fewer than one for every 4,000 black parishioners).[18]

These and other internal problems will cause U.S. Catholic leaders to reach for the Pepto-Bismol often during the coming decade. Tensions with Rome, upheavals over teaching, financial woes, and a growing "pick-and-choose" style of faith—particularly in matters of morals and sexuality—will upset even cast-iron constitutions.

No Surplus in the Surplices

Many mainline Protestant denominations are experiencing a surplus of clergy, but in the U.S. Catholic Church the shortage of priests is the largest threat to traditional Catholic parish administration. Yet, the problem may hold the seeds for a new and previously unexperienced vitality.

First the bad news:

- Since 1966, the number of seminarians seeking the priesthood has plummeted from 48,000 to 7,500. The number in the final four-year-program leading to ordination has dropped to only about 4,000.
- By 2001, the projected decline from resignations, deaths, and fewer ordinations will leave only 15,000 active parish priests—about the same number as in 1925 and less than half as many as in 1966.
- The average age of these priests at the turn of the century will be 65.
- Within twenty-five years of ordination, 42 percent of priests will resign, and younger priests are resigning in greater proportion

than older ones. The church's requirement of celibacy and a permanent commitment are the most frequently given reasons for not entering the priesthood or for leaving it.

- In the past twenty years, an estimated 19,000 U.S. priests have married, although the church forbids it and rescinds their right to perform priestly duties. Half of all priests under age sixty have married. About 90 percent of all priests who resign eventually marry. By the mid-1990s, the number of married priests is expected to equal or surpass the 26,000 unmarried active parish priests.[19]

"The vocation shortage is long-term, not just temporary, and the church is powerless to reverse . . . the social pressures causing the downturn," declared Dean Hoge, a sociology professor at the Catholic University of America in Washington.[20]

Now for the good news. Sort of.

A recent survey of priests in their late thirties found them to be happier than commonly thought. Eighty percent were satisfied with their vocation and would enter the priesthood if they had it to do over again. Ninety percent said they enjoy working with sisters and lay leaders.

"This is a new attitude," said Father Gene Hemrick, who researched the project with Hoge. "The spirituality of the laity is helping them [the priests] in their own lives. . . . It's supposed to be the other way around. In the past, priests would never say they're inspired by the laity they're serving."[21]

At the same time, most of the "thirtysomething" priests said they disliked being assigned to rectories. They would prefer to choose where they live.

At least 5,000 priests who have chosen to marry would serve their church in an ordained capacity if allowed to do so. Thirty to forty of the nation's 188 dioceses *do* permit married priests to function in church jobs but do not allow them to administer the sacraments. Another eighty to 100 married priests teach theology at the university level—half of them at Catholic schools.[22]

Some seminary officials consider their schools more than just a training ground for priests. They see them as a way to equip Catholic laymen for leadership that doesn't require ordination.[23]

Some attending seminary never plan on ordination. Sister Katarina

Schuth, OSF, coordinator of a Lilly Endowment-funded study, notes that about 4,000 nuns and lay people are pursuing graduate degrees in theology in seminaries across the country. Twenty years ago, there were none. Training the laity to take on religious tasks frees the clergy to concentrate on sacramental duties like saying Mass.

Then, too, more paid lay parish managers are presiding over business and administrative tasks once performed only by priests. In the future, these lay professionals may oversee three or four parishes, both priestless and staffed, church planners say.

Some innovative efforts are in place now. In Indianapolis, a laity-founded cooperative connects parishes by shared staffing. It's doing "a good Band-Aid job—keeping the parishes from falling apart," commented Father Clarence Waldon of Holy Angels Parish in the center city.[24]

Bishop Raymond Lucker of New Ulm, Minnesota, a pioneer in dealing with priestless parishes, predicts that even if priests were to become plentiful again, the emphasis on lay ministry would continue. The church can't go back to the days when "Father did it all," he said. "What started as an answer to a practical problem has opened up a new vision."

But he has also warned his fellow bishops that they can no longer ignore the ordination question.[25]

Sociologist Hoge speculates that if priests were given the option to marry, the number of candidates would quadruple. In a massive study, he found that 16 percent of college-age Catholic men would be interested in the priesthood if the celibacy requirement were removed. The number of candidates "would go up so high, the church would have to institute quality standards and could be more selective," he said.[26]

There seem to be three possible solutions to the priest shortage: ordain women priests; relax the celibacy standard for men; allow and encourage more laity participation. It doesn't take a crystal ball to figure out which one they'll try first.

Cafeteria Catholics

Although the Pope isn't ready for married priests, many U.S. Catholics are. Recent polls show that more than half of the priests and at least 60 percent of the laity favor optional celibacy for priests. A slight majority of Catholics also favor the ordination of women priests.[27]

But then, lack of uniform opinion is a hallmark of Americanism in the 1990s, and the diversity of our society has become a characteristic of the U.S. Catholic Church as well—to the consternation of hardline Vatican officials. Pope John Paul II cautioned American Catholics in 1987 that dissent had its limits, to which a few brave Catholics politely but firmly responded that the pontiff didn't understand America.

"Today there is no longer a single Catholic culture or even a single vision of church in the United States," wrote Jane Redmont, who has been a campus and parish minister in a variety of Catholic settings. "A diversity of opinion exists about moral and social questions, about church authority and ministry. The language of prayer itself is no longer uniform, but reflects a plurality of cultures, styles and spiritualities."[28]

American Catholics are more likely to follow their own conscience or personal preference than to assent unquestioningly to papal pronouncements. In no area is this more true than matters of sex and lifestyle. Not only do a large majority of U.S. Catholics disapprove of the church's teaching against contraception, they also favor a limited pro-choice position on abortion.[29]

And many Catholics agree with dissident theologian Father Charles Curran who says that homosexual behavior, masturbation, premarital sex, and divorce aren't always sinful.[30] (About one-fourth of U.S. Catholics have been divorced and half of these have remarried.)[31]

Curran, who was fired from his teaching post at Catholic University for his unorthodox views on sexual ethics, predicts that the role of women in the church "will be the most divisive internal issue facing Roman Catholicism" this decade.[32]

While the Pope keeps calling for traditional values, American Catholics keep finding their own. But they still consider themselves "good" Catholics, loyal to the church as they see it.

"Roman Catholics continue to be devout, believe in God and Jesus and go to church," priest-novelist Andrew Greeley declared. "But they no longer trust their leadership." He added wryly: "If we [clerics] haven't driven the lay people out in the last 25 years, then we'll never be able to."[33]

Future Directions

One new feature of Catholicism—the "magnet" parish—is drawing lay people in rather than driving them away. Magnet parishes, the Catholic equivalent of Protestant megachurches, are faith communities that attract people with common interests, not a common residence. These interests may be social activism, style of worship, or the charisma of a certain pastor.

Church canon defines a parish as a community of people. This simple definition allows Catholics to find parishes where they feel comfortable, said Jesuit Father Pat Carroll, pastor of St. Leo's in Tacoma, Washington, a magnet community that draws from far beyond its immediate borders.

"The scary thing is that if people don't like what's going on they just go away," Carroll added. "That's been one of the curses [of] the Protestant churches."[34]

Religion expert Jeffrey Hadden believes continuing conflict within American Catholicism will stem from Pope John Paul II's desire to replace liberal U.S. priests with conservatives.[35] Tensions between Rome and liberals in the U.S. hierarchy reached crisis proportions in 1986 when the Vatican disciplined Seattle Archbishop Raymond G. Hunthausen for laxness in pastoral administration—a situation many bishops thought could have been settled without Vatican intervention. Though that imbroglio was resolved, others wait in the wings.

In the decade's closing years, academic freedom and fidelity to church teaching at Catholic institutions, particularly higher education, will be publicly debated.

The Catholic parochial system will provide an important alternative to public schooling for the next century. These schools will be staffed mostly with lay teachers rather than clergy or persons in religious orders. Half or more of students in inner-city parochial schools will be non-Catholic, and large majorities will belong to ethnic minorities.

In Southern California, 93 percent of Catholic inner-city school enrollments in 1991 were children of color. The Archdiocese of Los Angeles's school system—second-largest of all systems, public and private, in the state—has a dropout rate of less than 1 percent. And 86 percent of Southern California students who graduate from Catholic high schools—where they perform two grade levels above the national average—go on to college.[36]

But throughout the nation, financial and personnel cutbacks have forced Catholic schools and parishes to close. Nationwide, Catholic schools still enroll about 2.5 million students, but that's down about 45 percent from the peak of 4.5 million in 1964.[37] Consolidations and closures that have already hit Detroit and Chicago will spread to other big cities unless new sources of income and leadership are recruited.

Meanwhile, the church will be hard-pressed to come up with enough money to provide decent retirement programs for a growing flock of retired and elderly priests, nuns, and brothers.

Greeley points with alarm to continuing cash squeezes and lighter collection plates. Back in the 1960s, Americans were giving about 2.2 percent of their income to the church. Protestants still give that much, but Catholics give a paltry .9 percent—resulting in an income loss of about $7 billion annually.[38] Sister Sharon Euart, RSM, who helps the U.S. Catholic Conference make long-range plans, agrees the church is in for a time "of diminishing resources in terms of finances and shifting personnel."[39]

Perhaps Clarentian priest Rosendo Urrabazo, president of the Mexican-American Cultural Center in San Antonio, Texas, sums up the best-hope scenario for a "reformed" American Catholicism of the 21st century. He believes the church must challenge the social structures of the nation and take the side of the poor—which includes immigrants and large segments of the black and Latino communities. And, he says, the services need to be adapted to the Hispanic community and culture. "The festive community that celebrates and sings and is joyful wants to express that worship, and, for many, in Spanish."[40]

Blacks to the Future

Many Pentecostals and charismatics know the name and the place: Azusa Street Mission in Los Angeles, California. That's where, in 1906, "Holy Ghost power" fell in a "new Pentecost."

But few know that African-Americans were at the heart of that revival. William J. Seymour, the pastor and spiritual leader at 312 Azusa Street, was black. So was the majority of his congregation.

Soon, however, the spiritual firestorm swept across racial lines, making multiracial fellowship and leadership the dominant mark of Pentecostalism during the early years of this century.

Before long, the races went separate ways, segregating into the predominantly black Pentecostal denominations, such as the Church of God in Christ, and the predominantly white ones, like the Assemblies of God.[1]

As the century nears an end, there are signs that people of color are once again at the forefront of a wave of spiritual power. A new survey of America's black congregations reveals that black Americans will increasingly look to forms of Pentecostalism for spiritual vitality. Sometime in the 21st century, the survey shows, half of all black churchgoers will be Pentecostals.[2]

Speaking with cautious optimism, the two scholars who conducted the survey, C. Eric Lincoln and Lawrence H. Mamiya, say that despite its many toils, tribulations, and cares, black religion is viable and showing signs of renewal and change.[3]

They are not alone in their assessment. Roof and McKinney project that black Protestantism "should continue to grow numerically and increase in importance as a societal force" into the next century.[4]

Black Church Vitality

The black Pentecostal and Baptist denominations in particular should extend their growth through the 1990s because of high fertility rates among members, strong communal bonds, and the black churches' tenacious commitment to civil rights.

Lincoln and Mamiya focus on the seven largest U.S. black denominations. These groups claim 80 percent of the nation's aggregate total of 24 million black churchgoers, about 77 percent of whom are Protestant. The largest U.S. black organization of *any* kind is the 7.5 million-member National Baptist Convention, U.S.A., Inc.[5]

Although the National Council of Churches' *Yearbooks* have little current statistical information about the black churches, figures for the Pentecostal and Baptist denominations in the 1950s and 1960s (the most recent available) place their combined membership at more than 3 million.[6] If they have grown by even 2 percent a year they would now total four or five million.

The oldest black denominations are the African Methodist Episcopal (A.M.E.) Church and the African Methodist Episcopal Zion Church, which were founded after the Revolutionary War by free blacks influenced by John Wesley's Methodist revival movement. Closely related is the Christian Methodist Episcopal Church. Together, these three churches during the early 1980s had more than 4 million members.[7]

The seventh major black denomination is the Church of God in Christ, which grew out of the Azusa Street revival. It claims about 3.8 million members.[8] According to *Time* religion editor Richard Ostling, it's the fastest-growing black denomination and "probably the fastest-growing major denomination of any kind" in America.[9]

The largest church sanctuary in the United States is owned by the Crenshaw Christian Center, a mostly black congregation in Los Angeles. With a seating capacity of 10,400, a campus of thirty-two acres, and a constituency said to top 16,000, the charismatic congregation pastored by Frederick Price is truly in the "metachurch" class.[10]

Price's U.S. crusades and nationally broadcast television ministry have given him a high profile. He is regarded as "a role model for many young pastors of the emerging independent churches," according to *Charisma* magazine.[11]

But Price's success isn't one-of-a-kind.

Nine of the top fifteen U.S. churches with the fastest-growing attendance are predominantly black congregations, according to a 1990 survey by church growth specialist John N. Vaughan of Southwest Baptist University in Bolivar, Missouri.[12]

The black charismatic wave of the 1990s includes at least half a dozen congregations in the multiple-thousands class. Many draw a majority of members in their twenties and thirties. A colorful variety of spirited music and hand-lifting worship, "word-of-faith" preaching, and old-time Bible teaching characterize these congregations. The unifying element appears to be an upbeat message of hope and self-esteem.

And that is good news indeed for a community that has often been downtrodden and cast to the margins of society during the past 400 years.

Roots and Fruits

Two-thirds of American black Protestants trace their ancestry to Africa.[13] But as their African culture receded over the decades, they forged a distinctive religious history and group identity. Black Protestants—especially those with Methodist and Baptist backgrounds—came to define and interpret their experience in this country through "revivalistic Protestantism."

"Early on, the black church emerged as an important institution, second only to the family, as a symbol and embodiment of racial solidarity and the quest for freedom and justice," say Roof and McKinney.[14]

Though it has been—and will be—under strain and assault, the black church is still the central institution in the African-American community and the best hope for its future. The black church is one of the few stable and coherent institutions to emerge from slavery.[15]

William Pannell, who directs the study program for black pastors at Fuller Seminary, said the black church "occupies a more central place in the lives, traditions, and day-to-day struggles" of black people than the church does for other racial groups. "The black church is both integrated into the African-American culture, and it is a source of strength for leadership and community development. . . . It's the one constant," Pannell said.[16]

Black churches are not only the focal point for organizing civil-rights and black political movements; they are also the cradle nurturing what is arguably the most religious race of people in the world.[17]

Surveys by Barna and Gallup, among others, consistently show that U.S. blacks hold stronger, more evangelical and traditional beliefs about the inspiration of Scripture, the divinity of Jesus, the presence of God, and the evidence of miracles than do Christians of other races. Blacks also are far more likely to put their beliefs into practice in terms of church membership, attendance, and denominational loyalty. And they pray and study the Bible more.[18]

All in the Black Family

The families of the country's 65,000 black congregations need strong faith to face the day-to-day struggles confronting them.

"Urban congregations are surrounded by neighborhoods demoralized by spiraling drug use, crime and family disintegration; the churches face a looming shortage of qualified clergy; and the very relevance of many congregations is being challenged," writes Ostling.[19]

But there is good reason for hope for the black church. Many positive models can take blacks to the future of God's kingdom.

Robert Franklin, dean of black church studies at Colgate Rochester Divinity School, foresees several trends for black churches in the 1990s:

- Black churches will put more emphasis on ministries dedicated to family stability.
- Many educated, affluent, black boomers will return to the churches they temporarily turned their backs on while in college or while starting to advance professionally. "As upwardly

mobile blacks abandon the inner-core central city," Franklin said, "they will retain attachment to their home church, even though they move to the suburbs. But, unlike their white counterparts, these buppies will drive back to the inner city to worship on Sundays." Even pastors will be a part of this commuter pattern.

- Because of the federal government's withdrawal of the "social safety net," inner-city folk are becoming wards of the church. This will put increased pressure on churches to provide basic services to the inner-city poor. "I'm hopeful this will . . . [produce] an increased ministry to the homeless, substance abusers, people who are hungry . . . ," Franklin said. "A cadre of young black women and men are preparing to minister in these areas."[20]

C. Eric Lincoln, professor of religion and culture at Duke, anticipates a decisive movement of the larger black churches into black economic development. These churches are building schools and apartment complexes, and sometimes developing supermarkets and plazas, he said.

Though this is "not yet what you'd call a trend," Lincoln told me, "it is reminiscent of the early days of the black church before slavery. Then the church was the only agent of relief for black people anywhere."

Lincoln points to the work of the Congress of National Black Churches, composed of the seven largest U.S. black denominations, as a signpost for decade direction. The congress is experimenting with group insurance, a common banking pool, and common purchasing for clusters of churches.

Other cooperative ventures hold promise. In Brooklyn, fifty-five churches have banded together to help clear neighborhoods of slum housing taken over by narcotics trade. Volunteers rennovate the reclaimed houses for low-income families.

"This is very definitely the direction the black church will be moving," Lincoln says with enthusiasm. "But it takes longer for smaller churches to get involved."[21]

Bridge Street African Methodist Episcopal (A.M.E.) Church in the Bedford-Stuyvesant section of Brooklyn includes a growing number of buppies. They are, says pastor Fred Lucas, "looking for the spiritual piece in their lives. They want to channel something back into the community."

And they do, reports Jane Redmont in *Progressions,* the Lilly Endowment report:

> Doctors, lawyers and other professionals have organized service-delivery organizations. The church helps operate a shelter for homeless men, provides pastoral care to people with AIDS, and offers walk-in counseling. Its credit union is the fastest-growing in the United States.[22]

The Graying of Black Clergy

But the black church turns gray when the focus changes to the clergy. The median age of the nation's black pastors is fifty-two, meaning that fewer young blacks are entering the ministry.[23]

"In the past, the black pastor was the best-educated and most articulate person in the community," Lincoln explained. "Then came the resurgence of black education in the civil rights movement. . . . So, many young men who would have gone into the clergy twenty years ago don't look in that direction today if they're bright and able; they look forward to careers in other fields. No longer do the seminaries get the best candidates."[24]

At the same time, the black church doesn't provide significant health or retirement benefits for its underpaid clergy. Just to survive, the typical pastor must stay on long after he'd normally retire. "This means the most prestigious churches are in the hands of superannuated people," Lincoln added, "and the young, aspiring clergy have nowhere to go. It's a waiting game."[25]

Lincoln thinks the problem ultimately will right itself. The number of black seminarians rose nearly 500 percent between 1970 and 1989—from 808 to 3,814.[26] Also, increasing numbers of black women are going to seminary. But so far, most black churches, especially Baptists (the largest group of black churches) and the Church of God in Christ, have been unwilling to call many women as pastors—even though the active membership of the typical black Christian congregation is 70 percent female![27]

Integrating Integration

The possibility of black clergy appointments is greater in white mainline churches, Lincoln says. "But they're disillusioned with those prospects because they are considered 'showplace pieces' and exotic. . . . They resent being put on display."[28]

In the past, major black church leaders have promoted integration, visualizing a society in which black and white live together in equality and peace. But black churchgoers may choose a different path. For some, that will mean choosing to attend a distant black congregation rather than a nearby integrated church.

In the North and the West, "blacks are no longer drifting into white churches when they move up the social scale," writes Richard Ostling. He quotes John Hurst Adams, senior bishop of the A.M.E. church in Atlanta: "We are not buying the integration route. We never have and never will. We seek an inclusive society that need not be integrated but values diversity and respects it."[29]

Others, like Anthony Evans, pastor of Oak Cliff Bible Fellowship, a large black congregation in Dallas, Texas, seeks to build bridges across the color line. Joint urban ventures link black and white churches: "Intact" families in white churches relate directly through guidance, spiritual support, and ministry to single-parent families in black congregations.[30]

Carlton Pearson, founding pastor of 3,500-member Higher Dimensions Evangelistic Center in Tulsa, is convinced that God will bring whites and blacks to the future that started in 1906. "What God intended to happen at the dawn of the century was an integration of the people at the Azusa [Street Mission] outpouring," he told *Charisma* magazine. "I believe we will at last accomplish that goal at the close of the century."[31]

Muslims, Jews, Mormons, and More

When the United States and its allies declared war on a predominantly Muslim nation in January of 1991, a spate of books and articles about the mysterious religion of Islam hit the bookstores and newsstands almost overnight. It was as if America had discovered for the first time a world faith of 900 million members.

The roots of this basically anti-Western and anti-Christian religion go back to a cave at the foot of Mount Hira near Mecca in present-day Saudi Arabia. There, in A.D. 610, Ibn Abd Allah had a vision, and the prophet-to-be, Muhammad, began to preach the word of Allah and transcribe the first verses of the *Koran,* the Muslim holy book.

"As a result, this man and his work transformed the lives of millions of people and affected significantly the history of the modern world," writes Michael Youssef in *America, Oil, and the Islamic Mind.*[1]

The bad image evoked by Saddam Hussein in his exploitation of the Muslim faith for his own perverted ends will largely be forgotten or forgiven, slowing the growth of Islam in the United States only momentarily.

Islamic mosques are being built by the hundreds throughout the U.S., and Islamic teachings are being propagated vigorously. The American Council of Mosques was preparing the way in 1990 for a nationwide missionary crusade. And Saudi Arabia and other Muslim countries are spending tens of millions of dollars in community development and other projects in America in order to help Muslim communities expand.[2]

Lawud Assad, president of the Council of Mosques of the United States, says there are more than 1,000 Muslim community organizations in his group alone, some worshiping in basements and other makeshift places.

Declared Gutbi E. Ahmed, director of the Moslem World League: "We are at a new stage in which we cease to be a religion on the margins, but [are] a religion of American people related to American life." In the fall of 1990, national Islamic representatives became official members of Religion in American Life, a major interfaith group. Muslims are "now ready," Ahmed said, "to interact with the rest of the American people, particularly in relation to its religious communities."[3]

Black Muslims

Nowhere are the Muslims edging more fully into American life than in the black community. Many there, says Youssef, "are rejecting values and ideals they consider outgrowths of a hypocritical white Christian society."[4]

"Islam is particularly attractive to young black males," asserts C. Eric Lincoln. "Many . . . see Christianity as a racist religion. And they're looking for an alternative to the black church of their mothers and fathers. . . . The black church is not yet aware of this potential threat."[5]

Lincoln estimates that as many as 1 million of America's Muslims are black. The militant Nation of Islam, led by iconoclastic black Muslim Louis Farrakhan, appeals to many black youths. The group evokes a strong image of male assertiveness, black supremacy, and ramrod discipline. But Lincoln and others think the enduring impact on blacks will not come from "cult-type" Muslims but from the orthodox "black Muslims" (a phrase coined by Lincoln) who follow the main body of worldwide Islamic teaching.

"This trend will intensify" during the 1990s, Lincoln thinks, "and the Christian black church will have to look to its laurels."[6]

Bolstered by immigration of committed Muslims and by younger American-born converts, Islam will be a factor in black politics in the next century, Lincoln says.

Yet, as Islam moves into the mainstream of American religion through increased numbers, recognition, and interfaith cooperation, Muslims will remain a heterogeneous group, often with little in common. The devout will continue to avoid pork, abstain from liquor, fast during the month of Ramadan, pay the "alms-tax," and pray five times daily. But, like Christianity, Islam is divided into splinters and sects. And, like other religions, it has extremist fanatics as well as moderate ecumenists.

Still Kosher to Be Kosher

Some Jews are worried that a great rise of Islam in the United States will pose a formidable challenge to Jews because the Koran makes it clear that Islam is to triumph over Christianity and Judaism.[7]

As a sign of the new times, however, American Jewish and Christian leaders, on March 1, 1991, issued a call to cease all verbal abuse and violence against Arab-Americans, Muslims, and their houses of worship.[8]

"Islam hasn't had the same tradition of pluralism that Christianity has had," observed Jonathan Farna, professor of Jewish history at Hebrew Union College in Cincinnati. "So we're in for a period of interreligious tension in America." Jews will have to deal with Muslim groups that "begin from a point of hostility to Judaism," Farna explained.[9]

Nor is Farna sanguine about Jewish prospects in a heterogeneous America of the 1990s.

Sometime this decade, Islam may surpass Judaism as the nation's largest minority religion. The rapidly expanding numbers of Muslims will eclipse the 2 percent of Americans who are Jews, a proportion that has held steady since the early 1970s, according to Gallup and Castelli.[10] The 5.9 million members of Jewish religious organizations listed in the 1990 *Yearbook of American and Canadian Churches* were a slight decline from the previous year's figures.[11]

Rabbi Yechiel Eckstein of Chicago, a bridge-builder between the Jewish and Christian communities, foresees divisions between the major branches of Judaism (Orthodox, Conservative, Reform, and Reconstructionist). These divisions will widen during the decade, he fears. The rifts will involve technical questions, like "who is a Jew?" Will standards of cooperation be developed to define who is a Jew and who has religious authority? Eckstein asks.

> We're going to have to find new ways to help Jews define what it means to be a Jew. . . . How to live in this world without melting down into some pot of stew . . . conveying values that we feel are distinctive without becoming an island unto ourselves. These are key questions for Jews of the 1990s.[12]

Jewish leaders are also concerned about the low birth and conversion rates among Jews. And they are disturbed by low rates of attendance at religious services and high rates of marriage to non-Jews. Brooklyn College sociologist Egon Mayer's extensive studies show that during the last two decades, fewer than half of Jews under forty married another Jew.[13] For these reasons, more than a few Jewish leaders are into a "survivalism" mode, seeking to confront these serious losses to assimilation, intermarriage, and indifference.

But Steven Bayme, director of Jewish Communal Affairs for the American Jewish Committee, says the challenge to today's Jewish leaders "is to move beyond survivalism; to continue to guard against threats to Jewish interests but also to develop the content of Jewish life; to form a Jewish community so compellingly attractive that others will wish to join it."[14]

Eckstein is among Jewish leaders who are optimistic about what they see as a nascent resurgence of Jewish spirituality: "a faith-oriented identity."

Along with the conservative growth trend within Protestantism, there is a concomitant swing among Jews who grew up in secular or alienated homes to return to their religious roots. This "re-Jew-venation" is particularly strong within the *Baal Tshuvah* (a person who repents or returns) movement.

"I see this new fresh blood coming into Jewish life—Jews who are recouping their Jewish identity or who are coming into it through conversion," said Eckstein. "They are providing a fresh basis for the next decade or two . . . [giving] a fresh leadership and appreciation to Judaism."[15]

Speaking about New York's Jewish Theological Seminary, fountainhead of the nation's conservative Judaism and "an institution that always prided itself on its intellectual vigor and steered clear of the mystical side of religion," Rabbi Neil Gillman says "we can now talk of what everybody calls 'spirituality.' I don't know what the word means, but to students today it means they don't want to be Jews and rabbis just for the rituals, just for symbolism, but in order to come closer to God."[16]

Jewish Baby Boomers

Some Jewish baby boomers are returning to an orthodox religion of dietary practices, daily prayers, and Scripture reading after experimenting with and rejecting other lifestyles. There's been a surge in kosher food sales, says Steve Ostrow, who published a guide to 850 kosher restaurants in the United States, Canada, and Mexico. Queens College sociologist Steven Cohen estimates that about 10 percent of U.S. Jews are Orthodox, and kosher-keeping kitchens number somewhere between 500,000 and 1.8 million, depending on who's defining kosher.[17]

Despite contentions of Cohen and Gillman that Jews across the religious spectrum feel more intensely Jewish, *Newsweek* religion editor Ken Woodward concludes that Jews have yet to recover 70 percent of their "lost" baby-boomer generation.[18]

So what will American Judaism of the 21st century be like, already?

Farna predicts American Jewry will be "one of the great centers of the Jewish diaspora." By that he means that Jews will become isolated in several major population centers—North America, Western Europe, the Soviet Union, and Israel—with larger and larger pockets having no Jews at all.

"Judaism will become more of a regional religion," he summarized. "A major change that we really haven't thought of."

Maybe we should.

Mormon Magnification

Like the Jews, the Mormons also hold down a 2 percent share of the U.S. population. But there is hardly a place in this country—or abroad, for that matter—where members of the Church of Jesus Christ of Latter-day Saints have not trod. Although they are still based predominantly in the western states, their worldwide missionary movement has had startling penetration in the last generation.

At the end of 1989, there were 7.3 million Mormons in the world; by early 1991 the number had increased to about 7.7 million, according to communications spokesman Jerry Cahill in Salt Lake City. At the end of 1989, U.S. Mormon membership stood at 4,175,000, a significant increase since reaching the 1 million mark in 1950.[19]

In 1989 alone "the church baptized 393,940 people into the faith, or an average of 1,082 *every day!*"[20]

What has made the LDS explode? According to Timothy J. Chandler, "the two biggest reasons for Mormonism's success have been their identification of themselves as a culture, and their remarkable missionary program. The first of these accounts for their success in the United States, and the second explains the millions of converts in foreign countries."[21]

Demographic considerations also have played a role in this religion's remarkable magnification. These include a higher proportion of Mormon women than men; the tendency to marry young and have an average of four children (about twice the national average); the relatively young average age of LDS church members and converts; and longevity factors attributed to "clean living."

Further, the Mormon Church is known for the deep loyalty of its members, its stress upon family life, and its abstinence from intoxicants.[22]

It seems certain that more and more Mormons will be in the race toward 2001.

The Jehovah's Witnesses are another rapidly growing American-bred religious group. The Witnesses' aggressive door-to-door missionary zeal, biblical literalism, heavy proselytism among Latinos, and an unyielding certainty that theirs is the only true faith are among the reasons for its 10 percent growth to 804,600 between 1985 and 1988.[23]

Hindus, Buddhists, and Baha'is

Several world religions of Eastern origin are making gains during the 1990s as well.

Hindus comprise 690 million of the world population and their growth rate is about 2 percent a year. According to Tom Sine, their ranks will reach 859 million by the dawn of the millennium.[24] In 1990, there were about a half million Hindus in the United States.[25]

Naisbitt and Aburdene say there are more than forty Hindu temples and 500 Hindu religious organizations in the United States.[26]

Because of immigration from Asian countries, a current fascination with Eastern mysticism among many of this country's spiritual

SOME MAJOR RELIGIOUS GROUPS IN THE UNITED STATES (In Millions of Members)	
Protestant	83
Roman Catholic	56
Jewish	5.9
Muslim	5 (estimated)
Eastern Orthodox	4.5
Latter-day Saints (Mormons)	4.1
Hindu	.5
Buddhist	.2
Sources: University of Massachusetts; National Council of Churches; denominational officials; American Jewish Yearbook.	

seekers, and the influence of the New Age movement, Hinduism is likely to maintain a steady growth into the next century.

The same is true for Buddhism.

Worldwide, there are an estimated 320 million Buddhists. With a projected growth rate of 1.7 percent annually, they should top 359 million by 2001; an increasing number will reside in the West.[27]

Baha'i, an eclectic and independent world faith whose followers revere 19th-century prophet-founder Baha'u'llah of Persia, has an estimated membership of 4 million worldwide. Teaching "the oneness of God, the oneness of religion, the oneness of mankind," and that religious truth is relative, Baha'i's estimated 110,000 American followers gather in several thousand local houses of worship.[28]

Meanwhile, millions of Americans are turning to alternative altars. Many seekers are on quasi-spiritual quests representative of the non-traditional beliefs our nation will embrace in the coming century.

Alternative Altars

Next-Age Faiths

When Robert S. Ellwood, Jr. wrote *Alternative Altars: Unconventional and Eastern Spirituality in America*, the perspicacious professor at the University of Southern California School of Religion was clearly onto something.[1] While giving ample evidence that occult, mystical, and Eastern traditions in the United States were neither new nor alien, he was the first to view our nation's unconventional spirituality as a unique, coherent, and emerging movement. These alternative altars often go unnoticed by the general public, Ellwood says. And they create new forms as they change with each new generation.

The trickle of next-age faiths that Ellwood detected more than a decade ago is becoming a torrent, and their presence raises basic questions for us all: What is "spirituality"? And can we influence the modes of spirituality that will prevail?

"We will be spiritually alive in the 1990s, full of conflict over which spiritualities we will embrace," declared Jeffrey Hadden, a University of Virginia sociologist, religion expert, and author.[2]

Television journalist Bill Moyers believes the struggle to define what it means to be spiritual is the "biggest story of the century."[3]

And Steve Turner, a Christian poet and journalist in London, thinks we will be hearing more and more calls for a "return to spirituality.

Being 'spiritual' in the '90s," he writes, "could carry the weight that being 'politically aware' carried in the '60s." Yet the content of the word *spiritual,* he says, is being drained of its conventional meaning. Current definitions are long on deep breathing and Mongolian chanting, but short on authentic biblical faith:

> In secular discourse, *spiritual* can refer to anything that cannot either be tested in a laboratory or bolted to the floor. Rock musicians are "spiritual" if they play whimsical music; anyone with a fascination for the occult is "spiritual"; and, of course, anything New Age is automatically "spiritual."[4]

Turner sees a key difference between biblical and "contemporary" spirituality. The contemporary idea is that

> Spirituality, like sexuality, is inextricably woven into the fabric of our being and we can either foster it or neglect it. . . . We just need to arouse the latent force within us. This is why there is currently so much emphasis on techniques that promise to improve the spiritual life. The force can be aroused through deep breathing or Mongolian chanting, or it may need a jolt of psychic energy from a crystal. Some even report that jogging does the trick.[5]

Spiritual Transformation

The new emphasis on spiritual transformation has altered more than consciousness; it has transformed what we mean by "spiritual." The broad umbrella we call the New Age movement is responsible for much of this shift.[6] Beyond its faddish aspects, the New Age provides what Hadden calls a "respiritualization" for those who have been turning "secular."[7] In 1978, 61 million Americans had no church or synagogue affiliation, Gallup surveys showed, but ten years later the number of unaffiliated had swelled to 78 million.[8]

The failure of many mainline churches to ask for a higher level of commitment and their failure to teach members the tenets of the faith may explain why so many drop out. As I noted, Roof and

McKinney profess that liberal Protestantism's major "competition" of the 1990s will not be from "the conservatives it has spurned but the secularists it has spawned."[9]

In their benchmark 1987 book, *American Mainline Religion,* Roof and McKinney document the fact that for every person raised without religion who becomes a church member, three people forsake church for no religious institutional involvement. These new non-affiliates are young, predominantly male, well educated, more committed to alternative lifestyles, and "oriented generally to an ethic of personal growth and self-fulfillment," the authors observe.[10]

Yet many of them still consider themselves "spiritual" or "religious." An amazing 82 percent told Gallup interviewers in 1984 that "growing into a deeper relationship with God" (however defined) was important to them.[11] And three-fourths of all Americans in 1988 said one can be a good Christian or Jew without attending religious services. At the same time, 60 percent of those tested said they were *more* interested in "spiritual things" than they had been five years earlier.

Thus, there are legions of "believers, but not belongers," out there. "They have their own private religions. It's a cultural super-market. . . . They prepare their own menus of modern mystical activities and recipes for moral commitment," says Steve Tipton of the Candler School of Theology in Atlanta.[12]

Without brand-name loyalty to a denomination, they are apt to pick up anything from the expanding God shelf—anything that appeals at the moment or offers a "quick-fix."[13]

Looking ahead, Southern Baptist specialists on alternative faiths see a religious atmosphere of floating allegiances, blending of practices, and greater variety. "Individuals will increasingly feel free to construct their own worldview from many options present in society rather than being bound by the orthodoxy of their particular faith," Gary Leazer told a 1990 conference of Baptist chaplains.[14]

Spirituality, Cafeteria Style

The likely result of this self-directed approach to religion will be cafeteria doctrine and do-it-yourself rituals.

Of all the people Root has studied, he finds that 60 percent reject the idea that a person should be limited to a single faith.[15]

"People will go to a study group on Hinduism on Friday night and then come to church on Sunday and try to interject those ideas into Bible study," says Leazer.[16]

And that's no prediction; it's happening.

Community Congregational Church in Tiburon, California, has attracted a growing number of members through services featuring Tibetan prayer bells, Buddhist chants, and various forms of meditation. Others have done similarly: In 1989, churches in thirty-seven of the thirty-nine regional conferences of the United Church of Christ (UCC) stressed spirituality in such forms as meditation, journaling (keeping spiritual diaries), dream analysis using the teachings of psychologist Carl Jung, dancing, and "body prayer."[17]

Looking toward America's religious future, George Barna describes a synthetic faith:

> It will be fascinating to watch people develop these new religious philosophies. In all likelihood, they will seek a blend of elements that will give them a sense of control over life, personal comfort and acceptance and a laissez-faire life-style philosophy. It is likely that from Christianity they will borrow Jesus' philosophy of love and acceptance. From Eastern religions they will borrow ideas related to each person being his or her own god, the center of the universe, capable of creating and resolving issues through his or her own power and intelligence. From Mormonism they will extract the emphasis upon relationships and family, toward establishing a greater sense of community.[18]

If nothing else, future spirituality will be heady and diverse. And its practitioners, a sundry lot.

One person's vision of tongues of flames (or flaming tongues!) descending at Pentecost may be the equivalent of another person's weightless feeling while soaking for an hour in an isolation tank, wrote Turner in *Christianity Today*.[19]

Although many people no longer belong to any explicitly religious group, they do belong to any number of other groups which they consider "substitute faiths" and through which they participate in "religion-like" activities. For example, the Sierra Club, Common

Cause, counseling classes, group therapy, aerobic ballet, yoga, and martial arts. These may not sound very "spiritual," but to those who invest them with spiritual meaning, they are. Perhaps what we have here is just a new version of the old line, "I worship God in nature when I'm on the golf course instead of in church on Sunday."

In-Syncretism with the Eclectic Current

There is syncretism abroad in our land, and it has powerful implications for Christians. To understand it, we must first learn its vocabulary.

Ecology: "Green" phrases such as "Earthkeeping," the Earth as "Mother," and "creation spirituality" are part of a new emphasis on the spirituality of ecology. For instance, papers produced on "The Integrity of Creation" for the 1991 World Council of Churches' General Assembly had "syncretistic echoes" . . . "with a heavy dose of the pantheistic 'green' theology so popular in ecumenical circles."[20]

This viewpoint comes to life in folks like Monte Paulsen, a newspaper publisher in Portland, Maine, who abandoned his Baptist upbringing and his vocation as a missionary to give himself to his new mission: saving the environment. His new religion? "Deep ecology." Meanwhile, he is "struggling to overcome the assumption that humankind is the most important species on Earth—something which the Christianity he rejected insists on."[21]

Self-help: Several self-help psychologists who emphasize the spiritual draw adoring crowds and adulation, if not worship. John Bradshaw, a onetime Catholic novitiate, packs in people around the country to hear his lectures on confronting childhood pain. Millions more watch him on PBS and buy his books like *Healing the Shame That Binds You.* "For the growing number of people around the country grappling with dependencies on everything from alcohol and cocaine to food and sex, John Bradshaw's message has become gospel," declares *People's Weekly.*[22]

Or consider M. Scott Peck, the self-awareness psychotherapist best-known for his blockbuster book *The Road Less Traveled.* "Peck is a chapter heading in the lives of millions of readers, especially in the Bible Belt," says Robert Randall in *The Christian Century.* "The meaning of life is that we have to learn. Psychological-spiritual growth (there is no distinction in Peck's mind) is the process of becoming ever more self-conscious. The road less traveled that leads to salvation-mental health (again, there is no essential difference) is one of courageously questioning every feeling and action with the aim of increased self-awareness."[23]

As we reap the bitter fruit of this decade's dysfunctional families, substance abuse, and other addictive patterns, we will see an increased fuzzing of the lines between religion and transformational psychology and occultism.

Psychology as religion becomes an alternative altar, notes John Wimber, leader of Vineyard Christian Fellowship. He sounds the alarm against elements of the inner-healing movement and the proliferation of books teaching that spirituality is primarily an aid to self-esteem, self-worth, and better living. "In the '90s look for increased tension between Christians who see Christ as their helper and those who see him as their Master. I suspect that churches will split over these issues," Wimber predicts.[24]

Ken Woodward of *Newsweek* paints a vivid picture of clerics who cover sin like an artist with an airbrush:

> Having substituted therapy for spiritual discernment, they appeal to a nurturing God who helps His (or Her) people cope. Heaven, by this creed, is never having to say no to yourself, and God is never having to say you're sorry.[25]

Finally, a word about "Twelve Step Spirituality," the immensely popular—though low profile—psychology-religion hybrid. Many people who crowd church social halls and basements for drug, alcohol, and a host of other rehab meetings can, as a result, develop a strong personal faith in God. But Twelve Steppers can also step right out of any religious structure or traditional faith into Altars Anonymous. Faith in faith, not in God, may be the only substance at the bottom of the glass.

Goddess/Feminism: The goddess pathway to self-empowerment is an option for many 1990's feminists. The path often combines goddess-worship with witchcraft. Perhaps 100,000 Americans already worship the goddess,[26] and many more will "begin a joyous adventure into the rich past of women's spirituality and power," beckons an advertisement for "The Spirit of Aphrodite" program. "Discover the Goddess within as you realize your birthright as Woman," it promises.[27] "A Mighty Goddess Is Our Forte," quipped *The Christian Century* magazine.[28]

At the same time, controversy will brew in mainline denominations this decade over the strong feminist bent in some seminaries. The trend has led to the adoption of nontraditional references to God, such as "Mother God" or "Mother-Father God," thus encouraging a search for a goddess figure in the Bible. This development may find favor among church hierarchs and seminary professors, if not pew people. In any case, a cauldron of syncretism and feminism will be bubbling as we celebrate the witching hour of the new millennium.

Astrology: As we race toward 2001, more people will impute a spiritual quality to astrology, believing that the conjunction of metaphysics and astrology will give heavenly advice about earthly events.

"Perhaps what drives modern Americans to seek the stars is the innate human need to find meaning and transcendence behind the details of daily life," speculates David Neff, an editor of *Christianity Today.* "Science and the Enlightenment have given us the belief that human beings are responsible for their own destiny. They have stripped our lives of transcendence and put us in charge. But we certainly do not feel in control."[29]

Many will be looking to the stars—those impersonal forces of planetary motion—for signs of the future. Myopia will keep them from looking above and beyond the stars to the God who created them and set them on course.[30]

Science: The new gurus will be "scientific mystics," those who "are mystical in their science and scientific in their mysticism." So says John David Garcia, author of *Creative Transformation.* But Karla Poewe-Hexham and Irving Hexham, authorities on cults and new religions, denounce the theological impetus behind the faith-in-science "myths of the New Age." They say that "real knowledge of how science works has been replaced by blind, baseless faith, which must be exposed for what it is: a leap in the dark and nothing more."[31]

Paranormal Experiences: "Psychic healing" and holistic health techniques are already a substitute religion for many. Natural remedies and homeopathy may become preferred and legitimate treatments for 2001 and beyond. But spirituality can be distorted when "the search for spiritual experience drifts off into the misty land of paranormal experiences," warns Father Andrew Miles in a charismatic Catholic newsletter.[32]

Civil Religion: Cultural religion, that old bogey of Protestant mainline purveyors, isn't dead in the 1990s, and don't expect its funeral any time soon. Inevitably, there is and will be what missionary statesman Ken Bailey calls "some subtle fusion between the cross and the flag." We can catch ourselves at this dangerous game, he said, only when we give authentic hearing to people from other cultures. And what is true for American Christians is also true for Christians elsewhere.[33]

Because the United States and its allies so resoundingly won the 1991 War in the Persian Gulf and restored the prestige of the American military, nationalism may enjoy a renaissance. Patriots may kneel at the alternative altar of a national religion that substitutes for scriptural faith.

This has been only a syncretism sampler: There are many more alternative altars and next-age faiths. Some, like the Native American spirituality movement—always popular at New Age expos and psychic fairs—are actually Old Age faiths. Now, they're raising the consciousness of whites in the new ecological era of the 1990s.

As we move into the next century, syncretistic religion will coincide with the philosophic bent of the nation, Barna believes. Many people will prefer relative values, disavowing any absolutes in truth, reality, or morality. Those who lack a fundamental knowledge of the Christian faith will be the most susceptible to alternative altars and the pervasive influence of New Age pantheism.[34]

According to Jeff Hadden, the New Age movement will "gain momentum and some focus" through the 1990s. At the same time, he says, there will be strong opposition from "serious Christians who aren't going to stand still for that."[35]

A battle for the worldview is heating up. Between now and 2001 that battle will pose perhaps the most crucial challenge to historic Christianity since the Reformation. And the winner will have a major influence on our planet.

Clashing Cosmologies

Battle for the Worldview

The battle over worldviews—Christianity's sharpest test in nearly five centuries—is being waged in a cultural supermarket of competing beliefs and philosophies.[1]

- A banner headline in *USA Today* proclaimed: "Yoga, Vegetarian Diet Can Heal Your Heart." But what the American Heart Association session really said was that relieving stress, exercising, and eating low-fat foods can help reverse coronary blockages.[2]

- In the motion picture *Star Trek V*, the crew of the starship Enterprise visits the center of the galaxy, where God resides. The Ancient of Days appears in the middle of a Stonehenge-like ring of monoliths. He shows the visitors his "many faces," which they immediately recognize as the gods of their various cultures. Hero Captain Kirk sums it up later by observing that they had finally learned that the real "God" lies within themselves.[3]

- Miriam Starhawk, a self-proclaimed witch, speaking from the pulpit of San Francisco Theological Seminary's chapel, addressed students and faculty on "Feminist Perspectives." Seminary President J. Randolph Taylor said Starhawk's lecture was a "wide-ranging" presentation "focused primarily on creation spirituality and the interrelationship of all life." According to the *Presbyterian Layman* newspaper, Taylor said Starhawk "explained her personal philosophy with references to the pre-Hebrew creation myths of Mesopotamia, quoting excerpts from that ancient literature and illustrating its usage with ritual chants." But some students disagreed with their president. The "ritual chants" the witch offered in the seminary chapel, they said, were really prayers to "powers under the earth."[4]

- As part of "Women's Week," sponsored by the Perkins School of Theology and held at Highland Park United Methodist Church in Dallas, Linda Finnell, another practicing witch, conducted a seminar that included such occult practices as "tarot card reading, building an altar to the goddess Diana, channeling energy, and attempting to communicate with a personal spirit guide."[5]

- Lewis Thomas, scholar-in-residence at Cornell University Medical College, defended the "Gaia hypothesis," which he called the "new idea that the Earth itself is . . . a living thing." The Gaia idea of a living earth "is not at all the mystical notion that it would have seemed a few years back," Thomas wrote. "It is now becoming the most practical, down-to-earth thought ever thought." Thomas said he could not believe "that an organism so immense and complex, with so many interconnected and communicating central nervous systems at work, from crickets and fireflies to philosophers, should be itself mindless."[6]

- In a special "New Age" issue of *Publishers Weekly,* the trade journal of publishing, Jeremy Tarcher wrote an article calling for the "end" of New Age publishing. Not because he's against New Age, mind you. His company publishes an assortment of New Age books, including Marilyn Ferguson's systematic "bible" of the movement, *The Aquarian Conspiracy.* What Tarcher had in mind was that New Age publishing should be taken for granted as part of an accepted truth—in other words, in simply *being the culture.*[7]

The job of the '80s was to set the boundaries, establish an identity and pick up the gold that lay on the surface. The

New Age publisher's goal for the '90s is to find ways to integrate these ideas within the general culture rather than isolating them in a special category, and to market the product as the age-old wisdom and good advice that it really is. . . .

The New Age consciousness can already be seen in a continuing flow of books dealing with psychological development, women's issues, health, relationships and recovery from dysfunctional families. In the future more books will reflect the new consciousness about the ecology, economic problems, politics, humanistic business practices and a full range of social transformation issues. There's no end to the possibilities.[8]

Tarcher's 1989 goal of having "no New Age category as such" within five years is well ahead of schedule. Only one year later, *Publishers Weekly* reported that publishers and bookstores were scrambling to re-label New Age books, slipping them into slots of science, education, psychology, mythology, etc.

Barbara Moulton, an editor at Harper-San Francisco, noted that feminine spirituality books were doing especially well at Christmastime. "Very mainstream women's magazines are approaching us for excerpts" of books like *The Spiral Dance, The Great Cosmic Mother,* and *The Language of the Goddess,* she said. "It has broken out of the New Age market to the general well-educated reader."[9]

• One more item: The surprise best-selling book of the summer of 1988 and the talk of secular American intelligentsia was *The Power of Myth* by Joseph Campbell. For months, bookstores couldn't keep the book in stock. The late literature professor was popularized by PBS journalist Bill Moyers in a series of television interviews summed up in the book.

"For Americans alienated by Christian fundamentalism, Roman Catholic dogma or the soft under-belly of 'New Age' psycho-babble," wrote Don Lattin in the San Francisco Chronicle, "Campbell's ideas swept across the religious landscape like a fresh invigorating breeze."[10]

Campbell defends his secular mythology as a way of achieving meaning and direction, transcending earthly activity at the same time it gives it significance.

But certain "myths" are redlined by Campbell, particularly the personal lawgiver God of the Bible and the Christian idea of sin. Disdaining the concept of ultimate truth, Campbell nonetheless "asserts the ultimate truth of an impersonal and amoral divinity," notes author and New Age critic Douglas Groothuis.[11] The centrality of Campbell's worldview? "I know," said Campbell, "that good and evil are simply temporal aberrations and that, in God's view, there is no difference."[12]

Battle for Hearts and Minds

In the final years of this century we will witness an escalating battle for the hearts and minds of men and women.

Tom Sine agrees. In his book *Wild Hope* he says that "the greatest threat to our freedom . . . will not be from those who attempt to invade our shores or abridge our Constitution. Instead, it will come from those who become increasingly more sophisticated in manipulating our values, opinions and worldviews."[13]

If the Christian worldview is to prevail, Christian leaders must design strategies to assert the biblical perspective in the 1990s. If they wait until 2001 it will be too late.

We need to recognize divergent worldviews more clearly and discuss them more intelligently.

But first we need to clarify the meaning of "worldview."

One historian says it's "a conception of the nature of cosmic and human reality that discloses the meaning of life." According to another definition, worldviews "furnish answers to the largest questions human beings can have about their condition."[14] Toffler says a worldview is a mental model of the world. And in German, a worldview is a "weltanschauung," a conception of reality that solves the "mystery" or "riddle" of life. In *Understanding the New Age,* I define worldview as "cherished premises or assumptions you hold about ultimate reality."[15]

A worldview is like a giant filing cabinet in which you arrange your suppositions about how the universe is ordered.

Therefore, worldviews hold our presumptions about God.

Although the distinctions are somewhat arbitrary, three major worldviews have been generally recognized by historians, theologians, and philosophers. Rivals for thousands of years, these worldviews are spoken of in the Bible. Paul was well acquainted with them, as 1 Corinthians 1–2 attests.

The first view of the world is naturalism, or naturalistic humanism, sometimes associated with secularism. The second is mysticism, or what comes under the headings of monism, pantheism, and other philosophies with a New Age label. This worldview posits the unity and divinity of all beings. The third major worldview is theism/supernaturalism. The biblical, Judeo-Christian worldview is a subset of this.

All three are alive and well on Planet Earth. But will they remain healthy as we speed toward the next millennium?

Naturalistic Humanism, Naturalism, Scientism

Naturalistic humanism, naturalism, and scientism are the "wisdom of the world" that the Apostle Paul spoke about in 1 Corinthians. "For since in the wisdom of God, the world through its wisdom did not know him, God was pleased through the foolishness of what was preached to save those who believe . . . so that your faith might not rest on men's wisdom, but on God's power."[16]

Naturalistic humanism is the prevailing worldview on most secular campuses: human reason and scientific innovation are the final authority for life and thought.

Nihilism, the belief that there are no certainties—that everything is up for grabs—is the spirit of the times that Allan Bloom speaks about in *The Closing of the American Mind*, the best-selling book during the summer of 1987. He describes trends in American higher education that have led to a crumbling of the belief that truth exists—or that it matters.[17]

"Relativism is necessary to openness; and this is the virtue, the only virtue, which all primary education for more than 50 years has dedicated itself to inculcating," Bloom argues. "The true believer is the real danger."[18]

This is not to disparage science. We need science, which theologian Reinhold Niebuhr described as "the rational effort to understand the world's coherences and master its powers."[19] We need science as well as theology to see the harmony of things and their relationships.

But the danger is believing that if we tote up all the exact little coherences of science, we arrive at the sum truth of everything.

The wisdom of the world says it knows "God." And God is simply the "vast coherence of things." The rational order is "God," though most naturalists wouldn't use that word.

Mysticism

The New Age worldview holds that God is an impersonal force, or a field of energy that holds everything together. Joseph Campbell commits to a "trans-theological" image of divinity, "an undefinable, inconceivable mystery, thought of as a power, that is the source and end and supporting ground of all life and being."[20]

Campbell, Groothuis submits, may have become a kind of posthumous prophet for the New Age worldview. For Campbell is in essential agreement with New Age celebrities like Shirley MacLaine, Werner Erhard, and John Denver: "All is one, god is an impersonal and amoral force in which we participate; supernatural revelation and redemption are not needed."[21]

But the New Age worldview goes further and speaks about the wisdom of self-consciousness. "New Agers avoid the materialist's despair, not by affirming transcendent absolutes, but by destroying rationality and denying the reality of the material world. For them, subjective reality is all there is."[22]

We create our own truth, our own reality. "Normal thinking processes are replaced with a nonrational mystical awareness."[23] In essence, God is everything; everything is God; and humans are part of that process—so *we are God.*

"New Agers typically view themselves as operating on a 'higher' spiritual plane than other people and believe that the whole traditional dichotomy between right and wrong is merely the product of a degenerated aspect of life," says Kevin Garvey, a New Age analyst. If man is God, then any act is potentially a sacrament, any idea potentially sacred.[24]

The problem, according to the New Age worldview, is not sin or evil, but ignorance. The problem is that we have *forgotten* who we are—that we are divine.

And the way to return to Godhead? (to use the Hare Krishna

phrase). Through *psychotechnologies*—all designed to alter the mind's perceptions. This shift may occur through mind-altering drugs such as LSD, meditation techniques, intense group encounters, psychic experiences, or other routes. These techniques are intended to alter consciousness and lead to "Enlightenment," which is supposed to occur when we shut down the analytical, logical, "left" hemisphere of the brain in favor of the feeling, intuitive, "right" hemisphere.

Enlightenment is "merging" with God, becoming one with the One. All religious paths are valid roads to truth. In this mystical "knowing," we supposedly see the "many faces" of Deity, the same "Star Trek V" God that all religions purportedly worship.

The New Age depiction of God, wrote Donna Steichen, "is held to be the immanent consciousness of the evolving universe, which we can all know by direct experience, because we are part of it."[25]

In other words, the Gaia hypothesis. What controversial Jesuit Teilhard de Chardin called "the soul of the world." What mystic physicist Fritjov Capra terms "the cosmic dance of energy." What Jean Houston calls the "emerging evolutionary process." And what Matthew Fox speaks of as "the divine 'I am' in every person and creature."

The widespread and multifaceted New Age worldview subtly touches virtually every aspect of our lives. It is mainstreamed into our daily newspapers, alluded to in Congressional hearings, and written into the Congressional Record. From public school classes, business seminars, psychology and science texts, to health, music, art, entertainment, and politics—and even in churches and seminaries—New Age theories and self-actualization therapies abound.[26]

This meshing of the metaphysical and the material boils down to a pop psychology of self-affirmation, necromancy through "channeling," and a wholesale borrowing from Eastern belief in reincarnation and the notion that the cosmos is a universal energy field or life force.

The New Age worldview appeals because people are looking for something new. Berkeley sociologist Robert Bellah speaks of "vague spiritual orientations."[27] Those who have rejected traditional Christianity nonetheless feel there must be something more. They seek transcendence. And the New Age movement promises "quick fix" spirituality, global harmony, and self-empowerment from the "divine within"—without troublesome demands for personal moral account-ability.

New Age is creeping into Christian thought and into more than a few churches. Its worldview is perhaps subconsciously adopted by those looking for an alternative to the impotence and vague spiritual orientations of lackluster congregations.

Judeo-Christian Theism

The "wisdom of God" is radically different from the worldviews of both naturalistic humanism and the New Age.

God is Personal—not an "it." He has attributes. He is separate from his creation; the creation is not God but his handiwork. Human beings are created in God's likeness or image,[28] but we are not God or gods. As Søren Kierkegaard once put it, there is an "infinite qualitative difference" between the human and the divine.[29]

In the Judeo-Christian worldview there is a problem with human existence, but it is not "metaphysical amnesia," as in forgetting that we are divine.

In the biblical worldview, the problem is sin, human disobedience to the revealed moral demands of a merciful but righteous Father in heaven. The broken relationship cannot be mended through psycho-technologies that seek to unite us with a loose energy-ball God who is "all that is."

"Christian conversion is not a case of fanning that little spiritual spark in the human soul into a flame. It is a case of invading a dark and doomed soul with spiritual light from above," declares Steve Turner. Nor does Christian spirituality originate "in a small area of the human brain. It is a transference of God's personality into the human life, and it can only happen on the basis of repentance, faith and discipleship," he continues. "It cannot be coaxed, kick-started, or chanted into being."[30]

Restoration comes through repentance, forgiveness, and the atoning work of Jesus Christ on the cross of Calvary.

"Paul's successful establishment of the biblical worldview, and toppling of opposing worldviews, resulted directly from his cross-centered life, preaching and focus," says Norman R. Gulley, professor of systematic theology at Southern College of Seventh-day Adventists in Tennessee.[31]

The wisdom of God has always been foolishness to the world. The preaching of Christ crucified and resurrected is incompatible with worldly wisdom. But it is the timeless wisdom of God that Christians must proclaim in new and fresh ways if a hardy biblical and evangelical theology is to endure into the 21st century.

In today's pluralistic world, the imperative of a Gospel that insists Christ is the only way, truth, and life sounds arrogant. One of the most seductive and appealing features of the New Age worldview is that it is tolerant—or appears to be. It invites women and men to spread their wings and fly with godlike possibilities.

But the bottom line is that the New Age worldview is nothing more than the serpent's lie in Genesis 3:5: If you eat of the forbidden fruit "you will be like God."

Pass It On

How, then, can we pass on the Christian worldview to our children and grandchildren?

During a discussion between several dozen evangelical scholars in Washington, Gordon College sociologist Stan Gaede suggested that

> The real question . . . is, "Are we giving our students an alternative worldview to the one they are getting in the modern age? Are they learning to think biblically about all of life? Is the Creator at the center of their understanding of creation? Is God's glory the primary purpose behind their thinking and doing?" If the answers to these questions is "yes," then regardless of what our students come to think of the particulars within the evangelical tradition, they will be in a position to carry on the task of the Reformation, even in the modern world.[32]

"What concerns me, however," Gaede continued,

> is that most Christian educators are not in a position to foster such a worldview—because they have never developed one

themselves. One reason for this is that evangelicalism has been as much a reaction to something as an affirmation of something.[33]

Admittedly, cultivating a biblical worldview is difficult in a modern world where the "freedom" of intellectual pluralism tempts us to compromise.

My son T. J. attends what was once a Methodist-related university. In a required freshman class called "Worldviews," the professor urged his students to "be skeptical about everything. . . . Learning grows only from doubt." He concluded that "the university is one of the few places—or it ought to be—where doubt needs no defense."[34]

Today's university students are asking questions. Heavy questions about ultimate issues, and they surfaced in T. J.'s Worldview course:

- Is there a God?
- Why are we alive?
- What is death?
- How do we live?
- Why is North, north? What structures our thoughts?
- What about good versus evil?
- What is justice?
- Are all humans and life forms equal?
- What is our relationship to Nature and to the nature of the world?
- What parts of us are hereditary and what parts are environmental?

The answers depend on your worldview.

Which worldview will we communicate to the generations of the next century?

Questioning, thinking for oneself, is absolutely essential for vigorous faith. But to think that truth is unknowable, that moral values must be held forever in suspension, is to fall into the trap of the world's wisdom—the world that does not understand the power and wisdom of God.

The biblical worldview needs to be defended against all others. The Bible is trustworthy and unique in historical character. The Jewish Scriptures alone, as religion and as history, are supreme over every other ancient writing. They are personally honest and factually accurate.

The Gospel is "hard news," and its cornerstone is laid in history, with consequences in history. The uniqueness of the Christian worldview is that the Christ drama really happened, while the myths about other world religions did not. The mythic imagination called for by Joseph Campbell is tempting, but it must be rejected. As Groothuis observes, Campbell "chokes on the hard historicity of Christianity, and is not comfortable until he recasts it in metaphorical terms."[35]

But metaphors contain no saving power.

The Christian worldview is oriented toward fact and verification, not subjective mysticism based on altered consciousness.

The other central support for the Christian worldview is the resurrection, as over against reincarnation. That is part of the historical Christ-event—fact, not theory.

The resurrection of Christ is the wisdom of God, and it is not known by the wisdom of the world, nor by the "wisdom" of the "universal mind." Faith grasps it even if we can't fully comprehend it. It is the realistic remedy for sin and the vanity of the human heart.

Christians need to say with clarity and conviction that human beings cannot know God when we make our humanity the ultimate end.

To understand the forces shaping the next age, the church must teach its people how to discern worldviews and separate clashing cosmologies.

Chapter 20

Shining the Pastoral Patina

Listen to Jim Dethmer speaking. He built from scratch a 1,500-member independent church in Baltimore and is now one of the teaching ministers at Willow Creek Community Church, the nation's second-largest congregation, in South Barrington, Illinois.

> The church of the 21st century will be a radical distribution of power to the laity. At present the laity exists to serve the clergy's program. The clergy will be important, but the heros of the twenty-first century will be laity who will shepherd small groups of six to ten people. These, fully empowered by the church, will make the difference. To get larger, churches will have to think smaller.
>
> The clergy will empower and equip the laity to do this, returning the ministry to the people. They won't be doing the bidding and will of the pastor but the work the laity are cut out to do. To have led and birthed small groups successfully would be a pre-requirement for seminary candidacy.

The seminaries have largely outgrown their capabilities to train leaders for the next century. Most seminaries are dysfunctional in training life-changing leaders. Life-change, through the Holy Spirit, doesn't usually mean you need to know Greek, exegesis, etcetera. This stymies people who want impact in their lives.

Today's typical seminarian will become absolutely irrelevant. He's become ghettoized. He needs to know the needs of modern man. Seminaries will be caught between an economic rock and a hard place. They'll be stuck with large campuses and libraries. But radical decentralization is the wave of the future. So a whole new paradigm in training is needed.

The educational model for the future will be decentralized to train an army of laity. It will happen through interactive TV, satellite disks, etcetera. Leaders will get content through their own home. But the major training won't be cognitive; it will be more on-the-job and in-service training. There are fifty skill sets needed for leadership in my opinion. Small-group leaders need to get these—intellectual development and character training from a coach—plus evaluations. This can happen while the trainee is being a commodities broker and raising the kids, for example.

We'll see an explosion of powerment of lay people like we've never seen. A second Reformation. The ministry is going to be returned to the people. The average church size is seventy-five. They're led by clerics, seminary trained, who are unwilling to give away ministry to other people. They must release power and leadership to others. Churches of seventy-five to 200 will become a thing of the past.[1]

Dethmer, who, by the way, is ordained, may be a visionary or just a dreamer. But he is not crying in the wilderness. Other leaders—largely those representing independent ministries rather than ones closely tied to denominations—are making similar sounds. And seminary administrators are starting to listen. More than a few denominational honchos may see their secure sinecures come apart at the seams (or sems) by the turn of the century.

The Seminary Scene

Mainline magnate William McKinney, director of education programs and professor of religion and society at Hartford Seminary, dares to ask:

> Where is it written that effective ministry always demands three years of post-college study in an accredited seminary? Where is it written that virtually all of our theological education funds must go to the preparation of ordained clergy and virtually none to the preparation of laity and their ministries in the world? Where is it written that every congregation must be able to support a full-time minister, or occupy a building with a steeple, or own an organ, or gather for worship for one hour a week beginning no earlier than 8 and no later than 11 on a Sunday morning?[2]

On the evangelical side of the aisle, Carl F. George, director of the Fuller Institute of Evangelism and Church Growth in Pasadena, goes so far as to recommend that a person shouldn't be allowed to enter seminary without demonstrating leadership over several small-group Bible studies for three to four years! Another seven to eight years of proven leadership should precede ordination, George believes.[3]

One recent study found that more than one-third of the senior ministers of megachurches (2,000 members and up) do not hold a seminary degree.[4] At the same time, many Protestant denominations are rethinking whether the ministry should be a full-time profession. Churches with less than 150 members probably won't be able to afford a full-time pastor by the end of the 1990s, in any case.

"We'll be working out new patterns whereby people can be both ministers of a church and hold another job," says Robert Lynn, retired senior president of Lilly Endowment. Lay people will be far more involved, Lynn added, partly because of shrinking church budgets and partly because there's "a new recognition of the diverse talents required in ministering." He questions whether one person can or should be expected to do all the things we assume a minister or priest should be able to handle.[5]

Parish consultant Lyle Schaller ponders the future of seminaries that educate students to serve a shrinking number of small churches barely able to afford a full-time pastor. But, he wonders, "Who will perpetuate the orthodox Christian faith if the large churches do not depend on seminaries for future ministerial leadership?"

The Knot at the End of the Church's Thread

Schaller puts his finger on another trend that threatens seminaries: large churches that cull their staff from volunteers. "Church leaders hand pick laypersons, then train and socialize them in megachurch culture rather than send them off to seminary. Will the megachurches, rather than the seminaries, be the primary source of both ordained and lay staff for tomorrow's megachurches?" Schaller asks.[6]

This is happening at churches like Willow Creek. And Frank Tillapaugh advocates this strategy in his book *Unleashing the Church.*

"It's amazing that we continue to put so much emphasis on a formal education for people in vocational ministry," Tillapaugh writes. "Educational resources are so numerous and available we can educate people on the job. We ought to be looking for ministry effectiveness and we're best able to spot them within our own churches.

"Allow the Body to determine what kind of staff the church needs," he adds. "The church unleashed can't afford to take a set approach to hiring its staff. It shouldn't look for people on the basis of resumes and paper credentials."[7]

David Barrett, a research consultant for the Southern Baptist Foreign Mission Board, says ministerial leadership is "a massive psychological problem; one has to find the leadership that clicks. And there is limited 'clickability.'"[8]

Another factor may shrink seminaries: diminishing job openings. A little arithmetic shows that if you have twenty congregations with 100 members, you have jobs for twenty pastors. But one megachurch of 2,000, though it might typically hire ten pastors, would provide only half as many ministerial jobs. Optimists answer, of course, that a thriving megachurch will reproduce itself several times, providing *more* jobs for pastors, not less, and that small churches seldom reproduce.

At any rate, it appears that many seminaries are training people for jobs that no longer exist. Or else failing to equip them for the tasks that *are* needed. They don't prepare clergy to market, manage, forge relationships, and lead, complains Barna. "Seminary should be the place where the average Christian can go and get equipped for fighting the fight of spiritual warfare," he says.[9]

At the beginning of this decade, at least, seminary enrollments weren't suffering. Yet shifts are occurring: more women students; more older, second-career students; and a lower proportion of students planning to enter pastoral ministry.

Although the 203 seminaries associated with the Association of Theological Schools grew in the early 1980s, they leveled off and dropped slightly in mid-decade. Then they started climbing again at the decade's end.

In 1990, women constituted 29.7 percent of seminary enrollment in the United States and Canada (17,501), more than three times as many as in 1974, when women accounted for only 5,255 of ATS enrollments.

The trend toward older students preparing for the ministry is likely to extend into the next century. A 1988 study by Shopshire and Ellis Larsen found that students age thirty and up represented 43 percent of all seminarians in Master of Divinity degree programs, the usual pastoral track. And at least one quarter of all seminarians were employed—many in a previously chosen career. So now it often takes a seminarian four to five years rather than three to complete M.Div. degree work.

Women in Ministry: Frustrated?

The Larsen-Shopshire study also showed that 65 percent of students over thirty intended to enter the parish ministry; of those under thirty, 60 percent did. Less than half (47 percent) of the women planned on parish ministry, compared to 62 percent of the men.

No doubt, Shopshire concludes, this is partly explained by the "barriers and discouragements" women in ministry face in almost all denominations.[10] (About 60 percent of all U.S. female clergy are within five denominations: Assemblies of God, Salvation Army, United Methodist, Presbyterian (USA), and United Church of Christ. In all, only about one-third of U.S. denominations currently ordain women.)[11]

The 1990 *Yearbook* lends support to Shopshire's thesis. A report based on women in four major Protestant denominations in Canada (Anglican, Baptist, Presbyterian, and United Church of Canada) notes that the women "are concentrated in the assistant and associate levels among the ranks of Christian education directors, as chaplains, [and] in the head offices of denominations as staff, executive assistant and secretary." Less than 30 percent of women in ministry are sole pastor, senior pastor, or co-minister, and less than one-sixth of all who have graduated from theological schools are pastors or co-pastors.[12]

Frustration may also undergird a powerful, female-driven revolution now quietly taking place behind the desks and in the dorms of seminaries and divinity schools across the country. Martin Marty says this religious feminism "represents the most comprehensive of the changes in the thinking and acting of church and synagogue in the past two decades."[13] And it is influencing theology, historical interpretation, and biblical scholarship.

This multifaceted feminine spirituality includes conservative evangelicals, radical lesbians, black "womanist" thinkers, Jewish and Roman Catholic women, goddess-worshipers, Marxists, liberal Protestants, atheists, and "pure scholars," according to *Christian Science Monitor* staff writer Robert Marquand.

Are you ready? Expect the fractious controversy to roil and polarize churches as the arguments are turned up to full volume. Marquand sees three main feminist groups affecting what happens at churches near you:

- Reformers who feel that church and theology can be changed from within.
- Radicals who often advocate a female separation from male culture or a wholesale rejection of "male-biased" Scripture in favor of a "post-Christian" spirituality.
- Loyalist-conservatives who adhere to older doctrine (a husband-centered family, for example), but feel it must be transformed in practice by a change of heart based on female virtues.[14]

Much of the shift in female religious perspectives is taking place at major universities and liberal seminaries, where theological tensions are likely to accelerate as we race toward 2001.

Liberal Protestant seminaries have become more like the graduate schools of religion at secular universities, notes Jeffrey Hadden, who wrote *Gathering Storm in the Churches* more than a decade ago. The kind of thinking that moves these seminaries away from the mainstream of their churches is continuing, he said. "For example, Illif [a United Methodist seminary] just hired a Buddhist. Who is going to stay around and teach what it means to be a Methodist? This makes about as much sense as a med school hiring a Christian Science practitioner."[15]

Clergy Confusion

By many estimates, the 1990s will be a time of continued confusion for the clergy. Ministers compose the "most frustrated profession" in the nation, according to management consultant Peter Drucker. George Barna says only a third of the clergy believe that their efforts to produce spiritual growth in members will succeed. The incidence of clergy stress and burnout is high, and the average career length for ministers is steadily decreasing.[16]

"After a decade of catching up to the behavioral patterns of the people they serve, clergy will have crisis conditions—divorce, alcoholism, drug abuse—at rates that approximate those of the population at large" by 2001, Barna predicts.[17]

Loren Mead, president of the Alban Institute, a research and development group that focuses on local church life, speaks about a "massive change in understanding" regarding "the role of clergy vis-a-vis the laity." This is bringing about sharp conflicts within congregations, intrachurch clashes, and "fights between staff. Our institute works with people within local churches to figure out what's going wrong and how to fix it. We're frequently called in when there are sharp conflicts," Mead said.[18]

Mead is busy these days.

A 1989 survey among Episcopal priests showed they were "confused and uncertain" about their jobs. The study, prepared under the auspices of the Episcopal Church Foundation, concluded that "many old and valued patterns for ordained leaders of the church are no longer working."[19]

Among clergy comments in the Episcopal study:

- The status of clergy is lower. There is less job security, more potential for being fired; you can be replaced.
- Clergy are no longer special people. In the past, clergy were taken care of.
- I feel pulled apart. Am I a priest or a businessman?

Many clergy, the report said, "are conceiving a role for themselves like chief executive officers of a multi-level organization, where skilled laity are middle managers."[20]

It appears this tension will be exacerbated as the call grows louder in many churches for greater lay training, participation, and leadership.

"Wounded Pastors" Talk

Stressed-out clergy do seem more willing to talk about their problems than they were a few years back. "Healing Our Wounded Pastors" was the title of a Denver conference in early 1991. A female minister in the audience said she'd been overwhelmed by the emotional and personal problems prevalent in modern society. "Am I co-dependent? Am I a workaholic?" she wondered aloud. "It used to be we just worried about whether we had sinned."[21]

Data compiled by church groups puts the problem into focus:

- Medication for stress-related illnesses ranks second only to maternity expenses in the Southern Baptist Convention's medical plan.
- A survey of fifty-seven Christian Church (Disciples of Christ) ministers who changed jobs between 1983 and 1989 found that 58 percent had left to escape stress.
- A four-year study released in 1990 revealed that 10 percent of ministers had sexual affairs with members of their congregations, and about one in four had some kind of sexual contact with a parishioner.
- A 1988 poll of Episcopal priests and spouses in six dioceses showed that one-quarter suffered from stress, anxiety, and insomnia; another fourth had eating disorders, and more than

one in ten had either severe depression or sexual, money, or alcohol problems. Forty percent said they felt lonely and isolated.[22]

A few commonsense measures may help ministers make it through the millennium. Things like learning to be involved in continuing education, setting boundaries for how much time they spend on the job, and taking vacations.[23]

From the lay side of the chancel, the Alban Institute suggests:

- Be sure your pastor gets *positive* feedback.
- Have a special group monitor the quality of life of the pastor and his or her family.
- Make sure your pastor is challenged by setting aside time (two weeks) and money (about $1,200) for continuing education each year, and encourage longer leaves every few years.
- Participate as a member of the congregation.[24]

If Jim Dethmer is right, the clergy will get more than a shoeshine from the laity as lay people assume responsibility for church leadership.

Chapter 21

Making Dollars and Sense of Missions and Ministry

Who gets more pay, your preacher or your plumber?

According to a 1990 Gallup Poll, Americans think the clergy should be paid less than plumbers. Less, in fact, than all the professions. Less than doctors and lawyers, engineers and mechanics, and a bunch of other people. Slightly more than one in three surveyed said the folks who fix your pipes should make at least $40,000 a year, while only one in four pegged $40,000 as an appropriate salary for those who try to save your soul.[1]

Appropriate or not, it's usually only the big churches that can afford that kind of money. (The U.S. Department of Labor estimated a $23,000 average annual salary for Protestant ministers in 1988.)[2] Finances are indeed one of the most formidable hurdles for religious groups in the 1990s.

In fact, the Rev. Dick Spencer, my Presbyterian minister friend, picks "longterm stewardship" as a key challenge for the turning of the century: "We must have a sustainable technology, a sustainable economy, and a sustainable church," he says.[3]

The good news about finances, missions, and church management is that religious faith has a firm foundation of charitable giving. With total contributions of $75 billion a year, U.S. religion would rank fifth on the Fortune 500 list of organizational income if philanthropy were included.[4]

The bad news is that most wealthy Americans are stingy when it comes to charity: contributing households earning $100,000 a year gave, on the average, 2.9 percent while households with incomes of less than $10,000 gave 5.5 percent, according to a 1990 report.[5] And some experts predict that future generations will give a smaller percentage of personal income to support mission and ministry.

Thus, the extent to which pastors and other religious leaders acquire management and monetary skills may spell the difference between the success or failure of their work.

The Greatest Depression Since the Great Depression

John and Sylvia Ronsvalle, a husband-wife team who run an organization called Empty Tomb in Champaign, Illinois, are pioneers in the field of congregational and missions giving. Their findings— the result of scientific tracking—are not entirely encouraging.

Back in 1933, at the depth of the Great Depression, church members were giving an estimated 3.3 percent of their disposable income to churches. But the proportion has fallen ever since.[6] The Ronsvalles project that if the 1990 trend continues, people at the beginning of the third millennium will be giving a scant 1.94 percent of their disposable income to their churches.[7]

If church members were to boost their giving to an average of 10 percent of their income (the tithe), the additional funds could eliminate the worst of world poverty, which James Grant, the executive director of UNICEF, says would require $65 billion. The 10 percent would provide that *plus* another $17 billion for domestic need—all while maintaining church activities at current levels![8]

Crisis fund-raising has already become a standard practice for many churches.

"The wolf at the door is actually welcome," said a pastor in one of six congregations studied by the Ronsvalles. "It gives you a valid excuse for talking about money"—a topic that is difficult for many congregations.

One parishioner, suggesting that church members have switched from being "stewards" to "consumers," said, "They no longer return a portion of their incomes to God. They buy certain services—like a youth program or a place to have ceremonies—from the church."[9]

Advertising, suggest the Ronsvalles, may influence giving habits as strongly as convictions or fund-raising pleas. "Advertising is addressing many of the same felt-needs that have been the church's area of concern over the years," said Sylvia. "Communication companies suggest that you will never be lonely if you use their service; vacation spots promise your family will be happy if you spend your money at their place; disappointments in life can be met by buying an expensive product."

God will meet all these needs, the church says, but he's definitely losing market share.

Boomer Boom or Bust?

The Ronsvalles hope their pilot project will demonstrate that giving downturn can be reversed and that members can be converted from consumers to stewards. But another expert in marketing, research, and strategy isn't so sure. Can the resources be generated to carry out the rallying cry to "Evangelize the World by A.D. 2000!"? wonders James F. Engel, a professor at Eastern College Graduate School.

Engel, who also heads the worldwide Institute of Leadership Development, says the generation of American Christians that has given time and money to support world missions is aging and shrinking and unable to meet new demands:

> We are at a time when the resource burden should be shift-
> ing to the pivotal . . . baby boomers. But there is real doubt
> that they will meet the challenge, because boomer priorities
> and interests diverge sharply from that of traditional mission-
> ary enterprise. They will be the missing link in the resource
> chain that could doom AD 2000 visions unless churches and

mission agencies radically change present resource mobilization strategies.[10]

As a generation, boomers are motivated by immediate gratification, the nontraditional, and the noninstitutional. Nevertheless, as Engel and social researcher Daniel Yankelovich indicate, boomers *could* be challenged to consider the cause of world missions if their interest in "holistic ministries encompassing economic development and social justice" were aroused.

"This means," says Engel, "that they will come aboard full steam when their entrepreneurial spirit can be channeled into direct, hands-on strategy development. They will not buy into someone else's program unless they have a hand in shaping it . . . short-term service is the key to the problem."[11]

As a matter of fact, the number of short-term missionaries sent from the United States has increased 13.2 percent annually during the past five years, according to the *14th Mission Handbook*.[12]

$igns of Generosity

Other assessments of boomer generosity show hope.

"The caring spirit is alive and very much growing, even [among] the so-called 'me generation' of baby boomers," said Brian O'Connell, president of Independent Sector, a coalition of 650 corporate, foundation, and volunteer organizations. A report released in October of 1990 said that three-fourths of American households contribute an average of $734 a year to charity—up 20 percent from 1988. And 98 million Americans were volunteering their time and talents to charitable endeavors, a gain of 23 percent from 1987.[13]

Respondents identified religion as a major motivating force in their giving, in line with other findings that from 50 to 70 percent of all charitable giving is directed to religious institutions.[14] (See chart at the end of this chapter.)

O'Connell pointed to the baby boomer generation as an important catalyst in the giving pattern. Noting that people usually give more as they age, he said the trends "make the picture for future giving and volunteering in this country very bright."[15]

Other plus signs from the report: both giving and volunteering in the black community show strong increases; 90 percent believe that charities are needed today more than ever.[16]

Meanwhile, in a survey by *Money* magazine, religion-related charities came away with flying colors, taking the top three spots and five of the top ten in a list of the nation's 100 largest charities. The magazine's criterion for performance was the percentage of funds raised that "actually went toward good works."[17]

Good press like that should help ease donor reservations about giving to religious causes; the 1990s are still a time of overcoming backlash from highly publicized religious financial scandals of the late 1980s.

Still, discernment and accountability will be the paramount watchwords for 1990's stewardship.

And there are mixed signals. Making dollars and sense out of the financial future of missions and ministry is no simple task. The fact that people are giving a smaller percentage of their disposable income to churches is a cause for concern, if not alarm.

Another disturbing statistic is that of all the money Christians give to charity, 99.9 percent is passed on to themselves or other churches! Of the $8 billion or so in missions budgets worldwide, "just one-tenth of 1 percent benefits the non-Christian world," said David Barrett, editor of *World Christian Encyclopedia*.[18] Another study showed that the average church in America allocates about 5 percent of its budget for evangelism but 30 percent for buildings and maintenance.[19]

Missions Strategies for 2001

So where are we—in the plus or minus category?

Barrett, on the plus side, thinks he's caught wind of "the largest spiritual revitalization in history" breaking loose. More than a million church members were involved in renewal movements in 1990.[20]

Thomas Wang, editor of *AD 2000 and Beyond*, agrees that statistics show initial signs of "a massive international Christian movement." He cites figures:[21]

- 3,500 new churches are opening somewhere in the world every week. (He doesn't say how many are closing, however.)

- The church in China is adding up to 28,000 converts daily. The estimated Christian population in the People's Republic is between 25 and 50 million.
- The church in Africa is adding about 20,000 people daily. Below the Sahara, the continent is believed to be about 40 percent Christian.
- South Korea is about 30 percent Christian. A hundred years ago, it had no Protestant churches and was thought to be unreachable.
- Indonesia may be 25 percent Christian by now. (But government leaders in the officially Islamic country won't print the statistics.)
- The remaining "unreached people groups" in the world are down to 12,000 from 17,000 in 1974. Missiologists project that churches could be planted among these populations by 2001, according to Wang.

If the planet is going to be won for Jesus Christ in the near future, the job most likely will be done by evangelical agencies. Eighty percent of Protestant missionaries spreading the Gospel abroad are affiliated with evangelical groups rather than mainline denominations. The same is true for overseas relief and development; contributions to Church World Service, the National Council of Churches' most successful agency, have fallen well below those to World Vision, the leading evangelical relief group.[22]

An end-of-the-century deadline for evangelizing the world has been set by many missions groups. Barrett, peering into his computer data bank, says there are 254 such plans, 3,030 population segments yet to be reached, and 230,000 martyrs dying for the cause of Christ each year, a figure he projects will zoom to 835,000 by 2050.[23]

Among the plans to preach the Gospel to all the world's people before the turn of the millennium:

- "Dawn 2000," founded by James Montgomery, brings evangelical leaders together to compare growth rates and has set the ambitious goal of establishing an additional 7 million churches in every unreached village and neighborhood.
- The Southern Baptist Convention's "Bold Mission Thrust."
- "Decade of Harvest," an Assemblies of God strategy to plant 5,000 churches during the 1990s.

- "The World by 2000," an international radio broadcasting scheme to blitz the world with Gospel programming in enough languages so that everyone can understand.
- "Vision 2000," the Evangelical Free Church's plan that includes deployment of 150 non-traditional missionaries in closed countries by the end of 1999.[24]

Other evangelistic trends to look for: more cooperation between missions agencies during the 1990s; a missions push by aggressive Korean Christians throughout the world; a surge of evangelism activity to the Muslim world; and the deployment of large numbers of "tentmaking" missionaries—skilled professionals like engineers, teachers, and communications specialists who are welcome in countries where missionaries are not.[25]

Paul Pierson, dean of the School of World Mission at Fuller Seminary, sees alternative training as another 1990's mission trend.

> While academic institutions are still valued, we see a growing number of informal and nonformal training programs, of which theological education by extension is only one. . . . With the rapid growth of the church in many parts of the world, there's no way an adequate number of leaders can be trained using academic models, which are too expensive, too limiting and tend to become elitist and eventually distance the church from the majority of the people.[26]

Alternative Training Programs

I saw a positive example of alternative training during a tour of the Soviet Union in the fall of 1990. In concert with American businessmen who supplied "seed-money," a successful, self-perpetuating enterprise is flourishing under the leadership and direction of Soviet Christians. It's capitalizing on *perestroika* for joint-venturing.

In the progressive southern area of this vast country, near the northern shore of the Black Sea, several dozen laymen, mostly members of the Evangelical Christian Baptist Church of Maikop, have pooled their capital and harnessed techniques of private enterprise to turn a profit. They are using the funds to establish and run a Bible college and gain a controlling interest in a new commercial bank.

A few years ago the Soviet laymen gathered together and decided to acquire a wood shop to make furniture moldings. They obtained contracts with larger furniture fabrication firms in major cities and then rented a state-built wood shop from the government. The group also rented the adjoining decrepit brick factory from the state. Slowly, they modernized it and have improved its efficiency so that it turns out 15,000 bricks a day.

The Dekor Brick Company is able to pay the workers nearly four times as much as they made when the Communists controlled the factory. The Christian management has built six new low-cost housing units for workers' families, runs a co-op where they can buy food at reduced prices, and allows workers to observe religious holidays.

The other piece in this Baptist scenario is Logos Bible School in Belorechensk—also a child of *perestroika.* For years, Logos has operated a biblical-theological program, based in Fresno, California, to train young Soviet Christians through extension courses. In 1990, the organization teamed up with the Soviet business leaders to sign a lease-purchase agreement for a former Communist youth camp on an abandoned collective farm.

The new school, one of the first resident Bible programs in Russia, welcomed about 100 Soviet students in the fall of 1990, using more than twenty teachers from the West to get started. Students concentrate for seven weeks on theology and three weeks on business principles.[27]

CHURCHGOERS GIVE MORE				
Attendance at religious services		Average household contribution	Average percentage of income contributed	Average hours volunteered/ week
Weekly or nearly every week	37.3%	$ 1,386	3.8%	3.4
Only a few times a year	24.6%	$ 423	1.3%	1.2
Do not attend	22.3%	$ 293	.8%	1.8
Source: Independent Sector, October, 1990.				

"The school . . . is a real miracle," declared Viktor Reimer, a Logos founder. "Many times we thought it would be closed because of tensions with local authorities and with the KGB. The school continues because it is God's will to prepare workers for the harvest."[28]

Joint-venturing is also involved in other Soviet projects, such as publishing badly needed Christian literature. "Our goal is to enable the Soviet Christians to make it on their own with training, support and encouragement from us in the West," explained Bill Greig, a board member of GLINT (Gospel Literature International), a Christian organization that has been involved in the translation and publication of 501 books in thirty-nine languages.[29]

Projects based on this type of philosophy can be copied in many parts of the world during the closing years of this century.

So we see-saw between the optimists and the pessimists.

One thing is certain, however: churches can no longer put out appeals and just expect the dollars to pour in simply because people have a fondness for giving to religious charities.

Those who will make the most dollars and sense out of missions and ministry will do so by showing the tangible, personal benefits of giving.[30] They will see themselves as delivery systems rather than as accumulators of human or monetary capital.[31]

Part 3

Models for the Millennium

Chapter 22

Goal Setting

Evangelical Lutherans

In the first two sections of this book we have assessed the forces shaping both society and religion as we race through the 1990s. Now it's time to look at some church models for the millennium—hardy perennials likely to endure well into the 21st century.

Church planners have been debating whether the strategies for the last of the 1990s can best be charted by studying the past or by forecasting the future. Jackson Carroll of Hartford Seminary thinks that for church executives "the big interest now is looking at the past."[1]

Tom Sine believes that churches are "doing long-range planning as if the future is going to be an extension of the present. We are going to be surprised by change as we were so often in the past. . . . Christian organizations are tremendously slow. . . . What we need is a renaissance of Christian creativity [applied to] the emerging issues of tomorrow's world."[2]

Indeed, in a decade when Christianity's position at the center of the religious stage is threatened, most churches are being "reactive" rather than "pro-active." The scholars among them read the present through the past. Combing case histories and tracing sociocultural change, they look backward for their understanding of current religious ferment.

There are, however, a few forward-looking denominations and some creative congregations that are devising innovative strategies to harness the forces of the 1990s.

The Evangelical Lutheran Church in America and the United Methodist Church, two mainline denominations, have focused on setting goals for the 1990s. A glimpse of these goals and the processes that brought them into being may bring insight into how these models could work in your church or community.

My focus on these two denominations—and on the Presbyterian Church in America and the Southern Baptist Convention, two evangelical denominations—is not meant to imply that they are the only church groups setting goals or creating innovative models for the future. They are simply representative. Also, they were off to an early start in the race toward 2001, so they have a slight head start.

Bible-toting, Tithing, and Inclusive

Though hampered by an acute budget crunch, the 5.25-million-member Evangelical Lutheran Church in America (ELCA) is taking bold steps to make the denomination—the fourth-largest U.S. Protestant body—a Bible-reading, tithing, "inclusive" church. Inclusive means having at least 10 percent of its members be non-white and/or non-English-speaking people by 2000. That would be a five-fold increase from the 2 percent of African-American, Asian, Hispanic, and Native American ELCA members in 1989.

By mid-1990, about 70 percent of the church's sixty-five synods either had adopted plans for meeting the racial/ethnic inclusiveness goals or had already met them.[3]

The inclusiveness goal was written into the founding documents of the ELCA when three Lutheran bodies merged to form the new denomination in 1987–88 (see chart on page 153, "Declining Membership in Mainline Denominations").

Mission 90, the ELCA's statement of commitment for the 1990s, was hammered out over a period of months after scores of meetings, assemblies, and consultations. Yet the statement was largely the work of the church's spiritual leader, Bishop Herbert W. Chilstrom. The plan came "pretty much out of my own observations," Chilstrom says.[4]

Mission 90 focuses on thirteen dimensions of "challenges and opportunities" for this decade. It calls for "seeing anew what it means to be Christian"; "growing in our witness to the faith, in our giving, in our intention to become a more diverse church," and "serving the world in the cause of peace, justice and the care of creation."[5]

The statement looks at worldwide forces, saying that "a church born to this decade needs to understand and effectively respond to these conditions." The thirteen dimensions are (1) an unevangelized world; (2) religious pluralism; (3) urbanization; (4) interdependence; (5) poverty and oppression; (6) emergent churches and theologies worldwide; (7) the changing role of women; (8) high-tech communication; (9) antagonistic nationalism; (10) environmental problems; (11) international economic disorder; (12) multicultural realities, and (13) racial discrimination.[6]

As outlined by Bishop Chilstrom, the ELCA intends to emphasize seven basic goals in light of these thirteen "challenges and opportunities":[7]

(1) Gathering to reflect on what it means to be a Christian. This goal is very popular; in early 1991 more than 9,000 of the denomination's 11,000 congregations had ordered Chilstrom's tapes, "What Does It Mean to Be a Christian?" a faith-development program based on biblical and Lutheran material.[8]

(2) A new venture to encourage daily Bible reading. "Ventures in Bible Reading" was coordinated with a new Revised Standard Version of the Bible.

(3) Bible-study witness. This involves a relatively brief but intense course to teach key biblical themes and prepare people to share their faith in daily living.

(4) An accent on tithing. Chilstrom said he was looking for a million tithers (those who give 10 percent of their income to the church), or about one out of every five ELCA members.

(5) Partners around the world. Mission 90 calls for every congregation and synod to link up with another ministry in the United States and one overseas. "That could be another church, a hospital, school or seminary," Chilstrom explained—"a very specific place where a congregation would connect itself and learn as much as possible as partners."

(6) Peace, justice, and creation issues. The goals also link churches

with the world, centering "on what we as believers can do to bring justice to the world and what we can do to preserve the Earth itself for future generations. . . . It's an effort to help people understand these issues and connect them with environmental concerns," Chilstrom said.

As an illustration of a tangible application of this goal, the ELCA is using its position as a shareholder and an investor to effect change in U.S. corporations. The church's pension board alone owns almost $1 billion in stock and equities. In 1990, the church council approved thirty-two different shareholder resolutions, filed with fifty-nine companies. These included the tobacco industry, firms that develop military products, and those that do business in South Africa. "We concentrated our effort on environmental issues and poor and minority communities issues," said Edgar G. Crane, director of the Lutheran Office for Corporate Social Responsibility.[9]

(7) The 10 percent "inclusiveness" goal. "Unless there is the commitment of significant amounts of time, prayer, money, talent and support for these goals, the ELCA will remain an overwhelmingly white denomination in the midst of an increasingly multicultural world," declared Martin Smith, an executive of the church's Commission for Multicultural Ministries.[10]

Black, Brown, Yellow, Red—and Green

Skeptics doubt that the 10 percent goal is feasible. The ELCA, 98 percent white and in 1991 snarled in budget deficits for the fourth straight year, can't put enough money where its mouth is, gibe the critics. To reach the goal, said one speaker at the ELCA's first biennial Multicultural Gathering, the church needs more than a scattering of black, brown, red, and yellow faces. It also needs a lot of green—in the offering plate.[11]

Indeed, wallet woes in the 1990s may hamstring the best intentions of many major denominations. The ELCA's national offices trimmed $5.2 million from its authorized 1991 budget of $95.5 million. And 1991's red ink came on top of a $1.4 million shortfall in 1990, a $4.2 million shortfall in 1989, and a whopping $16 million shortfall in 1988, the denomination's first year of operation.

Among the reasons cited by the national church for its low income were rising health insurance costs for local pastors and a trend for congregations to prefer supporting various ministries, such as helping the hungry and homeless, at the local level.[12]

Some bishops were placing the blame on the income side rather than on the budget. Said Bishop Harry S. Andersen of the Northern Great Lakes Synod: "The great need is to generate new dollars, and we are not going to do that if we do not get the interest of the people. We have to give them the wider picture."[13]

Could Andersen have been reading up on how to get boomers to buy in?

Chapter 23

Drug Busting

United Methodists

When the Rev. DarEll T. Weist sat down with a committee of fourteen other church leaders in 1986, no United Methodist group had ever tried to pull together a strategy for one of its districts. But three years later, after more than a dozen provocative—and sometimes soul-searching—sessions, goals for "The Los Angeles District in the Year 2000" finally emerged.

"The United Methodist Church has always been a middle-class church," said Weist, who wrote the report. "So if we're going to succeed, the challenge is to develop a ministry that meets the needs of the people living in poverty in South Central and East Los Angeles, as well as the emerging yuppies . . . who are moving into Hollywood and West Los Angeles."

Weist's committee also had to reckon with the fact that forty-eight of the sixty congregations in the district were aging; twenty-four had major building code violations. "We discovered we could no longer buy new property because of property costs, and because of building costs, it was no longer possible to build new churches from scratch," Weist explained.

So compromise goals were set: (1) Refurbish as many of the buildings as the district could afford. (2) Earmark the others for recycling to a different ministry. (3) Or sell them to provide an endowment for other ministries.[1]

Setting these kinds of goals was not easy; it was painful to realize that not all of the sixty congregations would make it into the new millennium.

"This will be very difficult," Weist's report noted, "since closing churches looks like failure rather than a natural part of the life cycle of being born and dying. Church grief work for the affected congregations will have to be done. A clear strategy will help us do the grief work with integrity and also conserve our resources."[2]

The case of the Los Angeles Methodists illustrates the importance of goals and strategy at the local and district level. They're pivotal also on the national front.

Drug Deaths on the Doorstep

The nine-million-member United Methodist Church has been a goal-setting pace-maker in the church war on drugs. The impetus for their drug program, which has become a model for religious groups around the country, began one night in 1989 when members of A. P. Shaw United Methodist Church in southeast Washington, D.C., were gathered for a prayer meeting. A drug turf war erupted outside, and the pastor went to investigate. On the church doorstep he found two teenagers shot dead.

That incident, recounts Pastor Bernard Keels, served as the "clarion call" for his congregation to enlist in the war against drugs. Soon the denomination appointed Felton E. May, a burly, energetic, black United Methodist bishop, to a year's special drug-busting assignment. "The plan was to work together much as we did on civil rights during the sixties," May told me. "This is basically a spiritual warfare."[3] The idea, May continued, was "to build solidarity in terms of life and death with folks right where they are."

May took up his battle station during 1990 in the nation's capital, where he developed a coordinated response. Shaw and thirteen other United Methodist congregations participated in a demonstration project. Five of them set up huge army-surplus tents they called "saving stations." Inside the tents were special outreach campaigns; children's activities; drug-education seminars; food, shelter, family programs, and counseling. The saving stations were advertised by large red-and-white signs in front of each church and staffed largely by volunteers. By summer's end, they had ministered to a thousand persons.

The saving stations produced "tremendous evangelistic benefits as well as helping the community," Pastor Keels testified. Meanwhile, Shaw Church developed "10 Steps to Deliverance," a scripturally based substance abuse program. The Methodist Board of Global Ministries later adopted it on a nationwide scale.[4]

"Scores of sermons, workshops, seminars, 'think tank' meetings, and symposiums also marked the drug war effort as May crisscrossed the nation, meeting with church and government leaders," reported United Methodist communications officer Robert Lear. In one gathering, 1,500 persons were urged by the Rev. Cecil Williams of San Francisco's Glide Memorial United Methodist Church to take the crusade to the streets.[5]

Gliding in with "Unconditional Love"

Glide folks did exactly that when 800 members and supporters tromped into the Valencia Gardens housing project in the drug-infested Tenderloin district, announcing that "recovery time" had arrived for addicts and their families.

Rather than simply forcing drug dealers to move a few blocks away, effervescent Williams told the pushers and users, "You stay here. The total community needs recovery. We're coming in with unconditional love. We're your family." Williams's remedial approach—faith and resistance—has successfully liberated many from drugs, according to Charles Jackson, counselor for San Francisco's Substance Abuse Referral Unit. Jackson particularly praised Glide's program for "young crack mothers."[6]

Williams, a close friend of May, has hosted several national conferences, bringing thousands of church and community drug-abuse workers together. In 1987 he started an informal daily rap session at Glide church called "Open Mike." Drug addicts come forward to share their stories and segue into recovery groups.

The message that help is available to overcome drug addictions and that housing projects are not the turf for dealers has also been proclaimed loud and clear at other United Methodist churches across the land.[7] And the concept of saving stations has spread to New York, Detroit, and other cities. Even to St. Luke's in Shady Gap, Pennsylvania, a rural community of 500.[8]

The Methodist bishops renewed the program under May's leadership for 1991. Goals also include a push for "realistic national policy" on substance abuse that allocates resources for education, prevention, and treatment as well as for law enforcement.

As an outgrowth of the United Methodist leadership, a consultation called for by the National Council of Churches brought together sixty-four denominational leaders in the fall of 1991 to set goals for a drug-free society. The participants discussed a "Declaration of Interdependence" among the churches. The plan calls for cooperation on drug issues, joint media projects that could compete with the commercial media's glamorization of alcohol and drug use, and an ecumenical substance-abuse think tank.[9]

Attacking crises as massive as substance abuse does indeed require cooperative effort—at the denominational level at the least. Best of all would be a combined spiritual, psychological, political, and local approach.

May thinks the government is unable to muster "an all-out assault" on drugs because of bureaucratic sluggishness and the "horrendous problem of coordination"; he believes churches can do a better job of "reaching people on the street."

The United Methodist Church alone has more churches than the U.S. Postal Service has post offices. May suggests that recovery groups could meet in church facilities, retreat centers, and closed army camps and hospitals.[10]

But, once again, chances of financing such a grand plan seem slim; the United Methodists had difficulty funding and staffing the fourteen-church summer project in southeast Washington.

May remains optimistic, however. "I'm convinced," he says, "that if the church were not involved, this country would be in chaos."[11]

Chapter 24

Perimeters and Satellites

Presbyterians and Baptists

Southern Baptists talk about "satellite" churches.[1] Elmer Towns, head of the Church Growth Institute in Lynchburg, Virginia, calls the concept "the geographical expanded parish church."[2] Others refer to it as the "perimeter" church.

Whatever we call the idea, churches practicing it are the pacesetting ministries on the leading edge of the coming millennium.

The Presbyterian Church in America

A pioneer in positioning churches from single to multicampus ministries is Randy Pope, pastor of Perimeter Church of Greater Atlanta, Georgia.

Some say perimeter churches are "minidenominations" in bud stage or actually small new denominations. But Pope's Perimeter remains firmly encircled by the doctrine and policies (polity) of the fast-growing Presbyterian Church in America (PCA).

With a strong commitment to missionary work, both at home and abroad, and to historic, creedal Presbyterianism, the PCA was organized in December, 1973, in Birmingham, Alabama. It jumped in size and expanded its geographic boundaries nine years later when it received the Reformed Presbyterian Church, Evangelical Synod, itself a merger of several Presbyterian bodies with antecedents in Colonial America.

The PCA also began picking up breakaway congregations and members disgruntled because of liberal leanings in the mainline Presbyterian denomination, now the Presbyterian Church (USA). Between 1987 and 1989, the PCA grew more than 13 percent, making it one of the fastest-growing denominations in the nation.[3]

The PCA believes the Bible is the inerrant Word of God and the only infallible rule of faith and practice. All officers are required to subscribe, without reservation, to the Reformed faith as declared in the Westminster Confession and Catechisms.[4]

"We are a conservative church," acknowledges Charles Dunahoo, the man in charge of the PCA's Christian education and publications, "but we're not old-fashioned. And we're very aggressive in our church growth department."[5]

When the denomination was founded less than two decades ago, it had 249 congregations and 40,000 members. Now, it has more than 217,000 members in over 1,200 congregations as well as 546 missionaries. And before the end of the century, the PCA seeks to add 875 new churches—200 of them ethnic. The PCA is concentrating on developing a cross-cultural "pioneering" ministry to Koreans and Latinos, Dunahoo added. In 1991, the denomination had ninety Korean congregations.[6]

Perimeter Church

The perimeter church is a PCA innovation. Dunahoo explained the concept as a "mother" congregation in a major city with satellites in the suburbs "reaching the yuppies under forty." The pastors are all associated with the main church, and once a month everyone joins in a festival of worship—a "big celebration"—at the hub church.

Pope's work in Atlanta has won high approval from his denomination. "We stay within the heritage of the Presbyterian Church, and we see our model as more biblical than any model in the contemporary church," Pope says.

Pope's original idea was to plant a church that would have 100 different locations on the perimeter highway that circles Atlanta—"sort of like having a pizza parlor at every other freeway exit," he joked.

Perimeter Church was designed to be one "local church," Pope told Towns, but with many locations "to reach the entire metropolitan area for Jesus." It would have one senior pastor and individual pastors in each congregation; one board made up of three elders from each congregation; and one program of outreach administered through each individual congregation.[7]

Pope, right out of seminary, sold his dream to PCA officials. They also bought the challenge that was to become the motto for Perimeter Church and Pope's personal credo: "Attempt something so great for God that it is doomed to failure unless God be in it."[8]

Pope began staking out Perimeter Church in the summer of 1977. After several events that he considered to be signs that God was supplying financial needs, the fledgling congregation rented a building and held its first Sunday morning service on September 25, 1977.

The second perimeter congregation was started in Marietta, about ten miles away, in 1980. Additional congregations have been born about every three years since. Another perimeter-style church has been spun off in the university town of Athens, Georgia, about ninety miles from Atlanta.[9]

As the network grew to eight congregations, administration became more difficult. So Pope reorganized his vision, creating an umbrella unit called Perimeter Christian Ministries, Inc. This is a "transchurch" organization making the eight local churches autonomous.

As Pope explains it, each congregation contributes 5 percent of its total income to Perimeter Christian Ministries. The primary goal is to plant other congregations of like faith and practice. Call it a paradenomination, if you will.

Local Identity, Shared Management

Towns defines an extended geographical parish church as multi-staff, multilocations, multiministries "with a single identity, single organization, single purpose, single force of leadership, yet governed by the entire members from all parts."[10]

In his book *Ten of Today's Most Innovative Churches*, Towns elaborates: "Each section of the extended geographical parish church has local leadership (full- or part-time) to promote local ministry and local identity, yet retains a central system of shared management." The perimeter church "resembles a business with a main office and regional offices, rather than the traditional denominational structure" or association of churches. "It has a single government for all the parts (churches) and a single staff to promote a unified ministry, unified vision and unified identity."

For example, when one part of a perimeter church ministers to unwed mothers or evangelizes a new suburb, "it is as though the whole church is operating through the one part."[11]

Towns points to the book of Acts as the biblical basis for the extended geographical parish church. The church at Jerusalem was one church (Acts 8:1), yet it was made up of several parts, or units: "All the believers were one in heart and mind" (Acts 4:32).

"Thus the large group in the Jerusalem church met for celebration, preaching, motivation and testimony . . . and in small cells for fellowship, accountability, instruction and identity (Acts 5:42)." From these observations, concludes Towns, "the norm for the New Testament church included both small cell groups and large celebration groups."[12]

Today this model seems natural because of sophisticated communication and rapid transportation. It's quite possible to plant a perimeter church with multiple congregations linked by easy travel and common information. And the perimeter church is well-suited for innovative, nontraditional styles of ministry.

Pope sees his role as equipping others for ministry, but in a pew-driven rather than a pulpit-driven mode. Instead of doing all the ministry himself or delegating his staff to do it, he equips the laity for these tasks. His intent is to involve every person in the church in ministry, helping them to identify and use their specific spiritual gifts.

Like Bill Hybels of Willow Creek Community Church, Pope is oriented toward the "unchurched." He feels that hymnals, chancel and choirs, singing the Doxology, and standing behind a pulpit to preach are put-offs to all but traditional pew people.

But Pope doesn't go as far as Hybels, who jettisons church

tradition altogether. Pope maintains the historic heritage of the Presbyterian faith. Once a month, on a Sunday evening, a traditional communion service is held for Christians at the 2,000-member Perimeter Church. Hymnals appear from a storage closet, a pulpit is dragged to the front of the chancel, and worshipers follow typical Presbyterian liturgy.[13]

Southern Baptist Satellite Churches

In the Southern Baptist version of the satellite church, worship may be contemporary, traditional, or a blend of both. Ordinarily, the satellite church staff and financial support are supplied by the sponsoring church or churches already established in the region.

Satellite churches studied in 1990 by the California Southern Baptist Convention were all "target focused"—that is, they sought to evangelize the unchurched population that existing area congregations hadn't been able to reach.

"Sponsoring churches learn from watching their satellites grow, and may make slower, less 'radical' changes in their own congregations," explained Harry Williams in the *California Southern Baptist* newspaper. "This, in turn, may make them more accessible to the California culture."[14]

One satellite church pastor, Mike Malody, left the staff of Grace Baptist Church in Antioch to form Lone Tree Community Church. A year later, the satellite, meeting in an elementary school, had an Easter attendance of 221, with 100 first-timers. The average age of the church's members was twenty-six, and the congregation had already purchased five acres of prime property to build its own campus.

And First Southern Baptist Church of Fresno launched Van Ness Community Church on Easter, 1988. Two years later, the congregation, meeting in a junior high school cafeteria, had grown to 188. It's a young group too: 81 percent under fifty years of age and 62 percent under forty.[15]

Wider Orbit of Satellites

As perimeter and satellite, or "hub-and-spoke," churches proliferate in the 1990s, a variety of adaptations and modifications will spring up to suit regional demographics and the preferences of leaders. Some of these emerging multicampus churches will become or remain connected to existing denominations; others will evolve into new "denomination-like" associations or fellowships.

Splinter and breakaway groups will be part of the constantly shifting paradigm. Strong voices in the embryonic denominations will establish their own Bible schools and conferences, and differing methods and expressions of missions and ministry will come into sharper definition—and division.

The organizing principle or hard core of these movements isn't doctrine, but "the standards by which effective ministry is measured."[16]

The day of the denomination is not dead, but the new passion, says Towns, is for "like ministry" as denominations change the way they play the game. "The new day . . . emphasizes moving toward a community of churches that are of like function and ministry."[17]

Chapter 25

Willow Creek Community Church

Imagine a church that[1]

- Doesn't have "church worship" on weekends, yet fills its 4,550-seat auditorium twice on Saturday nights and twice on Sunday mornings.
- Has no altar, cross, vestments, or other religious trappings, yet stresses "radical discipleship" to Jesus Christ.
- Has no choir, organ, hymnals, or song books, yet produces professional-quality music, ranging from rock to Bach and jazz to country.
- Does not use offering envelopes, ask for pledges, or hold fund-raising dinners, yet surpasses its budget and just completed a $20 million addition to its $15 million complex on 130 acres.

This strategy defies conventional methods, admits Bill Hybels, the founding pastor of Willow Creek Community Church in South Barrington, Illinois, a suburb thirty miles northwest of downtown Chicago.

"Our goal is to reach and teach 'non-churched Harrys and Marys' who have been turned off by the traditional church and are about to write off Christianity," Hybels explains. "Seekers can be anonymous here. You don't have to say anything, sing anything, sign anything, or give anything."

Willow Creek is one of the few churches in the nation shaped by a targeted "customer" survey. It is also a huge success: From a modest gathering of 125 people who first met in a rented movie theater in 1975, it has grown to become the nation's number two Protestant congregation in terms of weekend attendance. It is second only to Jack Hyles's independent First Baptist Church in Hammond, Indiana, which draws 15,000 to 30,000 attenders, depending on the season.[2]

Church analysts see Willow Creek as a prototype for successful churches of the future that will need to reach an increasingly secular and pluralistic society unfamiliar with traditional worship, music, and teachings.

The national religious magazine *Guideposts* named Willow Creek its 1989 Church of the Year "for meeting the needs of the 1990s by presenting timeless truth in a contemporary way."

Hybels is rhapsodic about the church's future: "We're on the verge of making kingdom history," he proclaims, "doing things a new way for a whole new generation. People all over the nation are looking at Willow Creek and calling it the church of the 21st century."

A simple explanation is that Willow Creek is cresting a high tide of growth that has swept up many evangelical churches during the past two decades. But it is Willow Creek's evangelism philosophy—rooted in its marketing survey, its dynamic pastor, and its 4,200 believers and 1,750 lay leaders—that has catapulted the independent congregation to the top. Espousing standard American evangelical Christianity, Willow Creek's statement of faith asserts the need for a personal conversion experience to Jesus Christ as Savior, the infallible authority of the Bible, and the obligation of believers to tell others about their faith.

Sounds simple, but it requires lots of organization.

652 Parking Cones

The church spends $75,000 a year just for traffic control, paying off-duty police to ease cars on and off busy Algonquin Road in the affluent Barrington-Palatine area. The church parking lot is so huge that signs marked with letters and numbers—airport style—were installed when members complained they couldn't find their cars after services.

But there is more to handling the traffic monster that snakes along the winding access road than setting out the church's 652 parking cones and waving red flashlights. Since they make the first and last impression on church visitors, parking attendants see themselves as an important part of the ministry. The motto for the large volunteer traffic safety team is "We get 'em first and we get 'em last."

"The main reason we are doing this is for the Lord," explains coordinator Rob Shearer, who wears an orange windbreaker and barks instructions to his team over a walkie-talkie as he surveys his kingdom from the church roof. "If the guy who's coming for the first time doesn't give us a thought, we're happy. We want to be inconspicuous. We are trying to get them into the church as quickly and safely as possible. We want people to remember what goes on inside, not outside. If we do that, God has been served."[3]

"We are represented by *extremely* diverse personalities and backgrounds on our team," confided another traffic volunteer. "The common denominator that knits us close, however, is God's gifts of helps and hospitality. Put these two gifts together and you discover how God gives people the tenacity to withstand the worst of cold (or heat or rain) and the tenderness to give special accommodations to the handicapped, the elderly, or to single parents."[4]

In fact, a specially designated area near the entrance is reserved for "single-parent parking." Children are abundant at Willow Creek. There are so many three-year-olds that nursery facilities are divided—those whose last names begin with A through L go to one room while the M's through Z's go to another.

Willow Creek's colorful, precisely planned, multimedia services attract 1,000 new churchgoers every year. Last year, 687 adults were baptized. And 1,800 members meet weekly in more than 200 small groups to study the Bible and pray.

Everything about Willow Creek Church—from the plain but massive sign on the highway to the "neutral corporate setting" of the campus—is designed to "impress seekers with excellence but not ostentatiousness," says Hybels, who for five years was chaplain to the Chicago Bears football team.

"How We Do It" Seminars

Church leaders throughout the nation and even overseas are taking notice of the Willow Creek model. Three times a year, up to 2,000 of them flock to Hybels' "how-we-do-it" seminars. He walks pastors through his seven-step program to bring non-churched Harrys and Marys full circle. Then they themselves go out and recruit "non-churched Larry and Cheri," as Hybels puts it.

In 1990, a team of nineteen Willow Creek leaders, including Hybels, held an "April in Paris" conference for 150 pastors, missionaries, and church planters from fourteen countries. The goal was to demonstrate how Willow Creek's approach might work in European cultures. "We are not coming here to establish Willow Creek clones or a denomination," declared Gilbert Bilezikian, a founder and former elder of Willow Creek.

Added Hybels: "You are going to have to figure out how to crack the code of your own particular culture. We are just trying to give you some tools."[5]

According to longtime trend watcher Lyle Schaller, the tool kit Hybels passes out seems to be just what's needed to jump start listless churches: a creative, imaginative pastor; extensive weekday programming; and greater emphasis on the teaching ministry of the church. Schaller also pointed to the radical reorientation of traditional Sunday services at Willow Creek as an example of what's typical for many growing megachurches.

"They are more attractive, less boring, more visual, and less audio. They are more the agenda of the people than that of the minister. This is especially reflected in the music, preaching, skits, and attention grabbers," he said. "Willow Creek is an extraordinary example of young adults coming back to church in big numbers. These people grew up in oldline churches, drifted away, and are now back—but not in the denomination or congregation they were in before."[6]

Hybels, who was raised in the Christian Reformed Church, sees the 25- to 45-year-old white-collar professionals who "grew up on television" as the primary target for his well-polished topical sermons. Wearing natty business suits with razor-sharp creases in the pants, Hybels delivers his messages from full notes as he stands behind a portable plexiglass lectern on the brown-carpeted Willow Creek stage. There is no pulpit, of course, and his audience sits in comfortable theater seats—not pews. The auditorium's massive windows look out on a large lagoon graced with willow trees and populated by wild ducks and geese.

After services, Hybels "works the bullpen"—an area just below the right front corner of the stage—where he chats individually with anyone who lingers.

His sermons usually last thirty minutes, and everything in the service meshes with his theme. Preceding a message about "The Changing American Dream"—on the illusory happiness of "having and doing it all"—Gilbert Bilezikian read Matthew 16:25–26: "For whoever wants to save his life will lose it, but whoever loses his life for me will find it. What good will it be for a man if he gains the whole world, yet forfeits his soul? Or what can a man give in exchange for his soul?"

Layman Bilezikian segued into the passage after speaking for several minutes on contemporary examples of "materialism and greed." Next, a humorous skit called "Confessions of an Ad-aholic," dramatized the pitfalls of a consumptive lifestyle. Though played by church volunteers, the skits—a staple of weekend services—are produced, choreographed, and rehearsed under the watchful eye of Willow Creek's fulltime drama director, Steve Pederson. Quality lighting and professional sound equipment back up each presentation. Large video screens give people in the balconies a better view of what's happening on stage.

At this particular service, the music included a prelude by ten flutists and a violinist, a number by three singers and a fifteen-piece combo—and a jazzed-up version of "Down by the Riverside" for the offertory.

Hybels eschews cliches, quotes news and financial magazines, and emphasizes "honesty, transparency" and "real life problems" in his sermons.

"Hybels is preaching a very upbeat message," said Stephen Warner, a sociologist at the University of Illinois in Chicago. "It's a salvationist message, but the idea is not so much being saved from the fires of hell. Rather, it's being saved from meaninglessness and aimlessness in this life. It's more of a soft-sell."[7]

Yet Hybels, who holds a bachelor's degree in biblical studies but is not seminary trained, pulls no punches: The "hidden cost" of the American dream may mean that dream chasers who "live spiritually alienated from God . . . pay the price in hell forever," he admonished, driving home his point from Matthew 16.

Weekend services are for beginners in the faith ("Christianity 101 and 201," says Hybels) and are not intended to provide worship for believers. But core members receive their spiritual "meat" ("Christianity 301 and 401") at Wednesday and Thursday night discipleship meetings. These services, called "New Community," plus some ninety "subministries"—everything from staffing Willow Creek's extensive food pantry for the needy and repairing autos for the indigent to producing Christian dramas for the elderly—make up the core of the church, according to the Rev. Don Cousins, Willow Creek's associate pastor for ministries.

"The weekend services are the front door, but the church inside has to be the real thing," he told a group of attentive church leaders at one of Willow Creek's conferences for pastors. "Or else people will go right on out the back door."

Selling Tomatoes Door to Door

Born the son of a produce executive from Kalamazoo, Michigan, Hybels, at age 22, felt the call to the ministry and walked out of the lucrative family business. Becoming a church youth leader, he focused on events to draw in non-believers and quickly built up the group from 25 to 1,000. Next, Hybels asked a few friends to help him canvas the Northwest Chicago suburbs to find out why adults didn't attend church.

"Boy, did we get an earful," Hybels recalls.

The answers, in order of frequency: The church is always bugging me for money; I don't like the music; I can't relate to the messages; the services are boring, predictable, and irrelevant; the pastor makes me feel guilty and ignorant, so I leave feeling worse than when I came.

CHAPTER TWENTY-FIVE

The follow-up question: What kind of church would attract you?

The survey respondents wanted a non-threatening environment, anonymity, elementary-level teaching, excellence, "high take-home value," and "time to decide."

Deciding they wanted to start *that* kind of church, Hybels and friends sold tomatoes door to door in the summer of 1975 to raise enough money to rent the Willow Creek Theater in Palatine. Rousing contemporary-style Christian music, quality drama, and low-key sermons lured newcomers—who were left alone and not asked for money.

Soon, the Palatine theater could not hold the crowds and the church was built in 1981. The facilities have been expanded to 355,000 square feet and a ministry center and gymnasium housing three basketball courts were added. Increasing the capacity of the auditorium—already larger than any theater in Chicago—is also under consideration.

But the initial philosophies still guide Willow Creek, where 1990 revenues were $9.1 million—$175,000 a week—and audited financial statements are made public.[8]

Just before the brown offering bags are passed at services, someone makes an announcement something like this: "If some of you came to give monetary thanks, the ushers will come by; if you didn't come prepared, that's OK. And if you're new today, we don't expect you to give because you're our guest."

But the inner circle of followers is taught the principle of tithing to the Lord's work.

The Hybels' Lifestyle

Bill, his wife, Lynne, and their two children live near the church in a posh subdivision where $500,000 homes surround a lake. But theirs, built in 1983, cost $200,000, and they own no vacation homes or other property and only one moderately priced car. Hybels has asked the church not to increase his annual salary beyond the 1990 figure of $67,000. Other income, he says, is from royalties from nine books he has written and honorariums from speaking and conducting funerals and weddings. He sets no fees for any of these services.

"I have no secrets," he says, adding that he has invited anyone who wants to look at his checkbook stubs to do so. Hybels told me he once turned down a $100,000 gift to the church "because it didn't fit with Willow Creek's purposes." He also mentioned that some Willow Creek members have turned down job promotions with large pay increases because they didn't want to have to move away from the church.

There's a tremendous price to keep what Hybels calls "the edge of excellence." He readily acknowledges his high intensity and strict discipline. He lifts weights, runs two to four miles a day, fasts a few days a week, eats health foods, and arrives at his office between five and six o'clock each morning.

The stress of bigtime ministry brought him dangerously close to "flipping out" a few years back. Ever since, he's insisted on a regimen of regular rest, physical exercise, spiritual reflection, time off with his family, and personal accountability.

The "accountability factor," says Schaller, is for many critics the crucial issue facing megachurches: "Who will hold these megachurches accountable for their actions? To whom are the senior pastor and his staff accountable?"[9]

Keenly aware of the credibility damage many independent church ministries have suffered as a result of financial and moral scandals, Hybels has shied away from putting his church on TV. Three male confidants to whom he reports informally would tell "in a heartbeat" if he strayed off the track, Hybels says. The chief pastor expects high performance from his associates as well.

Willow Creek's eight elders—three are women—put in eight to fifteen hours of volunteer work each week handling church business. The staff, too, feels the pressure of the pace. They understand what George Barna meant when he spoke about "Bill Hybels' . . . absolute dedication to see that everything must coincide with his vision . . . for a flourishing church."[10]

In 1990, Hybels and his board expanded the team-teaching ministry and management at Willow Creek to demonstrate to other churches that "shared leadership and teaching will work." Historically, no large church has ever been able to make the transition and "break the rule that unless the visible senior pastor teaches all the time, the church goes in the tank," Hybels said.[11]

In July, 1990, Jim Dethmer, a founding pastor of Grace Fellowship

Church—a Willow Creek-style congregation in Baltimore—joined Hybels, associate pastor Cousins, and director of communications Lee Strobel as the church's principal lectern speakers.[12]

"No one teacher can carry the burden of a megachurch," Dethmer told me. "It can't revolve around one charismatic or dominant leader."[13]

What hurts, Hybels confided, is being portrayed as "high profile, dictatorial, heavy handed. That's not true," he says, propping his feet atop his desk, "I'm an incurable team player."[14]

That's true, agree staff members, as long as he gets to play quarterback.

No Creek Clones

Hybels has not felt impelled to plant and staff satellite churches. Nevertheless, churches with similar formats and philosophies are popping up around the country. One in Southern California, Horizons Community Church of Glendora, "premiered" in 1991 in a theater in Diamond Bar.

"Some rules are meant to be broken," teased a flier inviting folks to Horizon's upcoming "Faithful Attractions." For example: Church is boring . . . church is not practical . . . church is not relevant . . .

> Horizons is for people who don't like church. Or for people who don't like some of the things that happen in churches. We will break some of these images, or perceived rules.

> High quality drama, music and multi-media will be used creatively as we look at how Christianity affects life in California in the 90s. . . . Come break some rules with us and help us reach the unchurched community with God's message of love.[15]

The nine Horizons start-up leaders attended a Willow Creek conference in 1989 and apparently took good notes!

South of Diamond Bar, in Orange County, Saddleback Valley Community Church is a flourishing congregation of more than 4,000 that was founded in 1980. Recently, it purchased a 113-acre site for expansion. While Saddleback has not directly borrowed from the Willow Creek model, pastor Rick Warren follows a style and outreach that is strikingly similar, reaching many previously unchurched boomers.

Not all church leaders buy the Willow Creek package—which is just fine with Hybels. He urges pastors to do their own marketing surveys and "listen to your people."

Some Willow Creekers have in fact departed because they miss the traditional hymns, rituals, and structures of denominational churches. Others have simply found the music too loud or the church too big.

Hybels is nettled by the perception of some critics that Willow Creek is a "lightweight" church: "the assumption that we present entertainment with a convenience-oriented gospel."

And staff members were not amused by a headline in the *USA Weekend* Sunday supplement on Easter, 1990. It read simply: "McChurch."

The ensuing story "read more like a Mac Attack" declaring that "happy customers are eating up our 'fast-food' religion," chided Rob Wilkins, editor of *Willow Creek*, the church's glossy, top-quality, full-color bimonthly magazine.[16]

In a kinder, gentler assessment, Anthony B. Robinson, senior pastor of Plymouth Congregational Church (UCC) in Seattle, made the following report in the *Christian Century* after his visit to Willow Creek:

"If Willow Creek is accessible to the unchurched," he asked, "is what it offers recognizable as the church? Or has the worshiping congregation been transformed into an audience? Are the weekly services more entertainment than worship?"[17]

Hybels bristles at the suggestion that Willow Creek demands anything less than deep discipleship: "I would say with a clear conscience that we challenge people to full commitment to Jesus Christ—95 percent commitment is not enough."[18]

Chapter 26

All Saints
Episcopal Church

Eleven o'clock Sunday morning, and the parking lot at All Saints Episcopal Church, a landmark for more than 100 years in downtown Pasadena, California, is full.[1]

A number of Porsches, Audis, Jaguars, Mercedes-Benzes, and Volvos stand fender to fender. Several sport bumper stickers, but they are not slogans of traditional piety such as "Jesus Is Coming Soon" or "Smile—God Loves You." The All Saints crowd prefers messages like "Question Authority," "Stop Apartheid," "Boycott Shell," and "Support Greenpeace."

If the parking lot tips off visitors to the essence of this growing, upscale parish, its buoyant rector, the Reverend George F. Regas, leaves no doubt that the church's emphasis during the more than twenty-four years he's been at the helm has been on liberal social causes.

"I felt my job was to lead the congregation into the battlefronts of Christian social justice," the sixty-year-old clergyman recalled as we talked over tea and scones in a fancy hotel.[2]

The Regas touch has been well rewarded: All Saints has become the largest Episcopal parish west of the Mississippi River. In fact, All Saints, tucked between the Moorish-style dome of city hall and a new twelve-story hotel, is one of very few growing liberal congregations within mainline denominations.

No wonder other congregations are eyeing its leadership profile as a model for the 1990s.

With the decline of denominational loyalty, church "shoppers" are congregating wherever they can find what they're looking for, says Robert Franklin, who served a stint as visiting professor of Afro-American religion at Harvard Divinity School. For many, that means "an exciting worship experience with good music, intelligent, socially prophetic preaching, and a variety of social ministries in which young professionals can employ their skills and knowledge," Franklin said.[3]

That's a pretty good summary of All Saints. Its success—particularly in balancing strong social action and creative forms of worship—provides a pattern for church strategists.

"Perhaps," says Donald E. Miller, a professor at the University of Southern California's School of Religion and an All Saints member, "the success of All Saints is that it is liberal in emphasis on social justice ministries, intellectual challenge, and openness to many diverse people and life styles, but it is also deeply conservative in its recognition of the importance of worship, pastoral care and personal spiritual disciplines."[4]

During the final years of the 1980s, net growth was about 750 people; there are now more than 6,300 baptized members, representing about 2,300 households. The church's annual operating budget doubled in five years to $2.4 million in 1990.

"There are enough Christians in the west San Gabriel Valley who want to take their Christianity seriously and combine it with liberal political causes so that this [church] appeals," says Peter Wagner, professor of evangelism at Fuller School of World Mission in Pasadena. "And George Regas is a good leader and preacher."

Mary Alice Spangler, a former Methodist who's been at All Saints since 1976, confirms Wagner's assessment. "It's the balance between strong social action, strong liturgy, and George. It's taking Christianity out into the world."

That hasn't always been easy, Regas is quick to admit.

There have struggles over taking liberal stands on such things as the Vietnam and Persian Gulf Wars, racism, disarmament, U.S. involvement in Central America, urban poverty, and acceptance of gays and lesbians into the congregation.

"Twenty years ago, people stayed in spite of All Saints' involvement [in liberal issues]. Today, they come because of it," Regas says with a smile.

Profile of All Saints

A survey taken in 1989 reveals All Saints to be a predominantly well-educated, wealthy, and white parish. Ninety-eight percent of the members have attended college, and 58 percent have education beyond a bachelor's degree. More than half the members earn more than $50,000 a year; 12 percent of the households have an income between $100,000 and $150,000, and a full 10 percent earn more than $150,000 annually.

Almost half the members are professionals and nearly 90 percent are white. Women make up 60 percent of the congregation; gays and lesbians account for 10 percent, and 15 percent of the members are divorced or separated. Less than a third (31 percent) were reared as Episcopalians; 15 percent were reared as Presbyterians and 10 percent as Roman Catholics. Half the members have lived in the area for at least twenty years.

"Most parishioners are extremely proud of the church's commitment to social activism," a report accompanying the survey said, "and the programs and sermons dealing with these issues are praised widely."

Despite general approval and high morale, there is disagreement and even disharmony on some issues. In fact, almost every survey question elicited negative responses from about one-third of parishioners who complained about such things as the church is too big, too rich, or too impersonal and elite.

Said Barry Jay Seltser, who prepared the parish survey: "It is not meant as a criticism of this church to suggest that most of the wonders and weaknesses of late twentieth-century liberal religiosity may be played out within its parish life."

All Saints' large membership, budget, and staff make it possible to provide ninety separate activities, reflecting the church's involvement with its people, the greater Los Angeles community, and the world. And that is exactly what draws many parishioners—and keeps them coming.

"All Saints is a place that integrates your life," says Sue Sprowls, a member since 1985.

A Multitude of Ministries

Among its many activities are these urban ministries:
- Union Station and the Depot, a hospitality center that offers free food, emergency shelter, counseling, and friendship to several hundred of Pasadena's most needy.
- The Office of Creative Connections, a network joining area leaders and resources to attack urban problems.
- Las Familias del Pueblo, a community center near Skid Row in Los Angeles that has helped more than 1,500 immigrant families relocate. Directed by the Rev. Alice Callaghan of All Saints, Las Familias is supported by individuals, corporations, and the church.
- Genesis Hotel, a thirty-unit residence, one of three downtown flophouses renovated in a $7-million project. It is run by a nonprofit corporation formed by members of All Saints and the Jewish Leo Baeck Temple of West Los Angeles.
- AIDS Service Center, with more than ten support groups in the area; it's the nation's largest, parish-based AIDS program.

Every Sunday on the church lawn, All Saints volunteers staff an AIDS information table—one of more than a dozen programs presented in a colorful potpourri of banners and booths to challenge the church family to get involved in everything from choirs to feminist agendas to peace and justice groups.

One of the best-known ministries is the Interfaith Center to Reverse the Arms Race, founded in 1979 by Regas. The center underlines All Saints' 1987 commitment to be a "peace church" and encourages protests at nuclear test sites and boycotts of goods produced by corporations making nuclear weapons.

All Saints declared itself a "sanctuary church" early in the 1980's sanctuary movement, disobeying U.S. immigration laws by pledging aid to illegal aliens and refugees.

Other ministries advocate justice for refugees in Los Angeles and the oppressed in Central America; the struggle against apartheid in South Africa; relief of world hunger; the advancement of environmentally sound life-styles; the promotion of U.S.-Soviet relations. And more.

"In short," observes Don Miller, "All Saints is an 'activist church.' It proclaims the Social Gospel vision of a hundred years ago, but with a modern understanding of the importance of coalitions, manipulation of the media, and social service projects that are funded by foundations as well as the church."[5]

There are welters of groups for those with special concerns or interests: (1) the Pro-Choice Task Force, whose mission is "to secure the right of procreative choice for all women"; (2) the All Saints Mastectomy Support Group; (3) a women's potluck discussion called "Sleep and How to Get It," on insomnia, dreams, and healthy rest; (4) GALAS (Gays and Lesbians All Saints); (5) EDEN (Environmental Defense of the Earth Now), and (6) SAFE, a support group for those being sexually harassed at work.[6]

Lest a visitor conclude, however, that All Saints is all works and no pray, a newcomer's information packet points to a plethora of "conventional" parish programs: family ministries, Christian education, youth classes and retreats, healing services with "the laying on of hands," a Bible study, "covenant" groups, and prayer fellowships.

On a recent Sunday, Associate Rector Denis O'Pray (his real name) devoted his sermon to "Now I Lay Me Down to Sleep and Other Simple Thoughts About Prayer."

O'Pray's advice on prayer? "Just do it."

Services at All Saints are rich and varied, and a printed order that often runs to twenty-five pages details every aspect.

"There's a tremendous diversity, and it's not stuffy worship," says Regas. "We may go from an elaborate expression of classical repertoire one week to all Hispanic music the next and black gospel after that."

There are also periodic "Rock Masses," a throwback to the 1970s when young people packed the sanctuary for monthly Sunday-night events of contemporary music coupled with anti-war demonstrations. A Rock Mass in March 1991 was a "supplication for peace" in the Persian Gulf as well as in America. The program featured music of The Who, Bob Dylan, and Tracy Chapman, among others.[7]

Regas, a theological liberal, says All Saints is "an open community" with "no theological straitjackets on anyone." Only 15 percent consider themselves "born-again" Christians, and 57 percent say they read the Bible or devotional literature "seldom or not at all."

Nevertheless, Regas says, "We're a Christ-centered church. We believe in the power of the living Christ to change lives."

At Easter, Regas preaches that the resurrection of Jesus, "the greatest story ever to break across the Earth," is the bedrock of Christian faith. "You take that away and the structure of the New Testament would collapse."

In his 1991 Easter message, he proclaimed, "In the magnificent triumph of life over death, we live in Christ's presence today. Take the victory of Easter into your soul and let it strengthen you for life anew."[8]

Regas studs his sermons with quotes from a wide gamut of sources: Martin Luther King Jr., Leo Tolstoy, Carl Sandberg, and Agatha Christie to "New Age" Dominican priest Matthew Fox, Peanuts cartoon characters, and *Los Angeles Times* sports columnists. These citations are at least as numerous as references to the Bible. That doesn't mean the Bible is unimportant at All Saints; it just doesn't play the central role it does in most conservative churches.

A condensation of Regas's controversial sermon espousing a pro-choice view of abortion was published in *The Los Angeles Times* and other newspapers. Subsequently, the church's elected lay leaders approved a pro-choice policy statement defending abortion from a religious perspective, saying that "no law should be enacted to force an unwilling woman to give birth to an unwanted child."

Regas made international headlines with his November 11, 1990, sermon announcing that he would begin performing "church blessings" for same-sex couples. "I strongly reject" the Episcopal Church's official policy opposing such recognition of gay and lesbian unions, he asserted. "[H]uman sexuality is the test case for communities of faith in our time," Regas said, putting his finger on what most likely will be the most explosive issue of the decade for mainline churches.

"Every human being has a God-given right to sexual love and

intimacy," he declared—"a right to be lived out in a way that is compatible with the spirit of Christ."[9]

Soon after the sermon, All Saints formed the God, Sex & Justice Task Force to discuss and plan for the blessing of same-sex unions.[10]

An "Honest to God" Greek

The son of a Greek immigrant, Regas attended a Greek Orthodox church as a youngster. He graduated from the Episcopal Divinity School in Cambridge, Massachusetts, and was ordained a priest in 1956. He first served "a little bitty mission" of fifty members in Pulaski, Tennessee, before spending seven years as rector of an 800-member church in Nyack, New York. He came to All Saints in 1967, where he now directs a staff of forty-five, including five full-time priests and seven professional lay associates.

Regas pursued graduate studies with his longtime friend and mentor, Anglican Bishop John A. T. Robinson, the late "Honest to God" theologian whose book by that name questioned most traditional Christian concepts. In 1972, Regas earned a doctor of religion degree at the School of Theology at Claremont.

Active at diocesan and national levels of the church, Regas was a key strategist in the denomination's 1976 vote permitting women priests. And in 1988, Regas was among finalists seeking the influential post of retiring liberal Bishop Paul Moore of New York.

USC's professor Miller thinks Regas is a "genius as a prophet" because he can "anticipate (and in part create) the consensus which then defines the view of many liberal clergy." This positions Regas as a leader, Miller wrote, "who is not crying in the wilderness, but who has a large and powerful congregation standing behind him."[11]

Regas's 1990 base salary was $70,000. He drives a church-leased BMW, and with his $30,000 housing allowance he is buying the All Saints' rectory. Regas also receives income from a family real estate enterprise, and his second wife, Mary, owns and operates a jewelry-making business. The couple give $14,000 a year to the church and have pledged another $32,000 to the church building fund.

Many in the All Saints family also give generously. According to the parish survey, 40 percent of pledging members in 1989 gave $2,000 or more a year; almost a quarter gave more than $3,500; and

10 percent donated more than $7,500 to the church. In the spring of 1991, All Saints embarked on a $10.8 million building project to add 22,500 square feet of space and to upgrade the existing facilities, including the 900-seat Gothic stone sanctuary.[12]

Ironically, the church's most attractive feature—strong preaching and commitment to social issues—was also singled out in the survey as the thing that made parishioners the most uncomfortable.

About a third of the All Saints family would like more balance between social activism and spirituality, with greater attention to worship, theological reflection, and spiritual depth.

"In some superficial respects," concluded Seltser, the survey analyst,

> All Saints fits the stereotype of the large, white, wealthy, mainline Protestant church: uncomfortable with dogma beyond the platitudes of peace and love; unafraid to speak out against racial or sexual discrimination but terrified of alienating members by taking theological positions and drawing lines about belief; open to diversity in membership and supportive of a pluralistic society but unable to identify precisely what makes it distinctively "Christian."

Presbyterian scholar John Leith writes, "the denominations that appear to be most optimistic about changing the policies of great nations, as well as economic and social systems, seem less concerned and optimistic about the possibility of significant transformation of the life of individuals in the congregations."[13]

Liberal mainline congregations that grow in the new century, then, will likely be sociologically strong rather than doctrinally strong. Somehow, they will demythologize the supernatural aspects of biblical faith while, at the same time, providing deep mystical experiences. They will have to maintain a precarious yet creative tension between the poles of worship and social action.

That will be a neat trick for the few that can do it.

Chapter 27

St. John the Baptist Roman Catholic Church

Monsignor Peter D. Nugent, pastor for nine years of St. John the Baptist Roman Catholic Church in Baldwin Park, played the hero in a melodramatic skit staged by a church-based community organization.[1]

The priest ripped the blindfolds off the Environmental Protection Agency's "watchdogs" so they could see and chase away the villains contaminating the ground water in Southern California's San Gabriel Valley.

Nugent plays a similar role in real life. His simple but strong biblical sermons, which he delivers without notes, relate to pressing social problems.

At St. John the Baptist, one of the largest parishes in the sprawling three-county Catholic Archdiocese of Los Angeles, he helped the church's 7,000-plus families, the vast majority of whom are Latinos and Filipinos, see opportunities to improve their lives and community.

"A lot of people here are ready to respond and develop and get into things if you give them half a chance," Nugent says. "My prime goal is leadership development."[2]

That goal is consonant with the vision of a leading Catholic Bishop, Donald Wuerl of Pittsburgh, Pennsylvania, who spoke recently on "Toward the Year 2000: Priests and the Laity." In the "increasing need for collaborative ministry," Wuerl said, "priesthood and lay ministry work hand in hand. . . . Increasingly, as more and more people recognize their own calling and respond to it, the tasks of the priest as leader of the faith community will more and more center on his ability to coordinate, oversee, and enable all of the members . . . to participate in the building up of the church."

Wuerl went on to describe the priest of the next millennium as one whose work is "less 'hands on' and more supervisory and empowering," allowing him to become "less the direct, omnipresent, sole minister in the church," and more able "to lead or shepherd the faithful."[3]

Nugent's successful service to his burgeoning flock is that kind of ministry. Church analysts say other priests in the 56-million-member U.S. Catholic Church will need to copy his style if the faith is to continue its growth and relevance through the 1990s and beyond.

Changing Population, Shifting Focus

Father Gene Hemrick, research director for the National Conference of Catholic Bishops, has predicted that by 2001 "immigration is going to turn the church upside down."[4] In Baldwin Park, it already has.

During the time Nugent—who is now in his mid-fifties and serves another Southern California parish—was in charge at St. John the Baptist, nothing influenced his focus more dramatically than Baldwin Park's shifting population. Once a semi-agricultural small town, it's now a rapidly growing semi-urban area with pockets of deep poverty and crime, gangs and drug problems.

Baldwin Park's population of 63,000 is about 77 percent Latino, 15 percent Filipino, 8 percent Anglo, and a smattering of others. The average annual income for individuals in 1989-90 was $16,000.

The ethnic diversity, generally low family incomes, and attendant social problems confound traditional patterns of parish leadership and worship.

"Incorporating the various ethnic groups into one parish is a challenging job," said St. John's music director, Tom Ratto. "We have a tremendous amount of turnover. It's a fast-moving place; it jumps."

St. John the Baptist parish is not untypical. Many in Southern California have experienced growth and a rapidly changing population in the past few years. In fact, virtually every parish west and southwest of downtown Los Angeles is experiencing what archdiocese communications director Bill Rivera calls "the Hispanic wave."

According to the 1990 census, Los Angeles County residents included 3.3 million Latinos, or 38 percent of the total population—up from 7 percent in 1950. Since 1980, 1.3 million persons of Spanish/Hispanic origin have been added to the county's population.[5]

St. John is a premier pioneer parish, according to Auxiliary Bishop Juan Arzube, who oversees parishes in the San Gabriel Valley. The "contemporary mentality" of its priests, its innovative programs, and Nugent's ability to "get things done" in the community combined to make St. John an attractive role model, Arzube said.

The parish is a prime example of what Jane Redmont, an authority on Catholic parish and campus ministries, says a congregation needs to do to remain vital: smoothly blend "prayer and social concern, spiritual nurture and a strong worship life, a commitment to religious education for adults and children, and a laity increasingly interested in making the connection between their religious faith and their daily lives."[6]

St. John's pastoral staff is certainly cosmopolitan: Nugent, a French Canadian, learned to speak Spanish when he was a student at St. John's Seminary in Camarillo, California. Associate Pastor Nick Ricalde is Filipino, and associate Guillermo Rodriguez is Salvadoran. An Italian priest learning to speak English joined the staff for the summer of 1989, and the year's seminary intern was Irish-German.

The swirling mix of languages and cultures is evident in everything from people to programs to the color of paint used in decorating.

Four of eight weekend Masses are said in Spanish. On a recent

Sunday, the morning Spanish Mass included music from a choir, organ, guitars, and an accordion. At the afternoon Mass, a choir sang—first in Filipino and then in English—"You'll Never Walk Alone."

Elizabeth Tapia, who grew up in the parish and now teaches English as a second language at the church, remembers when the 800-seat sanctuary had lots of marble and crucifixes. During extensive remodeling in 1984, the interior was done over in gold and coral pink.

"Many here have become acculturated," said Tapia, adding that St. John "really wants to serve all the needs of the people—all the cultures and perspectives."

That's an ingredient that makes effective contemporary parishes "work," according to The Notre Dame Study of Catholic Parish Life. The in-depth, decade-long research project looks at the combined impact of demographic change and the Second Vatican Council on local Catholic communities.

The most important components in building parish community, concluded David Leege, director of the study, are "the opportunity to serve in a wide variety of ministries, interest groups and activities; the accessibility and affirmation of pastors; and a participatory liturgy."

Also drawing a congregation together are sermons that relate to people's everyday lives, a Eucharistic celebration that recognizes those assembled as a "body of Christ" gathered around the Body of Christ, and hymns and responses.

Parishes that develop a strong sense of community also act as a "living catechesis" (religious instruction program), Leege said. "You can talk a lot about different programs to instruct people, but the strongest teacher is the way the parish goes about its business. It's through a sense of community that Catholics learn who they are and what they ought to do."[7]

Some changes have not been easy for the dwindling remnant of Anglos who originally formed St. John Parish and built the church and its school. Ruth Stein, who has been attending St. John since it was established in 1946, feels a little left out.

"We're the minority now," she sighed. "But when I go to church I go to pray to God, not to notice who's there. Things are going to have to change [more] and we're just going to go along with it."

Nugent, who often wears a Mexican-style shirt called a *guayabera*, was thirteen when his family moved to East Los Angeles from Canada. Ordained in 1962, he holds a master's degree in music from the University of Southern California, and he taught music at St. John's Seminary for fourteen years. After serving for two years as associate pastor at St. Pius X Parish in nearby Santa Fe Springs, he came to St. John the Baptist in 1981.

The soft-spoken, energetic Nugent belongs to a health club and likes music, reading, skiing, hiking, and the beach. He draws the standard salary for monsignors: $450 a month plus a car, meals, and lodging at the church rectory.

Moving Out for the Millennium

It's time, he says, for parishes to move into new strategies for the next century. "We've been a service church—baptisms, worship, weddings, education," he declared, noting that there had been 153 marriages, 412 baptisms, and 200 to 300 confirmations at St. John during the previous year. About 1,000 children and young adults were enrolled in the church's catechism program. "But I see the kids as they are growing up and they don't have the allegiances we had," he continued. "They are very free. Some don't necessarily believe [in the faith]. And that's not just the 'black sheep.' It's a way of growing up in modern America. Young adults, too. The church has to reach out."

Nugent's efforts to reach out included six-week home Bible study and prayer meetings that involved up to 500 people. And he held "friendly neighborhood encounters": home rosaries and occasional home Masses. "Our parish is the neighborhood; whoever is here is us," he said, spreading his hands. "That's in our tradition."

A growing tradition at St. John is a major youth emphasis sparked by full-time youth minister Lucy Boutte. She specializes in training high school young people to lead their own weekend retreats.

"These are often turning points. They encounter themselves, their parents, pain, each other, God, and Jesus," said Boutte, a former insurance underwriter. Estrangement between teens and their parents is the most frequent obstacle, so parents join in on the final night of the retreat, bringing "love letters" they have just written to their children. The young people respond by writing their parents. A family "reconciliation service" concludes the evening as the parents lay hands on their children in prayer.

"If we don't address the conflicts within families, they get passed on for generations and we get more broken relationships," Boutte explained.

Laura Garcia, sixteen, one of Boutte's twenty-five team leaders, said the retreats had helped her to be "more understanding and patient with people," but "some [young people] don't get involved because of peer pressure."

St. John tries to reach children early. Its school serves some 500 pupils from first through eighth grades. Students score an average of two-and-one-half to three years above the national achievement norms, according to Sister Assumpta Martinez, a teacher and principal at St. John's for sixteen years. About 95 percent go on to Catholic high schools and half to college, she said proudly.

The monthly tuition at St. John's School is a bargain: $92 per student for working parents, and $75 for non-working parents, who are expected to help with school supervision. Proceeds from weekly parish bingo games help keep fees low.

Although most children speak Spanish, only English is used at the school, in line with Sister Assumpta's conviction that bilingual classes hinder education in the long run.

"We have the most outstanding, caring, family environment here," said the sister, a member of the order of the Religious of the Love of God. The school has no problems with drugs, alcohol or tobacco, she added, crediting good discipline: "We cherish freedom . . . based on responsibility."

Counseling, Social Service, and Guidance

Sister Joan Keltus, who supervises Christian social service programs at St. John, sees another side of the parish and community. There is counseling for troubled marriages, assistance for battered women, groceries given to 1,000 families each month through an ecumenical food center, and guidance for immigrants navigating a maze of red tape and paperwork to obtain food stamps, medical benefits, and employment. And before the registration deadline,

Sister Joan helped 5,000 area families sign up for the immigration amnesty program.

"There's a lot of poverty and unemployment in this area," says the nun, a member of the Sisters of Social Service. She sees irony in the fact that she's pledged to poverty but her monthly stipend of $500 plus a car and apartment total more than what many in the parish make—half earn only the minimum wage of $4.25 an hour.

"Rents here are outrageous," huffed Sister Joan, pointing to an ill-kept housing development down the block where two or more families often share two-bedroom units at $560 a month.

She calls her ministry no more than "Band-Aiding—meeting immediate needs." And, she says, as the government cuts back on social services and counseling, "the church has to do more and more of this."

David Leege, overseer of the Notre Dame parish study, found that parish-connected Catholics want even more of these kinds of services from their local parishes: drug and alcohol counseling, marital help, programs for the separated and divorced, adult religious education, interfaith experiences, and social action projects.[8]

The staff of St. John's is indeed working to give the people a stronger voice in their own destinies. For example, Margarita Vargas, a leader in the powerful interdenominationally based East Valleys Organization, targeted 4,748 Baldwin Park residents eligible to vote. She got 2,100 of them registered and to the polls. And substantial portions of St. John's $700,000 annual budget help fund organizations like the interfaith food center and the East Valleys Organization.

The Rev. Donn Crail, pastor of Baldwin Park Presbyterian Church, had this to say about his neighboring parish: "St. John will continue to be a significant presence in the future . . . particularly for Hispanics, giving them empowerment and self-esteem. It does a very good job of reaching the 'whole person.'"

And the Notre Dame study offers this lesson from history for the millennial road ahead:

> The moment the [Second Vatican] Council defined the church as the "People of God," a change in thinking took place, and a change in acting as well; the concept of shared responsibility entered into church life, and with it came shared decision-

making. These elements have been developing for . . . [more than] 20 years and in ways most likely not envisioned by the bishops at the council. No one can predict the future, but release a powerful agent for change in a society undergoing rapid transformation, and the future is unlikely to imitate the past.[9]

If I were betting on the type of ministry to blaze the trail through the nineties and prepare the way for Jesus Christ in the millennium, I'd choose that of St. John the Baptist.

True Vine Missionary Baptist Church

The members of True Vine Missionary Baptist Church in West Oakland know the awesome power of an earthquake. The October, 1989, killer quake that wreaked havoc in the San Francisco Bay area leveled the double-decker freeway that ran just east of the modest cream-colored stucco church. Before the quake, True Vine was hidden from sight by the freeway. But when the earthquake flattened the double-decker highway, the church came into prominence.

True Vine members also know the awesome power of the Holy Spirit. They have seen it transform a neighborhood violently ruled and shaken by drug dealers. That potency, too, has brought the church into new prominence.

True Vine faithful, led by Sallie Carey, church evangelism director and the pastor's wife, drove the pushers out of the 750-unit Acorn Housing Project after praying, fasting, and marching around it seven times. Their bold act imitated the trumpet-blowing Israelites who circled the city of Jericho before its walls tumbled.

"The walls of Jericho didn't fall down because the Israelites marched," explained Pastor Newton Carey, Jr. "They fell because the people believed."

There are a lot of true believers at True Vine. That's the secret of the church's success. In fact, the church has been so successful that the congregation had to postpone a "Here's Hope" revival in 1990! Advance outreach had already brought in 1,250 new converts, overflowing the small sanctuary for the two Sunday morning worship services and the one on Friday night.[1]

True Vine is an example of what can happen in an inner-city ministry when a congregation catches on fire with the power of the Holy Spirit.

"The 21st-century way of winning souls is the first-century way—Jesus' way," exclaims Pastor Carey.[2]

The story of this black congregation isn't a Cinderella saga of megachurch proportions—that's why it's such an attractive, hopeful, "copyable" model for the coming millennium. It's a success story for "Any Church, U.S.A." But let some black believers tell you in their own words.

Testimony Time

A typical testimony goes like this:

> My sister has been coming to True Vine for a while, and she's always telling me I ought to come to church. I told her I didn't like going to church because people are more concerned with the clothes you have on than what you're supposed to be in church for. And then the preacher is always talking about stuff that ain't got no bearing on my life right now. I don't even have no Bible, and I don't understand what it's saying anyhow.
>
> But my sister kept telling me that if I come to True Vine, I could wear whatever I want and nobody was going to say nothing to me about it. And she said this preacher talks about the Lord in a way that makes you feel like he's some kind of personal friend who really listens to you. And then she gave me this *Here's Hope* New Testament Bible that was easy to read.[3]

Well I still wasn't too enthused about True Vine, but I noticed how since she's been coming here, my sister has changed. Every time I see her, she's talking about how the Lord has blessed her and how he can do the same for me. Even when she got laid off her job she was walking around talking about "praise the Lord." When I asked her why she was praising while she was out of work, didn't have no car and no money, she kept saying something about how the Lord would supply all her needs. And all the while she seemed like she was, you know, happy!

Now I know my sister doesn't use drugs, at least I don't believe she does, but she's, like, high all the time. When I asked her what kind of substance she had got hold of, she said "the Holy Ghost." That's when I knew it was time to come check out True Vine.

See, my life ain't going that great either, but I sure ain't happy about it. I've had problems with drugs and family life, and none of my relationships ever seem to work out. So I figured I'd just come and see what was going on at this church and if I can get some of this joy my sister talks about all the time.

I realize now that what is missing from my life is Jesus. And the way the preacher talked about him this morning, I know it's time for me to invite him in my life and get to know him for myself.[4]

This is the best part of a Sunday service, some True Viners say. It comes *after* the sermon, when folks of "any given racial, economic, and social persuasion step forward to accept Jesus Christ as their personal Lord and Savior," explains member Denise Williams. "Each new believer is given the opportunity to testify before the congregation about how he or she made that crucial, life-changing decision."

The commitment to witnessing is emphasized in everything they do, she continues, "from prayer meetings to Bible study classes to door-to-door witnessing to our Continuing Witness Training program."[5]

That's why True Vine added more than 300 new members in 1990, bringing the total on the rolls to 1,200. It isn't a buppie congregation, though the Careys estimate that 95 percent of True Vine members are under fifty.

The explosion really began with a training and sending program for members who go door-to-door throughout the neighborhoods one Saturday a month. They hand out free copies of the specially marked *Here's Hope* New Testaments and offer to point out some key salvation passages. In 1990, after True Vine had exhausted its supply of 12,000 marked testaments, their denomination, the Southern Baptist Convention, sent them another 10,000 copies.

Why True Vine Abides

True Vine got its start when Isaiah Liggins began holding home meetings in West Oakland in 1962. Soon, a small, storefront-type congregation was established. Newton and Sallie Carey came in 1974. With their easy-going style and affable sincerity, they were well-liked from the beginning. But the small, ordinary church remained small and ordinary. For years, it was just one of hundreds of Oakland-area congregations and one of sixteen black Southern Baptist churches in Oakland.

In 1975, Sallie Carey began faithfully leading a team that witnessed in the county prison twice a month. And an early spark was touched off in 1979 by Cheryl Burwell, a woman from Los Angeles who joined True Vine and taught 20 weeks of evangelism and discipleship training.

But it was the heartbreak of seeing the drug dealers, crime and poverty in the church's "backyard" that got to Newton and Sallie. As the urban jungle spread, single mothers with two or more children and living on public assistance were increasingly victimized at the Acorn Housing Project. A security guard was killed and several people were injured in a long string of drug-related incidents.

"You could see Al Capone all over again just by looking out the window," Newton told Cameron Crabtree of the *California Southern Baptist* newspaper. Still, Carey felt frustrated because he didn't know how to help hurting people.[6]

The change came when Carey went off to the Santa Cruz mountains alone and agonized with God over the problem. There, he "discovered how to really pray." When he returned a few days later, Carey started spending an hour a day in prayer and fasting one day a week.

"It wasn't nothing I did, really," the father of four grown children told me. (The Careys' son, Zachary, is True Vine's youth pastor.) "The Holy Spirit was able to come in and use us. It was praying and receiving the power of the Spirit-filled life." The Careys feel the Christian church has failed to teach that vital step: "The Holy Spirit is the power the church needs to get the job done for Jesus. The power of the Holy Spirit—that was the ultimate change."[7]

Now, other pastors are knocking on the Careys' door, asking what they are doing differently. Area churches are using True Vine-produced teaching materials. Folks from as far away as Santa Rosa, Sacramento, Salinas, and San Jose come to True Vine's "God, Help Me Stop!" addiction-busting classes on Monday nights.

Soon after Newton's mountain experience, the Careys organized a core of concerned members who steadfastly fasted and prayed about the drug-infested neighborhood. And then Sallie led the small band around Acorn seven times. They prayed on their knees at every corner. They asked God to give them the territory and drive out drug dealers from where the police wouldn't go.

The pushers split. The drug trade broke up. And amazingly, the church hasn't been hit with vandalism or reprisals.

"God shows us how to get power to pull down strongholds," says Denise Williams.[8]

Next, True Vine held a huge block party for Acorn residents, laying on the church's famous spread: barbecued chicken, potato salad, and baked beans.

"We're strong on food, fellowship, and hugging," laughs Sallie, who's apt to tell a perfect stranger on the phone, "I don't know you, but I love you," and convince the caller that, as a sister in Christ, she sincerely means it.

Adds Newton: "We don't go to people with junk; we treat 'em like kings and queens."

People at Acorn apparently liked more than the chicken and potato salad because they started coming to True Vine. Now, the church holds children's classes in the Acorn project three times a week.

Newton drove my wife and me past an abundance of small churches in the general area. All appeared to be barricaded behind high fences and locked gates on that weekday.

"Those ones aren't concerned about the hurting people," Carey said. "They minister to their own kind only. But Jesus' church shouldn't do that."

By contrast, True Vine was open and a stream of people came and went for counseling, appointments, meetings—or just to pop in and say "howdy" to Newton, Sallie, and other True Vine leaders.

"We go out and get the down-and-out, the hungry, the poor, and the sick, those on drugs, in jails, those that have demons," Carey declared. "People are excited about it."

True Vine is also "reclaiming for Christ" housing projects at Campbell Village and Kirkland Court. Each witnessing and teaching venture is undertaken with the permission of the local housing authorities. And True Vine has good connections with area detox and treatment programs for persons who need professional help.

"Adopt-A-Block" Busters

Similar reclamation tactics have worked elsewhere, too. In Ravendale, home to 4,000 mostly black and poor people in Detroit's inner city, the Joy of Jesus ministry joined forces with a small, stubborn group of people trying to reclaim their neighborhood from crack dealers. Links to the business and church communities helped Eddie Edwards's nondenominational Joy of Jesus organize twenty-three of Ravendale's thirty-eight blocks. The pride of residents is vastly improved and crime has been drastically cut.

Together, residents and Joy of Jesus

- convinced Detroit police to open a satellite station in the neighborhood.
- organized youth sports leagues.
- helped more than 115 residents find jobs.
- established a nightly volunteer radio patrol to report crime.
- started a regular shuttle service for youth, the elderly, the handicapped, and job seekers, using a donated van.

Edwards's latest project is "Adopt-A-Block," a plan for suburban congregations to match up with each of Ravendale's blocks, providing material, human, and spiritual help.[9]

Newton Carey would like to add more of that dimension to True Vine's outreach. At the end of 1990 he was eyeing a large building a few blocks from the church. It would provide meeting space for 1,200 and become a "trade center" where job training, such as computer skills, could be taught to young people to help them break out of the poverty cycle.

But True Vine needed to come up with $300,000 to close the $1.4 million deal, and cash was one thing Carey didn't have.

Visitation Teams

Probably the most vital portion of True Vine's evangelism is its street witnessing. On the fourth Saturday of the month, trained True Viners meet at 9:30 A.M. for prayer and Scripture reading. Then they form teams of three or four and spend several hours walking the neighborhoods and calling in homes.

"There's no better job than being out there on the streets," Carey said with a chuckle. "Most of what Jesus did was outside."

Receptive people are given a *Here's Hope* testament and prayed for on the spot. Southern Baptist Home Mission Board materials are also used, such as the tract, "Do You Know for Certain That You Have Eternal Life and That You Will Go to Heaven When You Die?"

The neighborhood thrust has built the church and won more than a thousand converts to Christ. True Vine street teams are so turned on that now they occasionally travel hundreds of miles on a weekend to do witnessing with churches in other cities.

"We went door-to-door witnessing in Bakersfield last weekend," reported deacon Elijah Onick. "The Holy Spirit just kept opening up the door" when people seemed resistant, he told us. "We shared verses from *Here's Hope* with them and 205 accepted the Lord. Most had never made a commitment before."

How many church members are able or willing to do this kind of evangelism, even occasionally—let alone on a regular basis? The mission efforts of Jehovah's Witnesses and Mormons pay big dividends. True Vine's experience shows that Bible-toting and quoting

Christians from a modest inner-city church can do the same without fancy degrees or years of preparation.

Fruit of the Vine

To train disciples to witness to hopeless, hurting, and dying people they first have to abide in the True Vine, which is Jesus, Carey says. So that is his main emphasis. An avid reader (about a book a day, he says) and a bold preacher, Carey covers such topics in his sermons as marriage, family, child-rearing, jealousy, and control of the mind through the power of God. "We stop performing and get down to the real world," he explains. Worship services include twenty to thirty minutes of "exalting the Savior." His teaching "puts the Gospel into people's life-styles." And so do the programs his church offers.

In the hall just outside the main doors to the sanctuary is a large chart where True Vine classes are listed in longhand:

God, Help Me Stop!
Bible Study
Prison Ministry
New Members
Prayer
Knowing Jesus
Assurance of Salvation
The Christian and Stewardship
Survival Kit I
Survival Kit II
Youth Survival Kit
Every Single Won
Bible Characters
Master Characters
MasterLife
Great Truths of the Bible
Through the Bible in One Year—Genesis to Revelation
Acorn Ministry Study
Continuing Witnessing Training
Lay Evangelism School
Training Faithful Men
Training Faithful Women

The fourteen-week "God, Help Me Stop!" class on addictions and compulsions is probably True Vine's most innovative program. Led by Don Sutton, who heads the Oakland Crack Task Force, it is based on a twelve-step program. At the time we talked to Sutton, the course was being taught in eight area churches and at a cocaine recovery house for women as well as at True Vine.

"Having family problems? Can't stop gambling? Sexual compulsion? Can't communicate with your children? Compulsive overspender? Can't stop lying? Are you an addict? An alcoholic? Do you love someone who has any of these problems?

"If you can't stop, then we have a class for you!" advertises a handout.

The curriculum has been compiled into a book, *God, Help Me Stop: Break Free From Addiction and Compulsion.*[10]

Once people stop their addictive behavior, Carey's church gets them started in a whole new direction.

True Vine is a millennial model to watch closely.

Chapter 29

Vineyard Christian Fellowship

After John Wimber stopped working as a music arranger for the Righteous Brothers rock group and became a pastor, he started leading a small prayer group, preaching from the gospel of Luke about healing the sick and casting out demons.

But for ten months in 1977 the fledgling church repeatedly prayed over the sick without seeing one person healed or a single demon expelled. Many people left in disgust. Wimber himself was about to give up when he was asked to pray at the bedside of a young woman with a high fever. When the woman jumped up, apparently cured, Wimber was slow to realize what had happened. In fact, he was halfway to his car before it dawned on him.

Then, at the top of his voice, he yelled, "We got one!"[1]

That experience galvanized Wimber's convictions that the spiritual gifts of healing, speaking in tongues, and "words of knowledge and prophecy" were still relevant and that he could defeat Satan, sin, and sickness with the ultimate power of God.

A trickle of reported healings became a flood, and in Southern California's fertile religious soil—already famous for innovative and entrepreneurial church leadership—John Wimber's Vineyard Christian Fellowship took root as the latest "boom church."

The Vineyard's origins hark back to the hippie-era "Jesus People" movement. Chuck Smith helped launch the Jesus People in the late 1960s and 1970s through his chain of Calvary Chapels, starting in Costa Mesa. But Wimber's emphasis seems to reach a different stratum: younger believers who want to wed an orthodox, Bible-believing faith with immediate and palpable spiritual power and emotional experience.

The Vineyard in Anaheim has grown to 6,000. A network of Vineyard churches with about 100,000 followers—most of them baby boomers—stretches across the nation and overseas. And thousands attend Wimber's conferences on worship, healing, and prophecy held around the world.

The Vineyard story underscores the findings of church growth experts: More and more Americans are reaching outside the traditional, established denominations to find spiritual identification.

"I was into organized religion most of my life—Presbyterian and Evangelical Free churches," said Sandy Younger, who has been attending the Anaheim Vineyard since 1986. "But something was always lacking until I heard John preach. It was so different, so down to earth."

A high percentage of the nation's fastest-growing congregations are either independent or affiliated with new and loosely formed movements. These include Vineyard Ministries International and Calvary Chapels. By 1991 more than 500 Vineyards had sprouted, and churches affiliated with Calvary Chapels numbered above 418.[2]

Movements like these will be the *new* denominations of the new millennium.

Undisputed Ministry Mogul

With the reddish-white beard and rugged features of a Kenny Rogers and the physique and twinkling eyes of a Santa Claus, Wimber is the undisputed mogul of what has come to be known as the "signs and wonders" ministry. To him, it's all very simple: A new wave of supernatural power is rolling in, and it is based on the Bible message that Jesus' followers would see "signs and wonders" from the Holy Spirit certifying Christ's ministry and resurrection.

The cutting edge of the Vineyard, says Todd Hunter, executive pastor of the Anaheim congregation, is that "ordinary Christians can be used by God to do extraordinary things."

So extraordinary, it seems, that Wimber has been accused of fostering excessive emotionalism and anti-intellectualism and of misinterpreting Scripture. But he waves aside skepticism, saying his critics rarely consult him about their accusations.

"I don't have time to refute all that anyway," he told me during a break at the Pritikin Longevity Center in Santa Monica, where he periodically goes to shed pounds and shuck stress.[3]

Wimber's friend, C. Peter Wagner, a diminutive dynamo who teaches church growth at Fuller Seminary, says the controversial signs-and-wonders phenomenon is the "third wave" of evangelical Christian renewal to occur this century. The first wave was the rise of Pentecostalism, the movement that sprang up in the early 1900s among churchgoers who were below average in wealth and education. It emphasized the baptism of the Holy Spirit and speaking in tongues.

The second wave was the growth of the charismatic renewal movement that burgeoned among Protestant mainliners and Catholics in the 1960s and 1970s as they adopted spiritual healing and other Pentecostal practices into their churches.[4]

The third wave, according to Wagner and others, emphasizes the kind of supernatural manifestations that appeal to fundamentalists and conservative evangelicals. Until recently, these Christians tended to deny modern-day faith healings and regarded prophetic "gifts" as theologically suspect.

Wimber's classical theology, informal and praise-centered worship style, and aggressive evangelism strategies "represent an interesting and effective synthesis of the evangelical and the charismatic," according to a study done by Robin D. Perrin of Seattle Pacific University and Armand L. Mauss of Washington State University.

The two sociologists reported in 1989 that the great majority of Vineyard recruits who listed a denominational background had been reared in mainline Protestant or Catholic homes. More recent Vineyard recruits, however, had left their liberal religious upbringing and had been "circulating" among the conservative denominations. Only 13 percent indicated that the Vineyard was the first church they attended after becoming a Christian.[5] Thus, there are more "switchers" than converts.

"John began to draw into the Vineyard the boomers of the late '70s," Wagner said. "Many were in their teens. . . . The median age was 19." Ten years later, the average age was 10 years older. And Wimber, in 1991, was 57. Vineyard congregations are composed mainly of middle- and working-class people.

"John is one of the very few pastors to say publicly that the Vineyard is a one-generation church," Wagner told me, adding: "The even-younger generation . . . may need a new church yet" because Vineyard is "too established" for them.

(On the other hand, perhaps they'll want something *more* structured and formal, even liturgical.)

A perplexing question for the churches of the coming century: Will future congregations tend to center on the particular life issues of a single generation?[6] Will churches be stratified by age? If so, how does this relate to the biblical concept of the larger family of God?

Presbyterian minister Dick Spencer, an outside observer of the Vineyard movement, worries that its one-generation appeal may lead to peer-group isolation. "When clues to identification and behavior are closely followed from one another, the movement may turn out in the end to become conformist in dress, worship, and theology," Spencer said.[7]

I see signs that's beginning to happen. Sacrificing the richness of an intergenerational mix would be a disturbing trend.

Praising God—Earnestly and Casually

Wimber and his Vineyards hardly reflect traditional church patterns. At the Anaheim Vineyard, nearly 4,000 worshipers jam into a boxy, flat building—formerly a Pacific Stereo warehouse—for two Sunday services, morning and evening. The crowd, casually dressed and most carrying Bibles, sits on folding chairs under long rows of florescent lights. Heat ducts and fire sprinklers hang beneath the low, brown ceiling.

"If you see a man wearing a tie or a woman a dress, they're probably visitors," quipped Kevin Springer, Wimber's publication director.

The focus of attention is a stage on one side of the square room, where youthful musicians play guitars, drums, and a keyboard to lead a nonstop forty-five-minute medley of congregational singing. There are no songbooks; the lyrics are projected on the front walls. Like Bill Hybels's Willow Creek Community Church, there is no altar, organ, cross, or other religious trappings. This setting is typical at the other Vineyards as well.

Many of the worshipers raise their arms, praising God earnestly as they sing the easy, repetitious melodies. Most songs have been composed by Vineyard members and extol spiritual empowerment and an intimate relationship with Jesus. A few worshipers kneel along the back wall with their heads in their hands, or touch their foreheads to the floor. A young woman, barefoot, gracefully dances to the music.

Although there are seventy Vineyard congregations in Southern California alone, this congregation is special because Wimber preaches here. In fact, he draws folks from other denominations, too: the evening I was there a van-load arrived from Bethany Chinese Presbyterian Church.

Wimber is on stage now; security personnel with earphones and walkie-talkies have cleared the aisles. The band sits back, and Wimber, standing behind a small wooden lectern, takes the mike.

If you expect a Pentecostal fireball delivery, you'll be disappointed. Wimber, dressed in cream-colored slacks and a print sport shirt, is talking about tonight's special offering for the poor and homeless. No emotion. No big pitch. Wimber weaves together a tapestry of Bible verses to make his case. Later it's announced that the day's contributions for this project total $180,000. That's on top of the $70,000 that comes in each week to run the church.

Wimber doesn't preach the "health and wealth" gospel—some have dubbed it "name it and claim it" or "blab it and grab it" theology—that makes God a convenient money genie: give a dollar to the Lord and he'll give you two.

Nor do the Wimbers live ostentatiously; their neatly kept ranch house in Yorba Linda and moderately priced cars bespeak middle class. Wimber's $80,000 combined salary and housing allowance are drawn from about $260,000 in annual royalties generated from sales of his many books and tapes. The balance goes to the Vineyard.

"I want a reward in heaven, not here," exclaims Wimber, drawing applause during his fifty-minute sermon.

A Vineyard regular who knew I was a newspaper reporter nudged me in the ribs during the offering and said, "He doesn't wear a Rolex either."

Working in the Vineyard

Although the Vineyard staples are ecstatic worship, prophecies, supernatural healing, and "deliverance from demon activity," Wimber and his twelve-pastor staff also take social action seriously. But the emphasis is far different from that of All Saints Episcopal Church in Pasadena!

The Anaheim Vineyard has been the meeting place and staging ground for Operation Rescue rallies and demonstrations against abortion. And staffer Monte Whitaker spearheads the Vineyard's benevolence arm, which distributes food and clothing to the area's needy and puts on a Saturday lunch and Bible service for about 300 transients and their children from the predominantly Latino neighborhood.

In the second quarter of 1990, Whitaker said, the Anaheim Vineyard provided 235,562 meals, handed out 17,163 pieces of clothing, and supplied 15,214 other items such as furniture and blankets.

Next door to the Anaheim Vineyard's bustling book, tape, and music store and a burgeoning mail-order department are the offices of Vineyard Ministries International. This division, among other things, coordinates prison ministries at twenty-five facilities throughout the state.

"We conduct worship services and do concerts and counseling," said Crystal Lee, who heads the prison ministry staff. "And Vineyard couples volunteer to be temporary foster parents to infants born to mothers while they are incarcerated."

Still another Vineyard-related work is Desert Stream, a Santa

Monica ministry to AIDS patients and homosexuals to help them overcome "expressions of sexual sin and brokenness."

Wimber claims he is often able to discern sexual sin through supernatural means. Once, for example, he saw the word "adultery" written across the face of a passenger opposite him on an airplane. "The letters, of course, were only perceptible to spiritual eyes," Wimber recalled, adding that a woman's name "came clearly to my mind."

Wimber confronted the man and told him God said he would "take him if he did not cease." According to Wimber, the man "melted on the spot and asked what he should do." Wimber led the man in a prayer of repentance, and he "received Christ" in front of a shocked stewardess and several passengers, who began to cry.

While Wimber is quick to admit that "only a few" of the people he prays for are healed of physical ailments and that "I am alive today because of the medical profession," he and Wagner launched a course at Fuller Seminary in 1982 that included an optional "laboratory" in divine healing. MC510, the class known as "Signs and Wonders," was the most popular course ever at Fuller—until a theological ruckus among faculty and trustees shut it down for a year in 1986.

How to explain why not all people are healed was foremost in the minds of many of the Fuller faculty, Presbyterian pastor Ben Patterson wrote in *Christianity Today* magazine. "Did Satan win one?" Patterson asked. "If so, then Satan holds a commanding lead in the game because the majority of people who are prayed for do not, in fact, get well physically. A subtle, but powerful, pressure therefore builds in the Signs and Wonders mentality to see miracles where there are none."[8]

After an evaluation, the class was reinstated, with Wimber taking a less prominent role. And Fuller officials released a 100-page report that urged caution in claiming miracle cures and attempting exorcisms of "evil spirits." In order to avoid "pious deception . . . the minister who engages in healing should publicize his or her failures as loudly as the successes," the report said, adding that "chronicles of healings should include failed attempts to heal, prayers for healing that were answered in death, apparent healings of people who soon relapsed into the disease from which they were healed—all of this alongside of the grateful reports of success."[9]

CHAPTER TWENTY-NINE

Roots of the Vineyard

Wimber was dramatically converted to Christianity at the age of twenty-nine from a show-biz, rock 'n' roll background. After completing three years of biblical study at Azusa Pacific University in 1970, he served as co-pastor of a Quaker church in Yorba Linda.

In 1977 he began shepherding the little home group that his wife, Carol, who had become a charismatic, had started. Soon he was preaching from Luke on signs and wonders. Then, after the feverish woman jumped from her sickbed, the Vineyard movement shot straight up as well.

The Vineyard movement got its start as part of Calvary Chapels. Kenn Gulliksen, a well-known Jesus movement pastor who had worked with Calvary Chapel founder Chuck Smith, established a home church in West Los Angeles in 1974.

"We called it the Vineyard," said Gulliksen, who now works with Wimber.[10] "Then we met for a year at Lifeguard Station No. 15 on the beach in Santa Monica. The third-graders gathered [for Sunday school] at trash can No. 3. We had the tannest church in the country! We were part of the Calvary Chapel movement then and were starting new churches out of Bible study groups so fast it was like unplanned parenthood."

Gulliksen and Wimber met in 1979 and became close friends. Three years later the two were pursuing the signs and wonders movement and the "gifts of the Spirit"—but more vigorously than Chuck Smith liked. After a meeting of Calvary Chapel leaders, Wimber's group was asked to join forces with Gulliksen's Vineyards and drop the Calvary Chapel connection. Some Calvary churches also switched over and later the Vineyard Christian Fellowship was formed.

Vineyard congregations typically multiply in one of two ways: An established Vineyard pastor and a cadre of his leaders select a new area and begin Bible studies and evangelistic meetings. Or an existing congregation petitions to be "adopted." One congregation that recently linked officially with the Vineyard—after a year's probation under Wimber's supervision—was the 3,000-member Kansas City Fellowship.

Church adoptions are in fact a major way these new movements of the 1990s are growing. In this sense, the new denominations will become the future "adoption agencies" for independent evangelical and charismatic churches that seek broader institutional identity.[11] They'll also become "foster parents" for congregational runaways who "can't take it anymore" when they feel the denominational family that nurtured them has drifted too far to the left.

By the early 1990s, the Vineyard movement was showing signs of becoming a denomination. It had trademarked its name, ordained about 500 men, licensed two or three women to preach (Wimber doesn't approve of women's ordination), and appointed regional and area pastoral coordinators. About 200 new pastors were to plant churches between 1991 and 1993.

In early 1991 Wimber purchased fifteen acres of prime Orange County real estate for a new headquarters, a "renewal center," and the county's largest sanctuary, which he said will have more seats than Robert Schuller's cavernous Crystal Cathedral in Garden Grove. The property, valued at $45 million in 1987, was obtained for about $20 million, Kevin Springer said.[12]

All of this growth has not come without some pain.

"We have fast growth, young pastors, and it's hard to develop structures to care for new members," assessed Springer, who edits Equipping the Saints, the Vineyard's slick quarterly magazine that has a circulation of 6,500. "People get lost in the crowd," he added, sounding very much like an executive of a budding denomination.[13]

Short Fuse or Tall Flame?

One burning question the new denominations must resolve is that of uniform training for pastors. No central school or Vineyard seminary exists, so which congregations and which ministers are accepted is pretty much up to Wimber's whims.

"I wield a lot of authority in the movement," Wimber acknowledges. "But I take instruction and counsel well."

So far, the Vineyard has avoided being trampled with major scandal, and Wimber, who seems to have gained wide respect, is clearly in control, keeping tabs on his staff and what they teach.

"I trust Wimber and the movement," said Charles Kraft, a professor at Fuller's School of World Mission who helps lead the "Signs and Wonders" class. "But there are a lot of very young people involved. . . . It's in its adolescence."

As movements like the Vineyard and Calvary Chapels enter the 21st century, the inevitable challenge will be: What happens when their charismatic and visionary founders pass on?

Les Parrott and Robin Perrin offer the following analysis of these new denominations: "On the one hand, their followers have been drawn by the anti-institutional, back-to-the-Bible fervor of their charismatic founders. On the other hand, the absence of institutionalization and structure leaves them with little to hold these movements together when the charismatic founders are gone."

Parrott and Perrin think the catch will be that the need for organization in the next decade will bring a decline in the emotional and spiritual fervor that fueled these movements: "The longer they burn, the smaller their flame."[14]

"What if Wimber should die?" I asked Jack Deere, Vineyard's international minister.

"Most of us think the movement would disintegrate," replied Deere, who was fired from the faculty of Dallas Theological Seminary in 1987 when he refused to renounce his identification with Wimber's beliefs. "There would be no force to hold it together; he's the cohesiveness, the central figure."

I tend to think that while the flame may sputter, it won't go out. Enough solid cohorts will keep it burning. But we'll have to wait at least till 2001 to know if John Wimber is a John Wesley.[15]

Other Models, Strategies, and Assessments

Thus far we have looked at both denominational and congregational models for the future, along with vignettes of innovative ideas, projections, programs, and organizations that seem poised to meet the challenges of the next century. In the final chapter of this section, I want to survey an additional sampling of innovations and ministry trends that, I believe, gives clues to America's future religious landscape.

Churches "in the new century will have a lot of innovation," speculates Win Arn of the Institute for American Church Growth. "Some will be successful, some won't. Those that will grow will have a philosophy of ministry and a clear target audience and will build in things to make that [philosophy] happen. Those doing business as usual are the ones that are going to go down."[1]

The survivors will be innovators.

Cell Groups

Small groups, or cells, make up the vibrant, throbbing pulse of what Elmer Towns calls the "Body-life" church.[2] In these cell groups, people get real. Caring happens. Spiritual growth surges. Members look to one another—not a pastor—for support, fellowship, and ministry.

Towns and George Gallup both see cell groups as the wave of the future. To be a whole church, it must have the *cell* as well as the *celebration,* Towns quipped at a conference on innovative church leadership.[3]

Gallup, speaking to a group of business and religious leaders, went so far as to say that small groups are "the most encouraging trend in religion today." For in them, he added, members learn the Bible and how to pray and are empowered for social service.[4]

"Covenant" cell groups are called together for a certain purpose and time period. Another style of small groups meets indefinitely. Perhaps the nation's most effective cell ministry of this type is administered by the Rev. Dale Galloway at New Hope Community Church. This megachurch has more than 5,000 members and a 3,000-seat sanctuary; its 110-foot cross towers above the Clackamas Town Center mall, dominating the skyline along the I-205 on the east side of Portland, Oregon.

The experts say boomers prefer short-term commitments, but New Hope members seem to be an exception. They like belonging to ongoing groups. Unlike people at Willow Creek Church, who are assigned to specific cell groups, people at Galloway's church can attend whatever TLC group they prefer.

"Cells are not another ministry of our church," Galloway told Towns. "Cells *are* the church." Indeed, in 1990, some 500 lay pastors directed TLC (Tender Loving Care) groups weekly. Galloway's goal is to have 1,000 lay pastors directing 10,000 cell-group members by 1995, holding to his vision of one cell group for every ten members.[5]

The threefold TLC purpose is discipling, evangelizing, and shepherding. Every group, Galloway explains, is expected to lead one new family to Christian faith every six months. The one-hour meetings begin with short conversational prayer and end with fellowship and food. Galloway writes the Bible-study lessons to go along with his sermon topics; the lay pastors teach the lessons in interactive style.[6]

The TLC group "makes" his week, one man told Towns: "The first thing we do is get caught up on the news of the week in everyone's lives. We talk to one another, then we pray for one another. Then we discuss the lesson. Everyone gets into it with their opinion. Finally, we order in pizza and keep on fellowshiping while we eat pizza and drink coffee. I wouldn't miss it for anything!"[7]

New Hope TLC leaders fill out weekly ministry reports which are discussed and analyzed at staff meetings. That's accountability for you.

Galloway, who comes from a Church of the Nazarene background, is convinced that his approach is the model for effective churches of the 1990s: "The successful church will be relational, need-oriented, relevant, and aimed at helping people."[8]

Affinity Groups

Green Valley Evangelical Free Church near San Diego, a 500-member congregation led by pastor-author Robert William Hull, has experimented with small cell groups based on *affinity*.

Affinity groups are tightly knit cells organized by age, interest, and marital status rather than by geographical location or schedule. For example, the church has had groups composed only of Sunday school teachers for toddlers, of men interested in sports, and of single parents of junior high-aged youngsters.

"A small group is a way of life all your life," declares Randy Knutson, who shared pastoral leadership with Hull after Green Valley was founded in 1983. "That's where the nurture comes from. The small group leader is the one who will show up at the hospital bed" when you're sick, Knutson explained. Each group meets a minimum of a year, but never longer than eighteen months, Knutson told me.[9] Then it may split or take on a different focus. The cells are small, and each cell leader has an apprentice. The leaders and apprentices are part of another group called "leadership community." Leaders with a "specific affinity" for special types of people are encouraged to develop their ministry gifts.

"We create evangelistic fishing poles . . . using affinity to draw people in," Knutson says. "We are trying to bring back to the cardio-vascular system of the church more biblical teaching and integrity."

Churches committed to the idea of cell ministry attempt to identify the "gifts" of members. Some use assessment devices, such as the Church Growth Institute's "Spiritual Gifts Inventory Questionnaire," to help people discover and understand their spiritual gifts. This can happen "in less time than it takes to drive to your nearest McDonalds," promises the accompanying literature.[10]

Ministries to Those with Disabilities

Because of the encroaching transformations in family life, it is no surprise that churches of the 1990s and beyond will need to revamp (and re-ramp) their ministries to persons with disabilities. "Families of persons with disabilities have come to expect something approaching the lifestyle of typical Americans," family ministry specialists Richard Olson and Joe Leonard point out.[11]

Also, technological advances as well as longevity extension have increased both the opportunities and the difficulties and dilemmas of living—and dying—with handicaps.

Olson and Leonard conservatively estimate that 10 percent of the U.S. population, or about 25 million persons, have some kind of disability. Perhaps as high as 20 percent of all families are affected to some extent. "Think about your congregation," they suggest. "Try to name the households in which someone is coping with physical disabilities or chronic illness or permanent injuries, caring for a frail elderly relative, concerned about a family member with long-standing psychiatric problems, or raising a child with developmental disabilities. How many can you identify?[12]

Churches and synagogues of the late 1990s and early 21st century will be pushed by conscience and advocacy groups to do a better job of counseling, supporting, and planning programs for persons with disabilities. These families are certainly entitled to their place on the church agenda!

Also, with new employment regulations mandated by the 1991 Americans With Disabilities Act in place, groups like the Christian Council on Persons With Disabilities will gain a significant and much-needed visibility. The organization is a national consortium of some 180 leaders and ministries that advocate a Christian perspective regarding people with disabilities and their part in the church.[13]

Targeting

Millennial ministries that address only a few specific needs in their area of influence—rather than trying to be all things to all people—will do well; those that don't, won't.

That's a key finding of a Barna survey about what successful churches have in common. According to the 1990 report, growing congregations "refused to be enticed into areas of ministry in which they discerned no special calling. Instead, they concentrated on doing what they were called to do," such as focusing on teen-agers, single adults, the disabled, or the elderly.[14]

That is a cornerstone philosophy of Willow Creek with its marketing survey. Target marketing is aiming the message and ministry at the group of people most likely to need and desire it, rather than broadsiding a larger, more heterogeneous audience. "Each church has been called to uniqueness and ought to explore ways of exploiting its uniqueness in service to God," the Barna report says.[15]

Metro Assembly

When Bill Wilson went to a Spanish Pentecostal Church in Brooklyn in 1979, he decided to relate to the street urchins in one of the nation's toughest, crack-infested ghettos. Fielding forty full-time and 200 volunteer staff, Metro now transports 8,000 children in thirty buses to Sunday school each week.

The staff and volunteers faithfully visit all the children and their families *every* week. The children are "mostly poor, mostly living in horrifyingly dangerous areas, many in families that don't care one way or the other whether their little church member lives or dies," writes John Gallagher, telling the story of Metro's street ministry.[16]

Wilson, a dynamic and moving speaker whose raspy voice betrays his frequent outdoor preaching, still drives one of the buses every weekend. When he picks up the little kids, he often says to himself, "That was me,"[17] for before his conversion at age fourteen, he was indeed one of them.

By targeting his ministry to a specific urban wasteland, one man and a small band of believers have built one of the largest Sunday schools in America—a ministry corps now influencing evangelical outreach around the world as the program is duplicated in other big-city ghettos.

Campbell Farm

On the opposite side of the continent is a unique ministry that is a combination farm and conference center.

Cragg and Barbara Gilbert, both graduates of Princeton Theological Seminary, grew up in the northwest, shared a background in northwestern agriculture, and wanted to start a nontraditional ministry. They got the chance in 1980 when a woman bequeathed a forty-acre farm to Central Washington Presbytery. They turned Nellie Campbell's legacy into a fruit and vegetable enterprise—with a difference.

The Gilberts also turned it into a conference ground where hundreds of youth and adults, up to thirty at a time, come to do farm work, study the Bible, worship, and "learn to recognize their place in creation a little better." The programs, explains Campbell Farm board member Judith Hill, "are always theological, agricultural, or global, often a combination. . . . And because of its congeniality and location, the Farm has hosted hard, gap-bridging discussions between farmers and farmworkers, farmers and consumers, and urban and rural dwellers in such issues as pesticides, hunger, and the church's role in America's rural crisis."[18]

After eleven harvest seasons, the Gilberts are reaping more than edible produce; their specially targeted ministry is yielding a bumper crop of applied theology. Ministries like Campbell Farm that combine areas of expertise with a need or opportunity won't expire in 2001.

Jesus People USA/Covenant Church

A very different example is the commune-style, inner-city ghetto ministry of Jesus People USA. At first impression it seems more a throw-back to the early Jesus movement of the late 1960s and 1970s than a model for 2001. I'm counting on it to endure, however, because it has tenaciously found its target niche.

Jesus People was started in 1972 with the arrival in Chicago of a West Coast couple who had "found Jesus." They began to minister to youth on drugs. Moving from its early housing in a former wrestling rink, the community, numbering about 450 in 1991, occupies a ten-story apartment building in the "Uptown" ghetto area. Members live communally.

"We lived together for years before discovering that what we were doing was called 'Christian community,'" says Jon Trott, assistant editor of *Cornerstone,* Jesus People's award-winning and artistically avant-garde magazine, which prints 100,000 copies. "Likewise, we began feeding the poor and housing the homeless without much reflection on the supposed dichotomy between evangelism and social action."[19]

JPUSA supports itself through a half-dozen or more community-run businesses (income is pooled for the community), and it sponsors a wide variety of local and national outreach ministries. These include:

- a "transitional" shelter for fifty-five homeless women and children
- a crisis pregnancy center
- ministries to AIDS patients, jail inmates, juvenile delinquents, and elderly shut-ins
- "Teen Moms," a program to train young mothers
- a neighborhood pantry and daily feeding program
- the annual Cornerstone Festival—an arts-and-issues-oriented celebration that draws an audience of 10,000 and some of the newest and hottest Christian artists in the nation.

"Music is almost continuous throughout the day from celtic bagpipes on the lawn to rap over by the skateboard ramp," according to handout material. "Cornerstone offers a unique combination of . . . punk, metal, hard-core, thrash, rap, 'nu' music, blues, urban dance, and straight-ahead rock 'n' roll."[20]

Jesus People's best-known outreach is probably its band REZ (short for Resurrection), a touring, recording quintet that grinds out startlingly raw music with blues-based hard rock and gut-wrenching vocals. The band, says lead singer Glenn Kaiser, is "intense rock 'n' roll with a conscience."[21]

Lately, Jesus People—if not REZ—has mellowed a bit, becoming an affiliate member of the Evangelical Covenant Church. The unlikely mixed marriage with the pietistic, largely middle-class denomination of about 100,000 has been amicable, both sides say.[22]

But JPUSA hasn't lost sight of its original goal—to reach the radical and often ragged fringes of society with a conservative, straight Bible message. Now twenty years old, JPUSA, like its heavy metal band, seems to have a way of reinventing itself to keep up with the times while never lifting an eye off the target.

Cooperation

The art and spirit of cooperation is another vital strategy for 2001. It will spell the difference between failure and success for ministries that want to gain new ground.

Cooperation worked recently in the rural hamlet of Deer Creek, Indiana (population 200). The town's only business, a gas station, had closed and the people of Deer Creek were isolated from one another. But Deer Creek Presbyterian and Faith Lutheran—two churches that had never joined in a project before—teamed up, with the help of a Lilly Endowment, to tap new resources for growth and change.

The town needed help, said Mary Blue, chairperson of the congregations' Active Care Develops Community project. "The [Presbyterian] church was one community and the town . . . was another. . . . Our paths never crossed. There was no central meeting place to get together to know each other."

When a couple decided to buy the abandoned gas station to start a community store, members of the project joined in. "Now," recounts John Long, "Betty's Stop & Shop, with its little tables for having coffee, links community and church together."[23]

A town sign with movable letters was set up in front of Betty's, a community newsletter was published, and the Presbyterian Church's annual mission bazaar was expanded into a yard sale for the whole town. Funds from a beautification campaign were used to buy dumpsters. And so on . . .

Community spirit and cooperation also touched the project's board of directors; once half Presbyterian and half Lutheran, it now is divided into thirds, with the new representation being from the community. And leaders were talking seriously about building a new community center in 1991.

Says Blue: "It doesn't take money to solve problems. It takes people . . . action by people who care." Says Long: "Now, other communities in the same region of Indiana are calling the folk in Deer Creek to find out how they did . . . [it]."[24]

Music and Entertainment

The greatest revolution in the modern church, in the opinion of Elmer Towns, is in worship. It's also the source of the greatest controversy, he says.[25] Nowhere is the dissonance greater than in discussions about what's "proper" in "Christian" music. Expect the syncopated tempo to pick up as we head for 2001.

"Praise" music like that of Vineyard Christian Fellowship has already worked its way into evangelical churches. Praise songs also have the charismatic Catholic community singing and swaying. In addition, the songs and "majesty worship" style of Jack Hayford, pastor of the booming Church on the Way in Van Nuys, California, is making an indelible imprint upon the way many churches integrate music with worship.

On that note, I am persuaded these trends and influences will play fortissimo beyond 2001, especially as new songbooks, lyrics, and Christian artists gain attention.

"If you take time to study the impact of music on our culture," writes pastor Doug Murren of Eastside Foursquare Church in Kirkland, Washington, "you will find that the music of the baby boomer generation [predominantly rock 'n' roll] is likely to dominate the culture of our society well into the next century. Even our children," adds Murren, himself a boomer, "are very comfortable with our musical tastes and identify easily with them."[26]

Murren and his staff have identified their target audience in the Pacific northwest: boomers who are "nominal Christians." The church's philosophy of ministry has integrated that target into its approach to music. In his book, *The Baby Boomerangs,* Murren says that all music in his congregation

- must be culturally relevant
- must be comparable in quality and excellence to what our target groups are listening to
- must communicate our values
- must enhance the atmosphere of worship.[27]

Eastside's music isn't just tuned to rock 'n' roll rhythm; the music leaders often take the tune of a popular hit from the last several decades—many in the service will recognize it—and rewrite the lyrics into a spiritual adaptation.

Meanwhile, over at Overlake Christian, another Kirkland megachurch, up to 40,000 people are drawn each year to performances of the church's annual Living Christmas Tree musical extravaganza. In 1990, the audience lapped up the Overlake spoof of the *Twelve Days of Christmas:*

"Ten Rosebowl tickets . . . five credit cards . . . two studded tires . . . and a ten-pound jar of Vick's VapoRub."

"This is our gift to the community," intoned tuxedo-clad Bob Moorehead, Overlake's pastor, speaking about the musical. Later, fifty church members took telephone orders for a free tape of Moorehead's sermon on the end of the world. The offer was also made on the air when the Christmas concert was broadcast on local TV.[28] Other musical outreach programs at Overlake include an Easter pageant and a patriotic celebration in July.

Bible-based preaching and first-rate entertainment are combined at Overlake. With more than 6,000 members, it is the largest congregation in all of Washington and Oregon.

Indeed, innovative music and entertainment may draw people to this and other enterprising churches of the future, but it takes something more to keep them coming. Moorehead says it's the unequivocal message of salvation he preaches that gets them in the fold.

My daughter-in-law, Lorie, who sang in the Living Christmas Tree, says it's also the friendliness, follow-up, and target ministering.

Lorie and Colin moved from a Southern California church, where they knew everyone, to one in the Northwest, where they knew no one. After visiting five congregations, they settled at Overlake for four reasons: It was the only place where people greeted them after the service; lay ministers called in their home within a week of their visit (though they filled out cards at the other four churches, no one called); the callers inquired about Colin's and Lorie's "spiritual status," which they appreciated; and Overlake was the only one of the five churches with a Sunday school class for young married couples.

For these reasons they put up with the traffic congestion, which— along with more restrictive zoning regulations for churches in suburban and residential areas—may hamper future big-church growth.

"It's a fun church," says Lorie. "It's not boring."[29]

And it's a worshiping church—which Pastor Hayford of the Church on the Way in Van Nuys says is the church of the future:

"The freedom to worship openly and expressively, with substance, depth, and joy, will become the hallmark of those whose liberty is due to their having grasped . . . that truth frees—and the dynamic of a church liberated to worship is a dynamic that liberates others. Vibrant worship is the key to vital evangelism."[30]

Part 4

The Finish Line

Chapter 31

Anticipating
the Next Age

We stand at the threshold of 2001. The new century will present a host of challenges; we're beginning to face many even now. Alvin Toffler calls the span from the mid-1950s to 2025 "the hinge of history." [1] Lance Morrow speaks of the coming millennium as a "cosmic divide." The 1990s are the "transforming boundary between one age and another, between a scheme of things that has disintegrated and another that is taking shape," Morrow says. [2]

We need to anticipate these new challenges and assess the values implicit in each before they overtake us.

We need to understand and anticipate the changes in an America that is ever more racially and ethnically diverse and composed of more elderly persons then ever before.

We need to relate to a culture in which communication and transportation have brought about "rurbanization" as the population spirals outward from the urban centers, replacing rural values with cosmopolitan ones. And in which new immigrants from the Third World are streaming into the big-city cores.

CHAPTER THIRTY-ONE

Core Concerns of the Century

But of all the challenges the coming changes portend for the twenty-first century, three areas seem to be the most crucial for America's religious future: communications and technology; the family and society; and spirituality.

Communications and technology: I return to the observations of Neil Postman whose contention is that television, "the new state religion," now controls the flow of public discourse in America. "We have less to fear from government restraints than from television glut," Postman declares in his book *Amusing Ourselves to Death*.[3]

To support his case, Postman draws from the writings of Aldous Huxley in *Brave New World* and *Brave New World Revisited*. Huxley feared those who would give us so much information that we would be "reduced to passivity and egoism." The truth, therefore, would be "drowned in a sea of irrelevance" as we became a trivialized culture. As Huxley saw it, people would come to "adore the technologies that undo their capacities to think," Postman says.[4]

Huxley foretold that "seemingly benign technologies devoted to providing the populace with a politics of image, instancy and therapy may disappear history just as effectively, perhaps more permanently, and without objection" than the state could do it through suppression. The Huxley warning, according to Postman, is that

> in the age of advanced technology, spiritual devastation is more likely to come from an enemy with a smiling face than from one whose countenance exudes suspicion and hate. . . . When a population becomes distracted by trivia, when cultural life is redefined as a perpetual round of entertainments, when serious public conversation becomes a form of baby-talk, when, in short, a people become an audience and their public business a vaudeville act, then a nation finds itself at risk; culture-death is a clear possibility.[5]

When religion takes on a civil role of self-indulgence and becomes a jaded consumerism, languishing in banality, then we find ourselves a culture wallowing in distractions. That is my concern about the media's seductive power over us as we race toward 2001.

The affliction of the people in *Brave New World* could all too easily beset us: It wasn't that they were laughing instead of thinking, Postman points out, "but that they did not know what they were laughing about and why they had stopped thinking."[6]

Entertainment and the news media sometimes go for the simple-minded in their haste and distraction. When content is "dumbed down" on the assumption that the audience—or reality itself—has grown more stupid, there is a kind of self-fulfilling cycle. "The stupider the public's source of information, the stupider the public must eventually become," observes Morrow in a *Time* essay entitled "Old Paradigm, New Paradigm."[7]

At the same time, television has destroyed childhood innocence by blurring the distinctions between the inside home of the family and the outside realm of the adult world. By presenting the same information directly to persons of all ages, TV will make parental screening of information for their children virtually impossible before the next century.

Social critic Joshua Meyrowitz explains how television has changed childhood and challenged parenting by taking kids "around the world before their parents let them cross the street."[8]

Short of permanently pulling the plug or investing in locking devices for TVs, VCRs, and video-games, there are some helpful things parents and community leaders can do. The Center for Media and Values has developed resource materials for home use, parenting classes, parent-teacher evenings, church programs, and the like.[9]

Two other aspects of the communications/technology futures market need to be addressed here. People increasingly turn to computers, video games, and TV to meet their needs for intimacy. As the line between the machine and our own personhood is blurred by implants, bionics, genetics and cybernetics, we will be faced with the difficult task of fundamentally redefining what human nature is.

Not only do technologies determine how we interact—even providing surrogate intimacy—they also threaten to replace God as an object of worship.

"In our post-industrial society," says Alan Jiggins, "nothing is sacred except the ideology of progress." The technological society is "arrogant and exploitative . . . corrupting our value system" and usurping the power of God.[10]

An article in the *New York Times* tells how a group of fifty Japanese engineers held a temple ceremony in 1990 to pay homage to worn-out computer chips. The chief priest, in deep purple robes, bowed low and chanted the *sutra.* Before him, at the feet of a giant cross-legged Buddha, sat a large lacquer tray overflowing with the used parts waiting to be exported to heaven.

In a few years, in addition to annual ceremonies, the engineers "hope to put up a monument to loyal, departed parts," wrote David E. Sanger. Shogen Kobayashi, the priest, said he had "no doubt that revering the chip will pay off for the Japanese people."[11]

The story is amusing, but it's a sad commentary on the extreme to which modern technology can take us. Values inherent in technology need to be critiqued from the perspective of biblical values.

Perhaps, as some analysts think, reaction against technological over-dependence may set in during the twenty-first century in the form of a "back to simplicity" movement. But I doubt it. Not as long as we're propelled by materialism and technology is in the driver's seat.

We must not bow down and worship at the altar of technology. Nor can we tamper with the basic nature that makes us human: the stamp that marks us "made in the image of God."

"The one attribute of human behavior that must be most scrupulously respected is the mutability of our nature," says Willard Gaylin, president of the Hastings Center. "While we may modify certain behavior we must *not* try to produce a human machine."[12]

Some lines must be drawn, and the bioethical, genetic one must be drawn at the point of respect for the uniquely human yet divine image—the spiritual side of individual existence. On the other side of that line is the real—and morally precarious—possibility that human enhancement engineering could obliterate the very image we most want to protect.

Family and Society: The world beyond 2001 may be physically easier. But it will be psychologically more difficult to live in. Family pressures, already battering at the door, may take over the house in the next decade because of changes in lifestyles, work, and leisure pursuits.

Much of the drama will revolve around the place and role of women, not only in the family and in the church, but also in the larger society. Not all the results will be depressing. As we cross into the next century, I think a leveling will occur in the women's movement. The shrill, radical voices will be muted as the movement matures. A more open, less-defensive and self-critical posture will take their place. More men will participate in the dialogue and the new empowering.

AIDS will strike or hit close to every American family by the first decade of the next millennium. Homosexuality will be the most complex, troubling, and divisive of the issues in mainline Protestant churches; in Roman Catholicism it will be second only to abortion.[13]

However, we may need the greatest discernment and help in our attempt to rein in conspicuous consumerism. It went galloping off in the 1970s and 1980s and is still unbridled in the 1990s. This is the decade, says James U. McNeal, a consumer behavior expert at Texas A&M University, of "parent-blessed mini-consumers." He's referring to the five- to twelve-year-old set spending $4.2 billion a year of their own money on their own desires.

"Saturday morning television, with its $100 million of child-focused advertising, is a moving monument to this new market," McNeal declares.[14]

Consumer watchdog Ralph Nader puts it bluntly: "Kids are big business, and big business needs youngsters compliant, vulnerable and hooked on their fads, fashions and addictions."[15]

I see few indications that parents are going to do very much very soon to reduce their children's consumptive habits. Many parents are all-too-willing accomplices in making their children easy targets for commercial abuses and greedy marketing campaigns that capitalize on peer pressure.

Parents in general, McNeal believes, seem determined that their children will become consumers at an early age. "Or, more fundamentally, become adult at an earlier age. Kids are marching toward adulthood at a much brisker pace than they used to and are wanting more mature things to go with this accelerated growth."[16]

The worship of materialism is idolatry, and parents will have to pay the price if they don't teach their kids that. Family values need righting, and parents need to fight exploitative videos for children and hammer home consumer savvy. Parents and children both need to learn not to buy things they don't need and to be suspicious of extravagant claims by merchants and advertisers.

The greatness of a people lies not in what and how much they buy, but in who they are, reminds *Media&Values*, a helpful quarterly resource for teaching media and consumer awareness.[17]

Spirituality: Several predictions about twenty-first century spirituality and the church:

- Large-rally evangelism in the Billy Graham mode will still be around. Some analysts have said stadium crusades would fall out of favor in the United States before the end of the century. Not so. In fact, crowds in five—even six—figures will be packing the arenas, domes, and bleachers for the foreseeable future. Televised, video-taped, and satellite-remote events will reach millions, but they won't eliminate the need for the big-scale evangelistic meetings.

- Church growth in the early decades of the next millennium will come largely through church-planting and mother churches birthing daughter churches. Far less numerical growth will arise from existing, mature congregations.

  Recent studies show that 90 percent of all churches reach their peak in attendance, outreach, and giving by their twelfth year. Among evangelical churches, those under three years old will win ten people to Christ per year for every 100 members; those in existence three to fifteen years will win five people per year. After age fifteen, the number drops to three a year, according to *Christianity Today*. About two-thirds of older, plateaued, or declining churches are not revitalized.[18]

- Liberal churches that "demythologize" Christianity in order to make it palatable to the "modern mentality"—i.e., well-educated people who value pluralism, diversity, and tolerance and stumble over the supernaturalism of the Bible and its "archaic" worldview—will find mythology creeping back under a different rubric. Despite a "this-worldly" interpretation of the Christian message in these churches, spiritual seekers will still encounter mysticism within liturgical expression and personal experience.

That's exactly what Don Miller found happening at All Saints Episcopal Church: people having "profoundly mystical experiences."[19] What they didn't seem to realize was that the "mythology" they think they are too sophisticated to accept comes sneaking in the back door. Faith is reinterpreted— "remythologized"—in their own form of mysticism. Thus the "plausibility problem" of a supernatural belief system is neatly circumvented. Supernaturalism, a la 2001!

• Bias against the historic Christian worldview will escalate. Such prejudice is already evident in academic circles and by major media. In 1991, more than 800 Christian leaders representing some fifty denominations petitioned television networks, stations, and film studios to end the "anti-Christian bigotry" in their programs and movies.

The statement called on the media to stop "unbalanced portrayal of . . . Christians," which, it said, is "unacceptable to all fair-minded Americans." Noting that the industry didn't tolerate anti-Semitism, the church leaders asked for the same standards against bigotry to be applied in portraying Christians.[20]

Despite such pleas, Christian-bashing is likely to be one of the few remaining discriminations acceptable in the twenty-first century. Robert Wuthnow, an establishment sociologist of Princeton University, has taken notice of the problem, telling stories of "how subvert and covert" some distinguished evangelical scholars "have had to be and sound in order not to be seen as strange."

"American higher education disdains Evangelical Christians," Wuthnow continued. "Few groups are as despised a minority. Jews certainly are not. African-Americans no longer are. Gays are not. Women are not. Roman Catholics once were, perhaps even very recently. But no groups arouse passions and prejudices more than Evangelicals and fundamentalists." Wuthnow has seen academic committees at Princeton reject prospective students simply because they classify themselves as evangelicals on their application forms.[21]

Martin Marty, meanwhile, has detected prejudice at the University of Chicago Divinity School. He is the faculty sponsor there for a group called Evangelical Divinity Students Eating Lunch (EDSEL). "Something in me says that such an association would need explaining in many academic circles in a way the role of a faculty backer for a Newman Club, Canterbury Club, or Hillel Foundation would not. Why?" asks Marty.[22] Why won't mistreated Christians, along with other abused groups, be widely defended in the coming decade by affirmative action, anti-defamation leagues, and other tolerance-promoting efforts? Wuthnow says it's because the conventional opinion is that being a Christian, unlike being a black, a woman, or a homosexual, is a choice rather than an unalterable part of one's identity.

Anti-Christian sentiment is also fueled by the excesses of some evangelical groups and an undiscerning tendency on the part of the general public to lump evangelicals and fundamentalists with cults and deceptive mind-control groups.

What's surprising, though, is the overwhelmingly Judeo-Christian character that our country has retained in its mainstream culture despite an immense, open diversity in our structures and institutions.

"That's what's uniquely American," said Barry A. Kosmin, the director of the City University of New York's broad survey of religion released in 1991. U.S. religion is "a cohesive element . . . a constant point of identification and commonality" ranged loosely in many different groups in an open "free market."[23]

The third millennium will see the strongest manifestation of the Christian church coalescing around a model foreseen by John A. Mackay, the late president of Princeton Theological Seminary. He made this forecast in the late 1950s: America's religious future will abide in "a reformed Catholicism and a matured Pentecostalism."

The End or the Beginning?

The meaning of millennium depends on how you look at it. It's the symbol of either an ending or a beginning. One millennium is drawing to a close while a new one is about to emerge. We can look back, or we can look forward. The threshold of 2001 marks a fresh opportunity to meet the most challenging—and exciting—forces of change ever to shape a century of civilization. The years between now and 2001 should be an important time not only to take stock but also to initiate renewal.

George Gallup has a prescription for making the 1990s a decade of deepening religious commitment. Ministry leaders, he says, need to

- LISTEN to the remarkable spiritual experiences of people and help them understand and build upon these experiences.
- TEACH people how to develop their faith, pray more effectively, bring the Bible into their daily lives, and become better trained in leadership skills.
- ENCOURAGE small-group fellowships, which serve as a means for people to enter the faith community as well as a way to support current members.
- INSPIRE people to reach out to others in appropriate and loving ways.
- TARGET key groups for spiritual nourishment and religious instruction: people in business, the professions, and other fields who constantly make ethical judgments; students, who receive an incomplete and distorted education if the vital role of religion is ignored; and people in the media, who often are ignorant about religion.[24]

Some Final Questions

There's more to racing toward 2001 than weaving together the multiple strands of our common future—as important a task as that is. We need anticipation and understanding, yes. Even more, we need help to harness the forces of change for our personal and collective journey.

The First Law of Wing Walking cautions, "Never let go of what you've got until you've got hold of something else."[25] But sometimes reaching for the future means spending some terrifying time in midair.

How many twenty-year-olds today know who they will be or what they will do when they are twenty-five? It's difficult to be good predictors of our own lives, much less of our children's. Economist Todd Buchholz reminds that parents must "learn to teach their children how to handle uncertainty—not how to ensure stability."[26]

Who *are* you? my son T.J. asked motorists as traffic crawled away from the Rose Bowl on the first day of the New Year. Who are *you*? I asked at the beginning of *Racing Toward 2001*. We need to ask the same question at the finish line: Who are you? To whom do you relate? Whom have you influenced the most in the past six months?

Who are *we*? Where are we going? Finally, what roadmap best guides our way into the unknown?

The final words of the apostle Paul's letter to the Christians in Ephesus were given on the edge of a new era for the people of God: "Finally then," Paul advised,

> find your strength in the Lord, in his mighty power. Put on all the armour which God provides, so that you may be able to stand firm. . . . For our fight is not against human foes, but against cosmic powers, against the authorities and potentates of this dark world, against the superhuman forces of evil in the heavens. Therefore, take up God's armour; then you will be able to stand your ground when things are at their worst, to complete every task and still to stand. Stand firm, I say.[27]

This is the place to stand. A place to assemble and marshal the forces for good and for God. A place from which to dismantle the strongholds poised to rule this nation. A place to seize the opportunities of the next age. And firm ground finally to rest upon.

Bibliography of Resources

Books

America 2000: What the Trends Mean for Christianity (Glendale, Calif.: Barna Research Group, 1989).

Anderson, Leith. *Dying for Change: An Arresting Look at the New Realities Confronting Church and Para-Church Ministries* (Minneapolis: Bethany House, 1990).

Barbour, Ian. *Religion in an Age of Science: The Gifford Lectures 1989–1991, vol. 1* (San Francisco: HarperCollins, 1990).

Barna, George. *User Friendly Churches: A Look at What Successful Churches Have in Common and Why Their Ideas Work* (Ventura, Calif.: Regal Books, 1991).

_____. *The Frog in the Kettle: What Christians Need to Know About Life in the Year 2000* (Ventura, Calif: Regal Books, 1990).

Barrett, David. *Our Globe and How to Reach It* (Birmingham, Ala.: New Hope, 1990). (Write to P.O. Box 12065, Birmingham, Alabama 35202.)

Bloom, Allan. *The Closing of the American Mind* (New York: Touchstone/Simon & Schuster, 1987).

Brown, Lester R., ed. *State of the World 1991: A Worldwatch Institute Report on Progress Toward a Sustainable Society* (New York: W. W. Norton & Company, 1991).

Buchholz, Todd G. *New Ideas From Dead Economists: An Introduction to Modern Economic Thought* (New York: Penguin Books, 1990).

Castelli, James and Gremillion, Joseph. *The Emerging Parish: The Notre Dame Study of Catholic Life Since Vatican II* (San Francisco: HarperCollins, 1988).

Cetron, Marvin and Davies, Owen. *American Renaissance: Our Life at the Turn of the Century* (New York: St. Martin's Press, 1989).

Chandler, Russell. Understanding the New Age (Dallas: Word Publishing, 1988).

Collins, Gail and Collins, Dan. *The Millennium Book* (New York: Doubleday, 1991).

Drucker, Peter F. *The New Realities: In Government and Politics, in Economics and Business, in Society and World View* (New York: HarperCollins, 1989).

Ellul, Jacques. *The Technological Bluff* (Grand Rapids, Michigan: Wm. B. Eerdmans Publishing Company, 1990).

Ellwood, Robert S. Jr. *Alternative Altars: Unconventional and Eastern Spirituality in America* (Chicago: University of Chicago Press, 1979).

Engel, James F. and Jones, Jerry D. *Baby Boomers and the Future of World Missions* (Orange Calif.: Management Development Associates, 1990).

Evans, Anthony. *Guiding Your Family in a Misguided World* (Pomona, Calif.: Focus on the Family, 1991).

Gallup, George Jr. and Castelli, Jim. *The People's Religion: American Faith in the 90's* (New York: Macmillan, 1989).

_____, and Jones, Sarah. *100 Questions & Answers: Religion in America* (Princeton, New Jersey: Princeton Religion Research Center, 1989).

Gerber, Jerry; Wolff, Janet; Klores, Walter, and Brown, Gene. *Lifetrends: The Future of Baby Boomers and Other Aging Americans: The Compelling Analysis of What They Will Have, Want and Need* (New York: Macmillan, 1989).

God, Help Me Stop: Break Free From Addiction and Compulsion (Glen Ellyn, Illinois, New Life Ministries). (Write to P.O. Box 343, Glen Ellyn, Illinois 60138; telephone 312-858-7878.)

Hunter, James Davison. *Evangelicalism: The Coming Generation* (Chicago: University of Chicago Press, 1987).

Jacquet, Constant H., Jr. *Yearbook of American & Canadian Churches, 1990* (Nashville: Abingdon, 1990).

Jiggins, Alan. *Human Future? Living as Christians in a High-Tech World* (London: Scripture Union, 1988).

Lane, Christopher and Melodie, *Parenting by Remote Control* (Ann Arbor, Mich.: Servant, 1991).

Meindl, James D., ed. *Brief Lessons in High Technology: Understanding the End of This Century to Capitalize on the Next* (Stanford, Calif.: Stanford Alumni Association, 1989).

Mohney, Ralph and Mohney, Nell. *Parable Churches: Stories of United Methodism's Ten Fastest Growing Churches* (Nashville: Discipleship Resources, 1989) (Write to P.O. Box 189, Nashville, Tennessee 37202.)

Murren, Doug. *The Baby Boomerang: Catching Baby Boomers as They Return to Church* (Ventura, Calif.: Regal Books,1990).

Naisbitt, John and Aburdene, Patricia. *Megatrends 2000: Ten New Directions for the 1990s* (New York: William Morrow and Co., 1990).

Olson, Richard P. and Leonard, Joe H. Jr. *Ministry With Families in Flux: The Church and Changing Patterns of Life* (Louisville: Westminster/John Knox Press, 1990).

Postman, Neil. *Amusing Ourselves to Death: Public Discourse in the Age of Show Business* (New York: Penguin Books, 1986).

Robertson, Pat. *The New Millennium* (Dallas: Word Publishing, 1990).

Sine, Tom. *Wild Hope* (Dallas: Word Publishing, 1991).

Smith, Shepherd and Smith, Anita Moreland. *Christians in the Age of AIDS* (Wheaton Illinois: Victor Books, 1990).

Successful Churches: What They Have in Common (Glendale, Calif.: Barna Research Group, 1990).

Tillapaugh, Frank R. *Unleashing the Church: Getting People Out of the Fortress and into Ministry* (Ventura, Calif.: Regal Books, 1982).

Tinder, Glenn. *The Political Meaning of Christianity: The Prophetic Stance* (New York: HarperCollins, 1991).

Toffler, Alvin. *Powershift: Knowledge, Wealth, and Violence at the Edge of the 21st Century* (New York: Bantam Books, 1990).

Towns, Elmer L. *Ten of Today's Most Innovative Churches* (Ventura, Calif.: Regal Books, 1991).

Vaughan, John N. *The World's 20 Largest Churches* (Grand Rapids: Baker Book House, 1986).

Wurman, Richard Saul. *Information Anxiety: What to Do When Information Doesn't Tell You What You Need to Know* (New York: Bantam Books, 1990).

Wuthnow, Robert. *The Restructuring of American Religion* (Princeton, New Jersey: Princeton University Press, 1988).

_____. *The Struggle for America's Soul: Evangelicals, Liberals, and Secularism* (Grand Rapids, Michigan: William B. Eerdmans, 1989).

Youssef, Michael. *Holy War, Oil, and the Islamic Mind* (Grand Rapids, Michigan: Zondervan Publishing House, 1991).

Articles

"21st Century Family," *Newsweek,* Winter/Spring, 1990.

"Ethics—Human Nature—Medical Progress," *Hastings Center Report* 20, no. 1 (January/February, 1990).

"The Second Century"—A Series on Future Issues and Trends Published in *The Wall Street Journal's* Centennial Year, *Wall Street Journal,* (beginning 23 January, 1989).

Bostian, David B., Jr. "Paradigms for Prosperity: Economic and Political Trends for the 1990s and Early 21st Century," *The Futurist,* (July–August, 1990): 33.

Coates, Joseph F. and Jarratt, Jennifer. "What Futurists Believe: Agreements and Disagreements," *The Futurist,* (November–December, 1990): 23–28.

Gross, David M. and Scott, Sophfronia. "Proceeding With Caution," *Time* (16 July, 1990): 56–62.

Lyles, Jean Caffey. "The Fading of Denominational Distinctiveness," *Progressions,* A Lilly Endowment Occasional Report 2, no. 1 (January, 1990): 16–17.

Marty, Martin E. "A Special Issue: the Human Genome Project," in *Context: A Commentary on the Interaction of Religion and Culture* 22, no. 21 (1 December, 1990).

Redmont, Jane. "Communities of Service, Families of Faith," *Progressions,* A Lilly Endowment Occasional Report 3, no. 1 (January, 1991): 15–16.

_____, "Future Challenges to American Catholicism," *Progressions,* A Lilly Endowment Occasional Report 1, no. 2 (June, 1989): 21–22.

Waldrop, Judith. "You'll Know it's the 21st Century When . . ." *American Demographics,* (December 1990): 23–27.

Journals and Newsletters

Church Growth Today, newsletter of the North American Society for Church Growth, Southwest Baptist University, Bolivar, Missouri 65613.

Connect, quarterly newsletter of the Center for Media and Values. Gives resources for critical awareness about media. 1962 South Shenandoah Street, Los Angeles, California 90034.

Context: A Commentary on the Interaction of Religion and Culture, newsletter by Martin E. Marty. Published 22 times-a-year by Claretian Publications, 205 West Monroe Street, Chicago, Illinois 60606.

Emerging Trends, monthly on polls in religion published by the Princeton Religion Research Center, P.O. Box 310, 53 Bank Street, Princeton, New Jersey 08542.

Evangelical Press News Service, weekly news service of the Evangelical Press Association, 1619 Portland Avenue South, Minneapolis, Minnesota 55404.

Hastings Center Report, bimonthly on ethical issues in medicine, the life sciences and the professions. The Hastings Center, 255 Elm Road, Briarcliff Manor, New York 10510.

National & International Religion Report, weekly newsletter edited by Edward E. Plowman. P.O. Box 21433, Roanoke, Virginia 24018.

Second Opinion, journal about faith-dimension in medical ethics, disease and health. Center for the Study of Health, Faith and Ethics, 676 North St. Clair Street, Suite 450, Chicago, Illinois 60611.

Organizations

Alban Institute, 4125 Nebraska Avenue N.W., Washington, D.C. 20016. (202) 244-7320; (800) 457-2674. Services congregations through research, publishing, training, education and consultation. Contact: Loren Mead.

American Church Lists, Inc., P.O. Box 1544, Arlington, Texas 76004-1544. (817) 261-6233; (800) 433-5301.

Americans for a Sound AIDS Policy (ASAP), P.O. Box 17433, Washington, D.C. 20041. (703) 471-7350. Resources, speakers. Contacts: Shepherd and Anita Smith.

Association of Christian Schools International, P.O. Box 4097, Whittier, California 90607-4097. (310) 694-4791. Contact: Paul Kienel.

Barna Research Group, 722 West Broadway, Glendale, California 91204. (818)241-9684. Independent, full-service marketing research firm. Contact: George Barna.

Center for Media and Values, 1962 South Shenandoah Street, Los Angeles, California 90034. (310) 559-2944. Contact: Elizabeth Thoman.

Charles E. Fuller Institute of Evangelism and Church Growth, 44 South Mentor Avenue, Pasadena, California 91101 (818) 449-0425. Contact: Carl George.

ChildS.H.A.R.E., 5400 Van Nuys Boulevard, Suite 412, Van Nuys, California 91401. (818) 784-9534. Videos and printed materials.

Christian Home Educators' Association, P.O. Box 28644, Santa Ana, California 92799-8644. (714) 537-5121. Newsletters, support network, manuals.

Christian Management Association, P.O. Box 4638, Diamond Bar, California 91765. (714) 861-8861; (800) 727-4262.

Christian Nature Federation, P.O. Box 33000, Fullerton, California 92644. (714) 447-9673. Promotes the Christian worldview within the natural sciences. Contact: Dean Ohlman.

Christian Women's International Network, 2232 S.E. Bristol, Suite 110, Santa Ana, California 92707. (714) 975-0776. Contact: Pat Rexroat.

Church Growth Institute, P.O. Box 4404, Lynchburg, Virginia, 24502 (800) 553-GROW. One-day seminars and briefings. Contact: Elmer Towns.

Church Information Development Services, 3001 Redhill Avenue, Suite 2-220A, Costa Mesa, California 92626-9664. (800) 442-6277.

Creative Futures Center, 7 Howe Street, Seattle, Washington 98109. (206) 284-1988. Contact: Tom Sine.

Cult Awareness Network, 2421 West Pratt Boulevard, Suite 1173, Chicago, Illinos 60645. (312) 267-7777.

Empty Tomb, Inc., 301 North 4th Street, P.O. Box 2404, Station A, Champaign, Illinois 61825-2404. (217) 356-2262. Stewardship and missions; congregational studies. Contacts: John and Sylvia Ronsvalle.

Environmental Challenge Fund, Radio City Station, P.O. Box 1138, New York, New York, 10101-1138. Uses contributions for recycling and scholarships for environmental education.

Hastings Center, 255 Elm Road, Briarcliff Manor, New York. 10510. (914) 762-8500. Studies ethical issues relating to aging, AIDS, care of the dying, chronic illness, artificial reproduction, genetic screening, rehabilitation medicine, and justice in health-care delivery. Contact: Daniel Callahan.

Health Ministries Association, 1306 Penn Avenue, Des Moines, Iowa 50316. (800) 852-5613. Newsletter and networking.

Holyland Fellowship of Christians and Jews, 36 South Wabash Street, Chicago, Illinois 60603. (312) 346-7693. Serves as educational bridge between the two faiths. (Rabbi Yechiel Eckstein)

Home School Legal Defense Association, Paeonian Springs, Virginia 22129. (703) 882-3838.

Institute for American Church Growth, 2670 South Myrtle Avenue, Suite 201, Monrovia, California 91016. (818) 447-2112. Contact: Win Arn.

Lavaggi, Steven, original and custom paintings, 10916 Peach Grove St., Suite 3, North Hollywood, California 91601. (818) 760-7770.

Lilly Endowment, Inc., P.O. Box 88068, Indianapolis, Indiana 46208. (317) 924-5471. Publishes *Progressions*, A Lilly Endowment Occasional Report related to endowment projects. (317) 921-7313.

National Foster Parent Association, 226 Kilts Drive, Houston, Texas 77024. (713) 467-1850.

North American Conference on Religion and Ecology, 5 Thomas Circle N.W., Washington, D.C. 20005. (202) 462-2591. Contact: Donald B. Conroy.

North American Society for Church Growth, Southwest Baptist University, 1601 S. Springfield, Bolivar, Missouri. 65613 (417) 326-5281. Contact: John Vaughan, who also directs International Megachurch Research Center.

Parish Nurse Resource Center, 1800 Dempster Street, Park Ridge, Illinois 60068. (708) 696-8773.

Princeton Religion Research Center, P.O. Box 310, Princeton, New Jersey 08542. (609) 924-9600. Contact: George Gallup, Jr.

Spiritual Counterfeits Project, P.O. Box 4308, Berkeley, California 94704. (415) 540-0300.

World Vision, 919 West Huntington Drive, Monrovia, California 91016. (818) 357-1111; 357-7979. Christian relief and education agency. Contact: Robert Seiple.

World Neighbors, 5116 North Portland Avenue, Oklahoma City, Oklahoma 73112. (405) 946-3333. Worldwide efforts to eliminate hunger, disease and poverty in Third World; educational programs, literature. Contact: William Brackett.

Yokefellow Institute, 920 Earlham Drive, Richmond, Indiana, 47374. (317) 983-1575. Parish studies, consultation. Contact: Lyle Schaller, now retired.

Churches

All Saints Episcopal Church, 132 North Euclid Avenue, Pasadena, California 91101. (818) 796-1172; (213) 681-9441.

Jesus People USA Evangelical Covenant Church, 4707 North Malden, Chicago, Illinois 60640. (312) 561-2450; (312) 989-2080.

Metro Assembly of God, P.O. Box 370-695/Wyckoff Station, Brooklyn, New York 11237-0015.

New Hope Community Church, 11731 South East Stevens Road, Portland, Oregon 97266. (503) 659-5683.

Overlake Christian Church, 9051 132nd Avenue N.E., Kirkland, Washington 98033. (206) 827-0303.

St. John the Baptist Roman Catholic Church, 3848 Stewart Avenue, Baldwin Park, California 91706. (818) 960-2795.

True Vine Missionary Baptist Church, 1125 West Street, Oakland, California 94607. (415) 444-4699.

Vineyard Ministries International, P.O. Box 65004, Anaheim, California 92815. (714) 533-9281; (800) 852-VINE.

Willow Creek Community Church, 67 East Algonquin Road, South Barrington, Illinois 60010. (708) 765-5000.

Notes

Introduction—The Starting Line

1. Quoted in Leslie Savan, "The Biggest Party Ever!" *Working Woman,* Jan. 1991, 72.

2. The survey was conducted through telephone interviews in 1989 and 1990 and was commissioned by the Graduate School of the City University of New York. Reported by David E. Anderson, United Press International religion writer, in "Survey Shows Americans a Religious People," wire story released 3 April 1991; *National & International Religion Report* 5, no. 8, 8 April 1991, 8; Ari L. Goldman, "Portrait of Religion in U.S. Holds Dozens of Surprises," *New York Times,* 10 April 1991, pt. A, p. 1.

3. "Are You a DINK or an OINK?" *Signs of the Times,* April 1991, 7.

Chapter 1—Keeping Up with the Joneses

1. Cited in Richard P. Olson and Joe H. Leonard, Jr., *Ministry With Families in Flux: The Church and Changing Patterns of Life* (Louisville, Ky.: Westminster/John Knox, 1990), 4.

2. Frank Tillapaugh, "Transformative Leadership in the '90s," audiotape of talk presented at "Take Hold of the '90s," a conference in Ventura, Calif., sponsored by Gospel Light Publications, 2 May 1990.

3. Felicity Barringer, "Census Data Show Sharp Rural Losses," *New York Times,* 30 Aug. 1990, pt. A, p. 1; Felicity Barringer, "What America Did After the War: A Tale Told by the Census," *New York Times,* 2 Sept. 1990, pt. E, p. 1.

4. Gary Farley, "The Death and Life of Rural America," *Joint Strategy and Action Committee Grapevine* 20, no. 9 (April 1989): np.

5. John Naisbitt and Patricia Aburdene, *Megatrends 2000: Ten New Directions for the 1990s* (New York: Morrow, 1990), 305.

6. William D. Gwinn, interview with author, Palm Springs, Calif., 16 Dec. 1990.

7. Quoted in William Dunn, "For Some Urban Escapees, Commuting Becomes Career," *USA Today,* 12 Dec. 1990, pt. A, p. 11.

8. Ibid.

9. Elmer Towns, "The Sunday School in the Future," audiotape of talk

presented at "Take Hold of the '90s," a conference in Ventura, Calif., sponsored by Gospel Light Publications, 1 May 1990.

10. Barringer, "What America Did After the War"; Judith Waldrop, "You'll Know It's the 21st Century When . . ." *American Demographics*, Dec. 1990, 27.

11. Waldrop, "You'll Know It's the 21st Century," 27.

12. "Population Growth and Shrinkage," *Adweek*, 11 Sept. 1989, 42; U.S. Department of Commerce, Bureau of the Census.

13. Naisbitt and Aburdene, *Megatrends 2000*, 178, 201.

14. Kevin Roderick, "Californians: 30 Million and Counting," *Los Angeles Times*, 16 May 1990, pt. A, p. 1.

15. Naisbitt and Aburdene, *Megatrends 2000*, 202–203.

16. Roderick, "Californians: 30 Million and Counting," 1.

17. Russell Chandler, "Californians: Spiritual but Not Conventional," *Progressions*, A Lilly Endowment Occasional Report 2, no. 1 (1990): 8–10.

18. Phillip E. Hammond, interview with author, Santa Barbara, Calif., 23 June 1989.

19. George Barna, *The Frog in the Kettle: What Christians Need to Know About Life in the Year 2000* (Ventura, Calif.: Regal, 1990), 185–87.

20. Cited in Barringer, "Census Data Show Sharp Rural Losses." Data from the Immigration and Naturalization Service and analysis by the Urban Institute in Washington, D.C.

21. Quoted in *National & International Religion Report* 3, no. 20 (1989).

22. Waldrop, "You'll Know It's the 21st Century," 27.

23. Frederick Rose, "The Second Century—California Babel: The City of the Future Is a Troubling Prospect if It's to Be Los Angeles," *Wall Street Journal*, 12 June 1989.

24. Waldrop, "You'll Know It's the 21st Century," 23.

Chapter 2—The Minority Majority

1. See Russell Chandler, "A Home for Diverse Faiths: A Stroll Around Downtown L.A. Shows off its Ubiquitous Houses of Worship," *Los Angeles Times*, 11 Aug. 1990, pt. F, p. 16.

2. "Ministry Strategy in the Los Angeles District for the 21st Century," *United Methodist Reporter* 135, no. 49 (1989).

3. According to a report from the Center for the Continuing Study of the California Economy; cited in Itabari Njeri, "'The World State': Californians Come From Just About Everywhere, Census Shows," *Los Angeles Times*, 13 Jan. 1991, pt. E, p. 8.

4. Waldrop, "You'll Know It's the 21st Century," 23–27.

5. Tom Sine, "Shifting Into the Future Tense," *Christianity Today*, 17 Nov. 1989, 21.

6. Barna, *The Frog in the Kettle*, 186.

7. *Context: A Commentary on the Interaction of Religion and Culture*, 15 Nov. 1989, 3.

8. Ibid.

9. William Dunn, "Asians Build New Lives as Immigrants," *USA Today*, 26 Nov. 1990, pt. A, p. 1.

10. Waldrop, "You'll Know It's the 21st Century," 23–27; Barringer, "What America Did After the War," 1; Dunn, "Asians Build New Lives as Immigrants."

11. Robert Pear, "Rich Got Richer in 80's; Others Held Even," *New York Times,* 10 Jan. 1991, pt. A, p. 1.

12. Cited in Pear, "Rich Got Richer," 1.

13. Cited in Tom Sine, *Wild Hope* (Dallas: Word, 1991), 140.

14. Sine, *Wild Hope,* 142.

15. Quoted in Jack Jones, "Slouching Toward the Millennium: Prognostications, Prophecies and Just Plain Guesses About What the Last Decade of the 20th Century Will Bring," *Los Angeles Times Magazine,* 24 Dec. 1989, 8.

16. Bob Fryling, telephone interview with author, 24 April 1989.

17. Alvin Toffler, *Powershift: Knowledge, Wealth, and Violence at the Edge of the 21st Century* (New York: Bantam, 1990), 249–50.

18. Ibid.

19. Father Eugene Hemrick, telephone interview with the author, 21 April 1989.

20. George Gallup, Jr. and Jim Castelli, *The People's Religion: American Faith in the 90's,* (New York: Macmillan, 1989), 119–20.

21. Barringer, "What America Did After the War," 1.

22. John H. Townsend, "The State of the Church—1989," *First Baptist News,* 8 May 1989, 3; Townsend, interview with author, 30 Aug. 1989. The First Baptist Church of Los Angeles is a member of the American Baptist Churches in the U.S.A.

Chapter 3—Gauges of Ages

1. Quoted in Wade Clark Roof, "The Spirit of the Elderculture," *Christian Century,* 16–23 May 1990, 530.

2. Joseph F. Coates and Jennifer Jarratt, "What Futurists Believe," *Futurist,* Nov.–Dec. 1990, 24.

3. Jerry Gerber et al., *Lifetrends: The Future of Baby Boomers and Other Aging Americans* (New York: Macmillan, 1989), 8.

4. Sine, *Wild Hope,* 143.

5. David M. Gross and Sophfronia Scott, "Proceeding With Caution," *Time,* 16 July 1990, 57.

6. Shari Roan, "How Long Can We Live?" *Los Angeles Times,* 4 Dec. 1990, pt. E, p. 1; Erik Eckholm, "An Aging Nation Grapples With Caring for the Frail," *New York Times,* 27 March 1990, pt. A, p. 1.

7. Ibid.

8. "21st Century Family," *Newsweek,* Winter/Spring 1990, 24–34, 48–49.

9. Richard D. Lamm, "Again, Age Beats Youth," *New York Times,* 2 Dec. 1990.

10. Gerber et al., *Lifetrends,* 48–49, 51.

11. Tamar Lewin, "As Alertness Outlives Vigor, New Kinds of Care for the Old," *New York Times,* 2 Dec. 1990, pt. A, p 1.

12. Ibid.; Tamar Lewin, "Strategies to Let Elderly Keep Some Control," *New York Times,* 28 March 1990, pt. A, p. 1.

13. Ibid.

14. Marsha Fowler, interview with author, 8 Jan. 1991.

15. Linda Hager Timberlake, "How's Your Health? Check on It at Church," *Presbyterian Survey,* Jan./Feb. 1991, 22.

16. Patricia Leigh Brown, "For Some, 'Retired' Is an Inaccurate Label," *New York Times,* 29 Nov. 1990, pt. B, p. 1.

17. Ibid.

18. George Gallup, Jr. and Jim Castelli, "Gallup Religion Poll: Older Americans Among the Most Religiously Active," *Los Angeles Times Syndicate,* 16 June 1989.

19. Sine, "Shifting Into the Future Tense," 21.

20. Elmer Towns, *Ten of Today's Most Innovative Churches* (Ventura, Calif.: Regal, 1991), 179.

21. Brown, "For Some, 'Retired' Is an Inaccurate Label," 1.

22. Michael Kiernan, "Best Jobs for the Future," *U.S. News & World Report,* 25 Sept. 1989, 60.

23. Naisbitt and Aburdene, *Megatrends 2000,* 232–33.

24. Paul C. Light, *Baby Boomers* (New York: Norton, 1988), 9.

25. James F. Engel, "We Are the World," *Christianity Today,* 24 Sept. 1990, 32.

26. Roof, "Spirit of the Elderculture," 530.

27. Diane Huie Balay, "National Gathering Finds Singles 'Mission Field' for Every Church," *United Methodist Reporter,* 10 Aug. 1990; George Barna, "Future Issues Affecting the Evangelical Press," audiotape of talk presented at the Evangelical Press Association, 7 May 1990, Colorado Springs, Colorado.

28. Gerber et al., *Lifetrends,* 14–36.

29. Wade Clark Roof, cited in Kenneth A. Briggs, "Baby Boomers: Boom or Bust for the Churches? *Progressions* 2, no. 1 (Jan. 1990): 5–6; Kenneth L. Woodward, "A Time to Seek: With Babes in Arms and Doubts in Mind, a Generation Looks to Religion," *Newsweek,* 17 Dec. 1990, 51.

30. Wade Clark Roof, "Return of the Baby Boomers to Organized Religion," *Yearbook of American and Canadian Churches 1990,* Publication of the National Council of Churches, ed. Constant H. Jacquet, Jr. (Nashville: Abingdon), 284–88.

31. Wade Clark Roof, telephone interview with author, 12 May 1989.

32. Mark Wingfield, "New Churches Key to Denomination's Future," *California Southern Baptist,* 8 March 1990, 1.

33. Kenneth L. Woodward, "Young Beyond Their Years," *Newsweek,* Winter/Spring 1990, 54.

34. Sine, *Wild Hope,* 160.

35. Gross and Scott, "Proceeding With Caution," 62.

36. Felicity Barringer, "What Is Youth Coming To?" *New York Times,* Week in Review, 19 Aug. 1990, pt. 4, p. 1.

37. Ibid.

38. "Church attendance and Other Polls," *Yearbook of Churches 1990,* 292.

39. George Barna, "Youth Ministry in Successful Churches," from a news release from the Barna Research Group, Glendale, Calif., April 1990.

Chapter 4—The Information Age

1. Toffler, *Powershift,* 20. Emphasis added.

2. James D. Meindl, ed., *Brief Lessons in High Technology: Understanding the End of This Century to Capitalize on the Next* (Stanford, Calif.: Stanford Alumni Association, 1989) xi–xii.

3. Sine, *Wild Hope,* 125.

4. Jacques Ellul, *The Technological Bluff* (Grand Rapids, Mich.: Eerdmans, 1990).

5. Neil Postman, *Amusing Ourselves to Death: Public Discourse in the Age of Show Business* (New York: Penguin, 1986), 157.

6. Julie Amparano Lopez and Mary Lu Carnevale, "Glassed Houses: Fiber Optics Promises a Revolution of Sorts, if the Sharks Don't Bite," *Wall Street Journal,* 10 July 1990, pt. A, p. 1.

7. Meindl, *Brief Lessons,* 31–61.

8. Toffler, *Powershift,* 139.

9. Barna Research Group, news release, Nov. 1989; Barna, *Frog in the Kettle,* 62.

10. Cecilio Morales, "This 'Electronic Church' Has No Walls," *United Methodist Reporter,* 24 Aug. 1990, 5.

11. "Christian Career-Matching Software Introduced," *EP News Service,* 17 Aug. 1990, 6.

12. Richard N. Ostling, "Many Are Called," *Time,* 27 Feb. 1989, 79.

13. "Television of the Future," *Newsweek,* 4 April 1988, 62–63.

14. Lopez and Carnevale, "Glassed Houses," 1.

15. Sine, *Wild Hope,* 47.

16. Waldrop, "You'll Know It's the 21st Century," 26.

17. Edmund L. Andrews, "F.C.C. Proposes a TV System That Interacts With Viewers," *New York Times,* 11 Jan. 1991, pt. A, p. 1.

18. Meindl, *Brief Lessons,* 37.

19. Barna, *Frog in the Kettle,* 59; Carla Lazzareschi, "Enough With the Gadgets," *Los Angeles Times,* 22 Aug. 1990, pt. A, p. 1.

20. Rose, "California Babel."

21. Sine, *Wild Hope,* 48.

22. Waldrop, "You'll Know It's the 21st Century," 26.

23. Kiernan, "Best Jobs for the Future," 60.

24. Timothy D. Schellhardt and Carol Hymowitz, "Economy—the Second Century: U.S. Manufacturers Gird for Competition," *Wall Street Journal,* 2 May 1989.

25. Mark R. Cutkosky, "Robotics: A Dream as Old as Antiquity," in Meindl, *Brief Lessons;* William J. Broad, "Proliferation of Sophisticated Robots Opens a New Age of Ocean Exploration," *New York Times,* 13 Nov. 1990, pt. B, p. 5.

26. From Gail Collins and Dan Collins, *The Millennium Book* (New York: Doubleday, 1991); cited in *Working Woman,* Jan. 1991, 74.

27. Cited in "Events and People," *Christian Century,* 19–26 Dec. 1990, 1192.

28. Sine, *Wild Hope,* 59.

29. Richard Saul Wurman, *Information Anxiety: What to Do When Information Doesn't Tell You What You Need to Know* (New York: Bantam, 1990), 158.

30. William A. Durbin, Jr., "Ramifications of Artificial Intelligence," *Christianity Today,* 4 April 1986, 48–49.

31. Peter D. Moore, "Networks That Mimic Thinking," *Los Angeles Times,* 29 Aug. 1990, pt. D, p. 3.

32. Philip Elmer-Dewitt, "In Search of Artificial Life," *Time,* 6 Aug. 1990, 64.

33. Ibid.; Garry Abrams, "Bugs With Byte," *Los Angeles Times,* 21 Sept. 1990, pt. E, p. 1.

34. "Artificial Intelligence: Will Computers Affect Our Relationship With God?" an interview with Dr. David Barnard, *Spirit!,* issue date unknown, 38.

35. Bill Bright, "A Potent Threat to Christianity," *Worldwide Challenge,* May/June 1986, 66.

36. Meindl, *Brief Lessons,* 38.

37. Richard C. Atkinson, quoted in Jones, "Slouching Toward the Millennium," 8.

38. Malcolm W. Browne, "New Directions in Physics: Back in Time," *New York Times,* 22 Aug. 1990, pt. B, p. 5.

39. Michael D. Lemonick, "Bang! A Big Theory May Be Shot," *Time,* 14 Jan. 1991, 63; John Noble Wilford, "Astronomers' New Data Jolt Vital Part of Big Bang Theory," *New York Times,* 3 Jan. 1991, pt. A, p. 1.

Chapter 5—Bioethics

1. A. James Rudin, "News from the American Jewish Committee," news release, Institute of Human Relations, New York, 13 April 1989.

2. Naisbitt and Aburdene, *Megatrends 2000,* 241.

3. Willard Gaylin, "Fooling With Mother Nature," *Hastings Center Report,* Jan./Feb. 1990, 18.

4. Martin E. Marty, "A Special Issue: the Human Genome Project," in *Context: A Commentary on the Interaction of Religion and Culture* 22, no. 21 (1990): 3.

5. Fay Angus, interview with author, 7 Dec. 1990.

6. Genesis 16. See also Genesis 30 for a reference to Rachel offering her maidservant to her husband, Jacob, to produce an offspring.

7. Carol Lawson, "Couples' Own Embryos Used in Birth Surrogacy," *New York Times,* 12 Aug. 1990, pt. A, p. 1.

8. Fay Angus, "The Promise and Perils of Genetic Meddling," *Christianity Today,* 8 May 1981, 27.

9. Ibid.

10. Shari Roan, "Ethics and the Science of Birth," *Los Angeles Times,* 8 Dec. 1990, pt. A, p. 1.

11. Quoted in ibid.

12. Matt Clark, Marianna Gosness and Mary Hager, "Should Medicine Use the Unborn?" *Newsweek,* 14 Sept. 1987, 62–63.

13. Quoted in Andrew Simons, "Brave New Harvest" *Christianity Today,* 19 Nov. 1990, 25.

14. Quoted in Andrew H. Malcolm, "Giving Death a Hand: Rending Issue," *New York Times,* 9 June 1990.

15. Otto Friedrich, "A Limited Right to Die," *Time,* 9 July 1990, 59.

16. Jerry Nachtigal, Associated Press, *Oregonian,* 27 Dec. 1990, pt. A, p. 1.

17. "Sad Farewells for Young Woman Starting on Road to Death," *New York Times,* 16 Dec. 1990.

18. Cited in Robert Steinbrook, "Support Grows for Euthanasia," *Los Angeles Times,* 19 April 1991, pt. A, p. 1.

19. Andrew H. Malcolm, "Judge Allows Removal of Woman's Feeding Tube," *New York Times,* 15 Dec. 1990, pt. A, p. 1.

20. Ibid.

21. Marsha Fowler, telephone interview with author, 7 Jan. 1991.

22. "Don't Jump into Designer Genes," *Christian Science Monitor,* 24 April 1988, 15.

23. Ian Barbour, *Religion in an Age of Science: The Gifford Lectures 1989–1991,* vol. 1 (San Francisco: HarperCollins, 1990), 215.

24. J. Madeleine Nash, "A Bumper Crop of Biotech," *Time,* 1 Oct. 1990, 92.

25. Naisbitt and Aburdene, *Megatrends 2000,* 251.

26. Collins and Collins, *Millennium Book,* 74.

27. Ibid., 257.

28. Marty, "A Special Issue," 1.

29. Ann Lammers and Ted Peters, "Genethics: Implications of the Human Genome Initiative," *Christian Century,* 3 Oct. 1990, 871.

30. W. French Anderson, "Genetics and Human Malleability," *Hastings Center Report* 20, no. 1 (1990): 24.

31. Fowler, interview with author.

32. Andrew Pollack, "Living Cells Enter Commerce; Now, Who Has a Claim to Profits?" *New York Times,* 12 Aug. 1990, pt. E, p. 6.

33. Ibid.

34. Owen Thomas, "Ethics Tries to Keep Pace With Medical Technology," *Christian Science Monitor,* 29 March 1988, p. 1.

35. Sine, *Wild Hope,* 57.

36. Pat Robertson, *The New Millennium* (Dallas: Word, 1990), 217; Angus, author interview; Michael W. Miller, "The Second Century—Digital Revolution," *Wall Street Journal,* 7 June 1989.

37. R.Z. Sheppard, "Splendor in the Grass," *Time,* 3 Sept. 1990, 78.

38. Angus, author interview.

39. Lammers and Peters, "Genethics," 869.

40. Richard Spencer, interview with author, 7 Dec. 1990.

41. Katherine Bouton, "Painful Decisions: The Role of the Medical Ethicist," *New York Times Magazine,* 5 Aug. 1990, 25.

42. Proverbs 9:10.

Chapter 6—Earth

1. Quoted in "UM Leader Says Creation Testifies to Grace of God," *United Methodist Reporter,* 2 March 1990, 4.

2. Genesis 1:28–29 KJV.

3. Thomas Berry, "Earth Day 1990," *Creation* 6, no. 2 (1990):10.

4. Quoted in Russell Chandler, "Religions Join the Crusade to Save Earth From Pollution," *Los Angeles Times,* 19 April 1990, pt. A, p. 3.

5. David R. Brower, quoted in Jones, "Slouching Toward the Millennium," 8.

6. Cited in *Only One Earth,* United Nations Environment Programme, United Nations, New York, March 1990.

7. Article by Gregg Easterbrook in *New Republic,* cited by Fred Barnes in "Media Issues of the '90s: Barnes Looks Ahead for EPA Gathering," *World,* 19 May 1990, 8; Sine, *Wild Hope,* 23.

8. Robertson, *New Millennium,* 233.

9. Jones, "Slouching Toward the Millennium."

10. Donald Woutat, "Substitute Car Fuels: a Tank Full of Choices," *Los Angeles Times,* 22 Aug. 1990, pt. A, p. 1.

11. Sine, *Wild Hope,* 32.

12. Ibid., 26.

13. *Only One Earth,* UNEP.

14. Ibid.

15. Ibid.

16. Quoted in Sheppard, "Splendor in the Grass."

17. Ad in *Time,* 4 Feb. 1991. The Environmental Challenge Fund, Radio City Station, P.O. Box 1138, New York, New York 10101-1138. Uses contributions for recycling and scholarships for environmental education.

18. Zondervan Publishing House, as cited in *Evangelical Press News Service,* 7 Dec. 1990, 12.

19. Leslie Whitaker, "Black, White and Green All Over," *Time,* 14 Jan. 1991, 47.

20. Kathie Durbin and Paul Koberstein, "Forests in Distress," Special Report, *Oregonian,* 15 Oct. 1990.

21. Robertson, *New Millennium,* 230.

22. *Only One Earth,* UNEP.

23. "Saving Our Soil, Saving Our Earth," *Neighbors,* Fall 1990, 4–5.

24. *Only One Earth,* UNEP.

25. Toffler, *Powershift,* 312.

26. *Only One Earth,* UNEP.

27. Ibid.

28. Ibid.

29. Sine, *Wild Hope,* 27–28.

30. William J. Broad, "A Mountain of Trouble," *New York Times Magazine,* 18 Nov. 1990, pt. 6, p. 37.

31. Ibid.

32. Robert Tomsho, "Indian Tribes Contend With Some of Worst of America's Pollution," *Wall Street Journal,* 29 Nov. 1990, 1.

33. Chandler, "Religions Join the Crusade."

34. Ibid.

35. William Bole, "Environment Chief Calls for 'Spiritual Vision' of Conservation," *Religious News Service,* 25 Jan. 1990.

36. "Global Forum on Environment and Development for Survival," Summary Report, South Coast Air Quality Management District, 3 Feb. 1990.

37. Frederick H. Borsch, "Our Fragile Island Home," *Episcopal News,* April 1990.

38. Mike Hamer and Nathaniel Mead, "Finding Heaven on Earth," *New Age Journal,* March/April 1990, 49.

39. Berit Kjos, "Earth Day 1990," *Focus on the Family,* April 1990, 11.

40. Martin Marty, *Context,* 1 July 1990, 4.

41. Dean Ohlman, telephone interview with author, 18 April 1990; "A Christian Voice for the Environment," news release, 1 March 1990.

Chapter 7—Designer Lifestyles

1. Tillapaugh, "Transformative Leadership."

2. Quoted in Russell Chandler, "Analysts See Evangelical Growth, Catholic Strength in the 1990s," *Los Angeles Times,* 23 Dec. 1989, pt. S, p. 1.

3. Ibid.

4. Barna, *Frog in the Kettle,* 41, 163.

5. Ibid., 34.

6. Chandler, "Analysts See Evangelical Growth," 1.

7. Barna, *Frog in the Kettle,* 83; Stuart Silverstein, "Tracking Life in the Fast Lane," *Los Angeles Times,* 30 April 1990, pt. A, p. 1.

8. Silverstein, "Tracking Life in the Fast Lane," 1.

9. Barna, "Future Issues."

10. Richard Zoglin, "Is TV Ruining Our Children?" *Time,* 15 Oct. 1990, 75.

11. Silverstein, "Tracking Life in the Fast Lane."

12. Quoted in Ron Alexander, "The Face and Fashions for the 90's," *New York Times* (Life Style), 25 June 1989, 35.

13. Ibid.

14. Jones, "Slouching Toward the Millennium," 8.

15. Naisbitt and Aburdene, *Megatrends 2000,* 133.

16. Jones, "Slouching Toward the Millennium," 8.

17. Alexander, "The Face and Fashions for the 90's," 35.

18. Quoted in David Briggs, "Religious Groups Join to Lobby for the Common Good," *Associated Press* series, "Unholy Wars: Religion in Public Life," no. IV; 20 Dec. 1990.

19. Barna, *Frog in the Kettle,* 158.

20. Fryling, author interview.

21. Mark Cutshall, interview with author, 21 Dec. 1990.

22. Robertson, *New Millennium,* 198.

23. Interview with George Gallup, Jr., in "Tracking America's Soul," *Christianity Today,* 17 Nov. 1989, 25.

24. Cited in transcript of sermon by George F. Regas, vicar, All Saints Episcopal Church, Pasadena, Calif., 11 Nov. 1990, p. 2.

25. Randy Frame, "The Evangelical Closet," *Christianity Today,* 5 Nov. 1990, 56.

26. Trish Hall, "Gay Travelers Find More Places to Vacation," *New York Times,* 22 Aug. 1990, pt. B, p. 1.

27. Bettijane Levine, "A Declaration," *Los Angeles Times,* 14 March 1990, pt. E, p. 1.

28. CBS Evening News, 24 Jan. 1991.

29. Shepherd Smith and Anita Moreland Smith, *Christians in the Age of AIDS* (Wheaton, Ill.: Victor, 1990), 17.

30. Shepherd Smith, telephone interview with author, 15 Jan. 1990.

31. Ibid.

32. From a study by the Alan Guttmacher Institute, cited in "Sexual Activity Jumps Among Teens in 1980s," *World,* 17 Nov. 1990.

33. Smith, author interview.

34. Ibid.

35. Materials provided author by Americans for a Sound AIDS Policy, Jan. 1991.

36. National Conference on HIV '89, sponsored by Americans for a Sound AIDS Policy; brochure, p. 23.

37. Earl E. Shelp, Edwin R. DuBose and Ronald H. Sutherland, "AIDS and the Church: A Status Report," *Christian Century,* 4 Dec. 1990, 1135.

38. Smith and Smith, *Christians in the Age of AIDS,* 9.

Chapter 8—Nuclear Family Fission

1. Advertisement for *Time* magazine television special, *Time*, 8 Oct. 1990, 83.

2. George Barna, "The American Family and Church Ministry," news release from the Barna Research Group, 30 July 1990, 3.

3. "America in 21st Century: A Demographic Overview," Population Reference Bureau, 1989, 6.

4. Felicity Barringer, "Changes in U.S. Households: Single Parents Among Solitude," *New York Times*, 7 June 1991, pt. A, p. 1.

5. Philip Elmer-DeWitt, "The Changing Family: The Great Experiment," *Time*, Fall 1990 (Special Edition), 73.

6. Barna, *Frog in the Kettle*, 66.

7. Robertson, *New Millennium*, 188–89.

8. Philip Elmer-DeWitt, "The Great Experiment," 73.

9. George L. Stelluto and Deborah P. Klein, "Compensation Trends Into the 21st Century," *Monthly Labor Review*, Feb. 1990, 38.

10. Waldrop, "You'll Know It's the 21st Century," 24, 26.

11. Howard V. Hayghe, "Family Members in the Work Force," *Monthly Labor Review*, March 1990, 14.

12. Jean Seligmann, "Variations on a Theme," *Newsweek*, Winter/Spring 1990 (Special Edition), 38.

13. Lynn Smith and Bob Sipchen, "2-Career Family Dilemma: Balancing Work and Home," *Los Angeles Times*, 12 Aug. 1990, pt. A, p. 1.

14. Dr. Joyce Brothers, "The New Man in the House," *Los Angeles Times*, 12 Aug. 1990, pt. E, p. 1.

15. Deirdre Fanning, "Fleeing the Office, and Its Distractions," *New York Times*, 12 Aug. 1990.

16. Barna, "Future Issues."

17. Gross and Scott, "Proceeding With Caution," 58.

18. Jack Balswick and Judith Balswick, "Adam and Eve in America," in *Christianity Today;* reported in *Evangelical Press News Service*, 17 Aug. 1990, 10–11.

19. Felicity Barringer, "Census Report Shows a Rise in Child Care and Its Costs," *New York Times*, 16 Aug. 1990, pt. A, p. 12.

20. Amanda Bennett, "In Future, Many May Provide Day Care, Education, Aid With Sundry Social Issues," *Wall Street Journal*, 8 May 1989.

21. Robertson, *New Millennium*, 206.

22. Olson and Leonard, *Ministry With Families in Flux*, 41; Robertson, *New Millennium*, 187.

23. Olson and Leonard, *Ministry With Families in Flux*, 41.

24. Philip Elmer-DeWitt, "The Great Experiment," 74–75.

25. "Single Parent Poverty," *Washington Times*, 9 Nov. 1989, pt. F, p. 2.

26. "The New Untouchables," *Newsweek*, Winter/Spring 1990 (Special Edition), 48.

27. Jill Smolowe, "Last Call for Motherhood," *Time*, Fall 1990 (Special Edition), 76.

28. Ibid.

29. Olson and Leonard, *Ministry With Families in Flux*, 85.

30. Balay, "Singles 'Mission Field.'"
31. Towns, *Innovative Churches,* 140–41.
32. Olson and Leonard, *Ministry With Families in Flux,* 109.
33. Darrell Turner, "Pa. Lawmaker Wants to Give Clergy Power to Divorce Couples," *Religious News Service,* 26 Nov. 1990.
34. Barna, "Future Issues."
35. *The American Family Under Siege* (Washington, D.C.: Family Research Council, 1989), 1.
36. Studies by Larry L. Bumpass and Teresa Castro Martin, published in the journal *Demography* and reported in "Study Says Two Marriages of Three Will Fall Apart," *World,* 25 March 1989, 4.
37. Fay Angus, interview with author, 12 Dec. 1990.
38. Barna, *Frog in the Kettle,* 72.
39. Gerber et al., *Lifetrends,* 38.
40. Gary B. Dixon, "Where Christian Education Is Going in the 90's," seminar presented at the Greater Los Angeles Sunday School Convention, Pasadena, Calif., 2 Nov. 1990.
41. Olson and Leonard, *Ministry With Families in Flux,* 139.
42. Marjorie Lee Chandler, "Foster Parents: Love to Spare," *Focus on the Family,* Aug. 1990, 3.
43. Ibid.
44. Ibid.
45. Smith and Smith, *Christians in the Age of AIDS,* 94.
46. Ken Dychtwald with Joe Flower, "The Third Age," *New Age Journal,* Jan./Feb. 1989, 52.
47. Olson and Leonard, *Ministry With Families in Flux,* 170.

Chapter 9—Educating Dick and Jane.
Ramon and Natasha.

1. Postman, *Amusing Ourselves to Death,* 146.
2. Ibid., 142–54.
3. Ibid., 143.
4. Josh Ozersky, "TV's Anti-Families: Married . . . With Malaise," *Tikkun: A Bimonthly Jewish Critique of Politics, Culture & Society,* Jan./Feb. 1991, 92.
5. Quoted in Toffler, *Powershift,* 367–68.
6. Quoted in Coates and Jarratt, "What Futurists Believe," 26.
7. Cited in James A. Mecklenburger, "The New Revolution," *Business Week,* (special advertising section), ED23, (no date).
8. Ibid., ED26.
9. See Ronald H. Nash, *The Closing of the American Heart: What's Really Wrong With America's Schools* (Dallas: Probe, 1990). Reviewed by David A. Horner, "Why Johnny Can't Think," *World,* 3 Nov. 1990, 15.
10. Jones, "Slouching Toward the Millennium," 8.
11. Susan Tifft, "Of, By and For—Whom?" *Time,* 24 Sept. 1990, 95.
12. Barna, *Frog in the Kettle,* 210.
13. Ibid., 215–16; Barna, "Future Issues."
14. "Enrollments Dip, Tuitions Rise," *Christianity Today,* 19 Nov. 1990, 52.

15. Ibid., 211.

16. Jones, "Slouching Toward the Millennium"; Jerrold K. Footlick, "Decade of the Student," *Newsweek,* 10 Dec. 1990, 72; Andrea Stone and Carol Castaneda, "Help Wanted: Educated 'Lightning Rod,'" *USA Today,* 12 Dec. 1990.

17. John K. Urice, "The Next Century: The Impact of Social and Economic Trends on the Arts in Education," *Design for Arts in Education,* May/June 1989, 40.

18. Naisbitt and Aburdene, *Megatrends 2000,* 198.

19. Footlick, "Decade of the Student," 71.

20. Urice, "The Next Century," 37.

21. Gerber et al., *Lifetrends,* 56.

22. Ibid., 235–36.

23. Waldrop, "You'll Know It's the 21st Century," 25.

24. Quoted in Daniel Cattau, "Education: A Problem Could Be a Solution," *Progressions,* A Lilly Endowment Occasional Report 2, no. 1 (1990): 20.

25. Carol Elrod, "Church Historian Analyzes Causes of Mainline Church Malaise," *Religious News Service,* 15 Nov. 1988.

26. Tom Sine, telephone interview with author, 21 Aug. 1990.

27. James Davison Hunter, *Evangelicalism: The Coming Generation* (Chicago: Univ. of Chicago Press, 1987).

28. Elmer Towns, "The Changing Role of Leadership," audiotape of presentation at "Take Hold of the '90s," a conference in Ventura, Calif., sponsored by Gospel Light Publications, 1 May 1990.

29. Amy L. Sherman, "Leaders Disagree on Future of the Church," *Christianity Today,* 21 April 1989, 42.

30. Gallup and Castelli, *People's Religion,* 179.

31. James Davison Hunter, "Evangelical Schools in Growth, Catholic Schools in Decline," *Wall Street Journal,* 8 March 1988, 34.

32. Paul Kienel, telephone interview with author, 7 Jan. 1991.

33. Culled from various written and oral sources.

34. Judy Daubenmier, Associated Press, "Education: Up to a Million American Families Maintain Home-Schools Where Their Children Are Taught," *Los Angeles Times* (Bulldog Edition), 11 March 1990, pt. A, p. 27

35. Pat Sikora, telephone interview with author, 7 Jan. 1991.

36. "In Silicon Valley, Home Schoolers Qualify for $1,000 Expense Accounts," *World,* 8 Dec. 1990, 8.

37. "Factors in Building Confidence," *The Teaching Home,* Oct./Nov. 1989, 54.

38. Personal correspondence from the Sikoras, Dec. 1990.

39. Robertson, *New Millennium,* 175–76.

40. Richard N. Ostling, "Those Mainline Blues," *Time,* 22 May 1989, 95.

41. Martin Marty, *Context,* 15 Oct. 1989, 5.

42. Robert Lynn, telephone interview with author, 19 April 1989.

43. Pat Wingert, "Exploring Childhood: Author Robert Coles Studies Spirituality," *Newsweek,* 10 Dec. 1990, 74; Alvin P. Sanoff, "Childhood's Chronicler," *U.S. News & World Report,* 3 Dec. 1990, 66–69. Coles' eighth and last book in his series about children is *The Spiritual Life of Children* (New York: Houghton Mifflin, 1990).

44. Cattau, "Education: A Problem Could Be a Solution," 21.

45. Peter L. Benson, "In the '90s: The Educational Challenge," *Alert,* Aug. 1990, 4.

46. "Study Highlights Importance of Christian Education," *Christianity Today,* 23 April 1990, 49.

47. "Study Highlights Importance of Christian Education," 48–49; Benson, "In the '90s," 2–5.

Chapter 10—Phantoms of Stage, Screen, and Canvas

1. Steven Lavaggi, interview with author, 4 Jan. 1991.

2. Edith Piczek and Isabel Piczek, interviews with author, 7 Jan. 1991.

3. Stephanie Allan, "Painging His Heart Out," Worldwide Challenge, Oct. 1988, 12–15.

4. Naisbitt and Aburdene, *Megatrends 2000,* 68.

5. Ibid., 62–92.

6. Urice, "The Next Century," 36–37.

7. Ibid., 37.

8. Ibid., 39.

9. "Taking Aim at Art," *Christianity Today,* 18 June 1990, 52; Doug Trouten "Religion in Review: 1990," *Evangelical Press News Service,* 21 Dec. 1990, 6.

10. I. Piczek, author interview.

11. Jerry Adler, "Truly Special Effects," *Newsweek,* 2 Oct. 1989, 45.

12. "Art as Transformation," UCLA Extension bulletin, Jan. 1991.

13. Naisbitt and Aburdene, *Megatrends 2000,* 87–88.

14. Barna, *Frog in the Kettle,* 90–91; Naisbitt and Aburdene, *Megatrends 2000,* 87.

15. Lyle Schaller in a Washington address to Southern Baptist ministers, quoted in "Things They Said," *World,* 16 June 1990, 4.

16. Ray Waddle, "Bill Moyers: Television Must Focus on Search for Spirituality," *Religious News Service,* 23 April 1990; "Defining Spirituality Called Century's Top Story," *Methodists Make News,* A United Methodist Weekly News Summary, 20 April 1990.

17. Michael Josephson, "Journalism: In the Year 2000," *Ethics: Easier Said Than Done,* Joseph & Edna Josephson Institute (no date), 63.

18. Ibid.

19. "Interactive TV Makes the Viewer a Director," *Connect,* Quarterly Newsletter for Members of the Center for Media and Values, Spring 1990, 2.

20. Toffler, *Powershift,* 360–61.

21. Michael W. Miller, "The Second Century—Digital Revolution: Vast Changes Loom as Computers Digest Words, Sound, Images," *Wall Street Journal,* 7 June 1989.

22. Donald Kurt, telephone interview with author, 15 Dec. 1991.

23. Bret Easton Ellis, author of *Less Than Zero, The Rules of Attraction,* and *American Psycho,* in "The Twentysomethings: Adrift in a Pop Landscape," *New York Times,* Arts & Leisure, 2 Dec. 1990, Sec. 2, p. 1.

24. Paul Thigpen, "Cleaning Up Hollywood," *Charisma,* Dec. 1991, 42.

25. Ibid.

26. Jon Pareles, "'Radical' Rap: Of Pride and Prejudice," *New York Times,* 16 Dec. 1990.

27. Gross and Scott, "Proceeding With Caution," 62.

28. Barna, *Frog in the Kettle,* 92.

29. Toffler, *Powershift,* 175.

30. Barna, "Future Issues."

31. Thomas B. Rosenstiel, "Media Study Finds 'Age of Indifference,'" *Los Angeles Times,* 28 June 1990, pt. A, p. 17; Richard Zoglin, "The Tuned-Out Generation," *Time,* 9 July 1990, 64.

32. Elizabeth Thoman, in "Interactive TV Makes the Viewer a Director," *Connect,* Quarterly Newsletter for Members of the Center for Media and Values, Spring 1990, 1.

33. Mel White, telephone interview with author, 12 Dec. 1991.

34. Ibid.

Chapter 11—Cash Flows and Flaws

1. "The Second Century: Journal's Panelists Role Play to Gaze Into 21st Century" (Part of a Series on Future Issues and Trends published in the *Journal's* Centennial Year), *Wall Street Journal,* 23 June 1989.

2. Todd G. Buchholz, *New Ideas From Dead Economists: An Introduction to Modern Economic Thought* (New York: Penguin, 1990), ix, 279.

3. Barna, *Frog in the Kettle,* 97.

4. Amanda Bennett, "The Second Century—Company School: As Pool of Skilled Help Tightens, Firms Move to Broaden Their Role," *Wall Street Journal,* 8 May 1989.

5. Janice Castro, "Get Set: Here They Come!" *Time,* Fall 1990 (Special Issue on Women), 50.

6. USA Snapshots, *USA Today,* 26 Nov. 1990.

7. Castro, "Get Set: Here They Come!," 50, 52; Naisbitt and Aburdene, *Megatrends 2000,* 226.

8. Barbara Rudolph, "Why Can't a Woman Manage More Like . . . a Woman?" *Time,* Fall 1990 (Special Edition), 53.

9. Buchholz, *New Ideas From Dead Economists,* 283.

10. Kiernan, "Best Jobs for the Future," 60.

11. Ibid.

12. "Homelessness in America: A Summary," *National Coalition for the Homeless,* Feb. 1991, 3.

13. William E. Schmidt, "Detroit Priest Preaches Hope Through Job Training," *New York Times,* 1 Jan. 1991, pt. A, p. 1.

14. Ibid., pt. A, p. 7.

15. Sine, *Wild Hope,* 92.

16. Cited in Sine, *Wild Hope,* 41; Pear, "Rich Got Richer," 1.

17. Alan Murray, "Many Americans Fear U.S. Living Standards Have Stopped Rising," *Wall Street Journal,* 1 May 1989.

18. Ibid.

19. Sine, *Wild Hope,* 76.

20. Robertson, *New Millennium,* 251.

21. Ibid.

22. Gerber et al., *Lifetrends,* 16.

23. Gerber et al., *Lifetrends,* 74–76, 113–14.

24. Waldrop, "You'll Know It's the 21st Century," 25.

25. Bennett, "The Second Century."

26. Mindy Fetterman and Martha T. Moore, "But Japan's Gain May Not Be USA's Loss," *USA Today,* 27 Nov. 1990, pt. A, p. 1.

27. Jones, "Slouching Toward the Millennium," 8.

28. Naisbitt and Aburdene, *Megatrends 2000,* 36, 212.

29. Kiernan, "Best Jobs for the Future," 60.

30. Toffler, *Powershift,* 226.

31. Robert J. Tamasy, "Now What? What Surprises Will the 1990s Have in Store for the World of American Business?" *Contact,* Dec. 1989, 5.

32. Barna, *Frog in the Kettle,* 172.

33. Toffler, *Powershift,* 179.

34. Castro, "Get Set: Here They Come!" 52.

35. David B. Bostian, Jr., "Paradigms for Prosperity: Economic and Political Trends for the 1990s and Early 21st Century," *Futurist,* July–Aug. 1990, 33.

36. William Bole, "Business Leaders Express Deep Concern Over Erosion of Ethics," *Religious News Service,* 12 Dec. 1990.

37. James M. Wall, "Scrambling for a Moral Vocabulary," *Christian Century,* 5 Dec. 1990, 1123.

38. Robertson, *New Millennium,* 244, 249.

39. Cited in Leonard Silk, "Why It's Too Soon to Predict Another Great Depression," *New York Times,* 11 Nov. 1990, Sec. 4, p. 1.

40. Ronald W. Blue, "Taking Stock of the Future," *Contact,* Dec. 1989, 15.

41. Toffler, *Powershift,* 447.

42. Naisbitt and Aburdene, *Megatrends 2000,* 33–35.

43. Robertson, *New Millennium,* 246.

44. Silk, "Why It's Too Soon to Predict Another Great Depression," 1.

45. Robertson, *New Millennium,* 245–47, 261.

46. Coates and Jarratt, "What Futurists Believe," 23.

47. Henry Grunwald, "The Second American Century," *Time,* 8 Oct. 1990, 48, 50.

48. Grunwald, "The Second American Century," 46–51.

Chapter 12—Political Spears? Or Plowshares?

1. Henry Grunwald, "The Second American Century," *Time,* 8 Oct. 1990, 50.

2. Coates and Jarratt, "What Futurists Believe," 23; Naisbitt and Aburdene, *Megatrends 2000,* 176.

3. Toffler, *Powershift,* 259, 244–45.

4. Ibid., 245.

5. Leighton Ford, "The End of History?" *Leighton Ford Ministries Hopeline,* 4, no. 4 (1990): 3.

6. Ibid.

7. Toffler, *Powershift,* 384–85.

8. Ibid.

9. Ibid., 386.

10. Oliver S. Thomas, telephone interview with author, 12 May 1989.

11. Toffler, *Powershift,* 331.

12. Sine, *Wild Hope.*

13. Samuel L. Dunn, "Christianity's Future," *The Futurist*, March–April 1989, 34.
14. Barna, *Frog in the Kettle*, 178, 180–81.
15. Thomas, author interview.
16. Rabbi Yechiel Eckstein, telephone interview with author, 18 April 1989.
17. Fred Clarkson, "HardCOR," *Church & State*, Jan. 1991, 9.
18. Ibid., 10–12.
19. Dunn, "Christianity's Future," 35.
20. Albert J. Menendez, "Traditional Patterns of Religious Groups Affirmed in '90s Vote," *Religious News Service*, 19 Nov. 1990; "Anti-Incumbent Mood Fizzles; Elections Bring Little Change," *Evangelical Press News Service* 39, no. 45 (1990): 1–3.
21. Gallup and Castelli, *People's Religion*, 201–18.
22. Ibid., 218.
23. George Cornell, Associated Press, in "Church 'Elite' Divided on Social-Political Issues," *World*, 8 April 1989, 8.
24. Gallup and Castelli, *People's Religion*, 219–21.
25. Ibid., 121; City University of New York survey, 1990, cited in David E. Anderson, "Survey Shows Americans a Religious People," *United Press International*, 3 April 1991.
26. Gallup and Castelli, *People's Religion*, 224.
27. *National & International Religion Report* 5, no. 1 (1990): 4; Gallup and Castelli, *People's Religion*, 230.
28. Albert J. Menendez, "The Voters, Candidates and Religion in the 1990 Races," *Religious News Service*, 19 Nov. 1990.
29. Ibid.
30. Gerber et al., *Lifetrends*, 134, 138.
31. Ibid., 142–48.
32. Barna, *Frog in the Kettle*, 89, 173–74, 177.
33. Ibid., 177, 179.
34. Waldrop, "You'll Know It's the 21st Century," 27.
35. Margaret Carlson, "It's Our Turn," *Time*, Fall 1990 (Special Edition), 16.
36. Waldrop, "You'll Know It's the 21st Century," 27.
37. Carlson, "It's Our Turn," 16.
38. Quoted in Mindy Belz, "Is Reaganism Ready for the Archives?" *World*, 17 Nov. 1990, 8.
39. "Two-Party Structure Frustrates Many Voters," *World*, 17 Nov. 1990, 5.
40. Glenn Tinder, "Can We Be Good Without God?" *The Atlantic Monthly*, Dec. 1989, 69–70.
41. Ibid.
42. Ibid, 82, 84–85.
43. Micah 4:3.

Chapter 13—Mainliners and Sideliners

1. William McKinney, "From the Center to the Margins," *Books & Religion*, Winter 1989, 3; David Briggs, "Religion Struggles for Role in American Society," Associated Press series, "Unholy Wars: Religion in Public Life," no. I, 17 Dec. 1990.

2. Wade Clark Roof and William McKinney, *American Mainline Religion: Its Changing Shape and Future* (New Brunswick, N.J.: Rutgers Univ. Press, 1987).

3. Ibid., 6.

4. The *Yearbook of Churches 1990* gave no new figures for the two major Orthodox churches with members in the United States. The last reported membership figure of the Greek Orthodox Archdiocese of North and South America, which includes Canada and Central America, was 1.9 million in 1977. The Orthodox Church in America, which includes Canada and is an offshoot of the Russian Orthodox Church, reported 1 million members in 1978. Other sources in 1989 projected a total U.S. membership of Eastern Orthodox churches at 4.5 million; Gary O'Guinn, "1990 Yearbook: Slow Drain from Mainline Churches Continues," *Religious News Service,* 11 Sept. 1990; "Religious Divisions in the U.S.," *United Methodist Reporter,* 14 April 1989.

5. Quoted in Gustav Spohn, "Authors Trace Mainline Protestant Decline to '60s and '70s," *Religious News Service,* 10 Jan. 1989.

6. From various editions of the *Yearbook of American and Canadian Churches.* The most recent available was for 1990, reflecting data for 1988.

7. Rodney Stark, telephone interview with author, 14 April 1989.

8. Mark Cutshall, "Looking Into the '90s," Everett (Wash.) *Herald,* 30 Dec. 1989, pt. C, p. 5; "United Methodist Snapshot," *United Methodist Reporter,* 4 Jan. 1991, 1; Ostling, "Those Mainline Blues," 95.

9. *Yearbook of Churches 1990.*

10. Lynn, author interview.

11. McKinney, "From the Center to the Margins," 3.

12. Thomas A. Stewart, "Turning Around the Lord's Business," *Fortune,* 25 Sept. 1989, 116.

13. Spohn, "Authors Trace Mainline Protestant Decline to '60s and '70s."

14. Jean Caffey Lyles, "The Fading of Denominational Distinctiveness," *Progressions,* Jan. 1990, 16–17.

15. *National & International Religion Report* 4, no. 23 (1990): 5.

16. "In This Issue," Joint Strategy and Action Committee *Grapevine* 20, no. 7 (1989): 1.

17. Ostling, "Those Mainline Blues," 94.

18. Gallup and Castelli, *People's Religion,* 264.

19. "The Spiritual Health of the Episcopal Church," *The Gallup Organization,* Princeton, N.J., 1990, 8.

20. Alan Wisdom, "The Meaning Behind Membership Decline," *Religion & Democracy,* Nov. 1990, 7–8.

21. Ibid., 7.

22. David Briggs, Associated Press, "Presbyterians Look for Comeback," *Washington Post,* 23 June 1990, pt. B, p. 7.

23. *National & International Religion Report,* 19 Nov. 1990, 6–7.

24. "Group Calls for New Understanding Between Pentecostals, Mainline," *Evangelical Press News Service,* 23 Nov. 1990, 3–4.

25. Randall L. Frame, "They'd Rather Fight Than Switch," *Christianity Today,* 5 March 1990, 25–28.

26. Briggs, "Presbyterians Look for Comeback," 7; John C. Long, "Presbyterians: A New Look at an Old Church," *Progressions,* Jan. 1990, 3.

27. John Mulder, telephone interview with author, 24 April 1989.
28. Roof and McKinney, *American Mainline Religion,* 242.
29. McKinney, "From the Center to the Margins," 4.
30. Lyles, "Denominational Distinctiveness," 17.
31. Jackson Carroll, telephone interview with author, April 1989.

Chapter 14—Frontliners and Headliners

1. John N. Vaughan, "North America's Fastest Growing Churches," *Church Growth Today* 5, no. 1 (1990): 1.
2. Juleen Turnage, telephone interview with author, 28 Feb. 1991.
3. *Yearbook of Churches 1990.*
4. Stark, author interview.
5. Vaughan, "North America's Fastest Growing Churches," 1.
6. *Yearbook of Churches 1990.*
7. Gallup and Castelli, *People's Religion,* 93.
8. Ibid., 93–94.
9. Naisbitt and Aburdene, *Megatrends 2000,* 279.
10. "Update on Action in American Churches," *Religion & Democracy,* Nov. 1990, 6.
11. Martin Marty, *Context,* 15 Aug. 1990, 2.
12. John Dart, "It's Not All in a Name for Some Churches," *Los Angeles Times,* 22 Dec. 1990, pt. S, p. 1.
13. John N. Vaughan, telephone interview with author, 3 May 1989.
14. Ibid.
15. Stewart, "Turning Around the Lord's Business," 128.
16. Lyle E. Schaller, "Megachurch!" *Christianity Today,* 5 March 1990, 20.
17. Jim Dethmer, telephone interview with author, 14 Jan. 1991.
18. Stewart, "Turning Around the Lord's Business, 128.
19. Lyle E. Schaller, telephone interview with author, 17 April 1989.
20. Schaller, "Megachurch!" 20–21.
21. Ibid., 24.
22. Ibid., 3.
23. Tom Sine, telephone interview with author, 11 April 1989.
24. Quoted in "Passing It On: Will Our Kids Recognize Our Faith?" *World,* 11 March 1989, 5–6.
25. "Study Finds Little Difference in Behavior of Born-Again Christians," *Evangelical Press News Service,* 21 Sept. 1990, 9.
26. Symposium, "Strategies of the 1990s," hosted by Gospel Light Publications, Pasadena, Calif., 18 May 1989.

Chapter 15—Roamin' Catholics

1. Russell Chandler, "Filling the 'Priestless Parishes,'" *Los Angeles Times,* 16 Dec. 1989, pt. A, p. 1.
2. Ibid.
3. Ibid.
4. Ibid.

5. Ibid.; *Yearbook*(s) *of American and Canadian Churches*; Roof and McKinney, *American Mainline Religion,* 15.

6. Naisbitt and Aburdene, *Megatrends 2000,* 288; in Gallup and Castelli, *People's Religion,* 126. The figure for charismatic Catholics is only 4 percent. Naisbitt's source for 20 percent is the National Catholic Renewal Center, South Bend, Indiana.

7. Gallup and Castelli, *People's Religion,* 93 (13 percent); George Gallup, Jr., and Sarah Jones, *100 Questions & Answers: Religion in America* (Princeton, N.J.: Princeton Religion Research Center, 1989), 167 (21 percent).

8. Chandler, "Analysts See Evangelical Growth," 1.

9. Roof and McKinney, *American Mainline Religion,* 237.

10. David Briggs, "Religious Groups Test Political Waters," *Associated Press,* series on "Unholy Wars: Religion in Public Life," no. II, 14 Dec. 1990.

11. Briggs, "Religion Struggles for Role in American Society."

12. Roberto Suro, "Switch by Hispanic Catholics Changes Face of U.S. Religion," *New York Times,* 14 May 1989, pt. A, p. 1.

13. Suro, "Switch by Hispanic Catholics," 1.

14. Anderson, "Survey Shows Americans a Religious People."

15. "Catholic Archbishop Says Evangelicals Lure Hispanics," *Evangelical Press News Service,* 23 June 1989, 7.

16. Lynn Smith and Russell Chandler, "Catholics, Evangelical Christians Battle for Latinos' Souls," *Los Angeles Times,* 2 Dec. 1989, pt. F, p. 18.

17. Gallup and Castelli, *The People's Religion,* 33.

18. Chandler, "Analysts See Evangelical Growth," 1.

19. Russell Chandler, "Flock Runs Short of Shepherds," *Los Angeles Times,* 1 March 1989, pt. A, p. 1; Russell Chandler, "Striving to Serve God and Family," *Los Angeles Times,* 19 Sept. 1990, pt. A, p. 1.

20. Chandler, "Flock Runs Short," 1.

21. "Survey of 'Thirtysomething' Priests Finds High Job Satisfaction and Happiness—But Most Would Opt Out of Rectory Life," *National Catholic Educational Association* news release, 18 March 1991; George Cornell, "Catholic Priests Found Happier Than Believed," *Associated Press,* 22 March 1991.

22. Chandler, "Striving to Serve God and Family," 1.

23. Russell Chandler, "Mahony Faces Challenge as Priestly Ranks Thin," *Los Angeles Times,* 2 March 1989, pt. A, p. 1.

24. Elizabeth Bookser Barkley, "Indianapolis's Urban Parishes Work Together," *St. Anthony Messenger,* Nov. 1990, 14–19.

25. Chandler, "Filling the 'Priestless Parishes.'"

26. Ibid.

27. Ibid; Gallup and Jones, *100 Questions & Answers,* 91.

28. Jane Redmont, "Future Challenges to American Catholicism," *Progressions,* A Lilly Endowment Occasional Report 1, no. 2 (1989): 21.

29. Gallup and Castelli, *The People's Religion,* 99.

30. Gallup and Jones, *100 Questions & Answers,* 67.

31. "The Essence of Parish-Connected Catholics," *Progressions,* June 1989, 5.

32. Terry McGuire, "Role of Women Will Be Major Church Issue, Says Theologian," *Progress* (weekly paper of the Archdiocese of Seattle), 5 July 1990, 11.

33. Father Andrew Greeley, telephone interview with author, 18 April 1989.

34. John Wolcott, "'Magnet' Parishes Draw Catholics from Afar," *Progress* (weekly newspaper of the Archdiocese of Seattle), 5 July 1990, 1.

35. Jeffrey Hadden, telephone interview with author, 12 April 1989.

36. Brochure, The Education Foundation, "An alliance for quality education for disadvantaged students and inner-city schools," Los Angeles, Calif., 1990.

37. "Eying Big Bucks, Catholics Knock Public Schools," *World,* 9 Feb. 1991, 16.

38. Greeley, author interview.

39. Sister Sharon Euart, telephone interview with author, 19 April 1989.

40. Father Rosendo Urrabazo, CMF, telephone interview with author, 19 April 1989.

Chapter 16—Blacks to the Future

1. Paul Thigpen, "The New Black Charismatics," *Charisma & Christian Life,* Nov. 1990, 58–59.

2. Richard N. Ostling, "Strains on the Heart," *Time,* 19 Nov. 1990, 88–90.

3. C. Eric Lincoln and Lawrence H. Mamiya, *The Black Church in the African American Experience* (Duke Univ. Press, 1990).

4. Roof and McKinney, *American Mainline Religion,* 232.

5. Ostling, "Strains on the Heart."

6. *Yearbook of American & Canadian Churches 1987,* Publication of the National Council of Churches, ed. Constant H. Jacquet, Jr. (Nashville: Abingdon), 244–45.

7. Ibid., 240–41.

8. *Yearbook of Churches 1990.*

9. Ostling, "Strains on the Heart," 88.

10. John Vaughan, "Megamyths," *Christianity Today,* 5 March 1990, 24.

11. Thigpen, "The New Black Charismatics," 59.

12. "Black Churches Now Among Top 15 Fastest-Growing Congregations," *Religious News Service,* 10 May 1991.

13. Gallup and Castelli, *People's Religion,* 122.

14. Roof and McKinney, *American Mainline Religion,* 90.

15. Quoted in Jane Redmont, "Communities of Service, Families of Faith," *Progressions,* A Lilly Endowment Occasional Report 3, no. 1 (1991): 15–16.

16. William Pannell, telephone interview with author, 12 Sept. 1990.

17. Gallup and Castelli, *People's Religion,* 122.

18. Ibid., 33, 97, 122–24, 260, 262; Roof and McKinney, *American Mainline Religion,* 91, 100–01; Gallup and Jones, *100 Questions & Answers,* 4, 6, 8, 10, 38, 72–74, 140, 162, 170, 176–77, 182–83; Russell Chandler, "Survey: A New Poll Also Finds that Blacks Are More Often Involved in Religion than Are the County's Whites and Latinos," *Los Angeles Times,* 15 Sept. 1990, pt. F, p. 16.

19. Ostling, "Strains on the Heart," 88.

20. Robert Franklin, telephone interview with author, 20 April 1989.

21. C. Eric Lincoln, telephone interview with author, 21 April 1989.

22. Redmont, "Communities of Service, Families of Faith," 16.

23. Ostling, "Strains on the Heart," 89.

24. Lincoln, author interview.

25. Ibid.

26. *Yearbook of Churches 1990.*
27. Ostling, "Strains on the Heart," 89.
28. Lincoln, author interview.
29. Ostling, "Strains on the Heart," 90.
30. Anthony Evans, "Alternative Philosophy," audiotape, *Focus on the Family,* 1989.
31. Thigpen, "The New Black Charismatics," 67.

Chapter 17—Muslims, Jews, Mormons, and More

1. Michael Youssef, *America, Oil, and the Islamic Mind* (Grand Rapids, Mich.: Zondervan, 1991), 49–50.
2. "Religion in Review: 1990," *Evangelical Press News Service* 39, no. 51 (1990): 4; Youssef, *America, Oil, and the Islamic Mind,* 28.
3. George Cornell, "Moslems Begin Edging into Interreligious Mainstream," *Associated Press,* 12 Oct. 1990.
4. Youssef, *America, Oil, and the Islamic Mind,* 28.
5. Lincoln, author interview.
6. Ibid.
7. David Dolan, quoted in "American Christians Lack Information Needed to Understand Roots of Gulf Crisis," *Evangelical Press News Service* 40, no. 7 (1991): 3.
8. "Jews and Christians Urge Respect for Muslims," *Religion in American Life* news release, Princeton, N.J., 1 March 1991.
9. Jonathan Farna, telephone interview with author, 24 April 1989.
10. Gallup and Castelli, *People's Religion,* 116.
11. *Yearbook of Churches 1990,* 75 (1988 figures); *Yearbook of Churches 1989,* 75 (1987 figures).
12. Eckstein, author interview.
13. Kenneth L. Woodward, "A Time to Seek," *Newsweek,* 17 Dec. 1990, 54.
14. "News From the Committee," *The American Jewish Committee,* New York, news release, 18 Feb. 1991, 3.
15. Eckstein, author interview.
16. Paul Wilkes, "The Hands That Would Shape Our Souls," *The Atlantic Monthly,* Dec. 1990, 70–71.
17. Ann Levin, Associated Press, "It's Kosher to Be Kosher Again," *Los Angeles Times,* 15 Dec. 1990, pt. F, p. 16.
18. Woodward, "A Time to Seek," 52.
19. Jerry Cahill, telephone interview with author, 1 March 1991.
20. Timothy J. Chandler, *Christian Science and Mormonism: Two Alternative Worldviews in American Religion,* manuscript delivered at the California Institute of Technology, Pasadena, Calif., 23 March 1991, 2.
21. Ibid., 16.
22. Roof and McKinney, *American Mainline Religion,* 98.
23. *Yearbook of Churches 1987,* 73; *Yearbook of Churches 1990,* 75.
24. Sine, *Wild Hope,* 174.
25. "Religious Division in the U.S.," *United Methodist Reporter,* 14 April 1989. The 500,000 figure squares with the City University of New York survey in 1990.
26. Ibid.; Naisbitt and Aburdene, *Megatrends 2000,* 276–77.

27. Sine, *Wild Hope,* 174.

28. Office of Public Information, Baha'i International Community, New York; Baha'i Public Information Service of Los Angeles, 3 Jan. 1991.

Chapter 18—Alternative Altars

1. Robert S. Ellwood, Jr., *Alternative Altars: Unconventional and Eastern Spirituality in America* (Chicago: Univ. of Chicago Press, 1979). Permission granted by Ellwood 13 March 1991 to use "Alternative Altars" as part of the title of this chapter, "Alternative Altars: Next-age Faiths."

2. Hadden, author interview.

3. "Defining Spirituality Called Century's Top Story," *Methodists Make News,* A United Methodist weekly news summary, 20 April 1990, 1.

4. Steve Turner, "Lean, Green, & Meaningless," *Christianity Today,* 24 Sept. 1990, 26–27.

5. Ibid.

6. See Russell Chandler, *Understanding the New Age* (Dallas: Word, 1988).

7. Hadden, author interview.

8. Gallup and Castelli, *People's Religion,* 136, 133. The apparent discrepancy between the Gallup findings and the City University of New York survey, which found that 90 percent of American adults identified with some form of religion, can be explained by the way the CUNY poll was conducted. That survey did not attempt to define faith or degree of practice; no questions were asked about church attendance, baptisms, financial contributions, or membership. The Gallup polls in 1978 and 1988 defined "unchurched" as those who said they were not members of any church or synagogue and had not attended a church or synagogue in the week before being interviewed. Many in this group considered themselves "religious," however.

9. Roof and McKinney, *American Mainline Religion,* 242.

10. Ibid., 181.

11. Gallup and Jones, *100 Questions & Answers,* 76–77, 178–79.

12. Steven Tipton, telephone interview with author, 18 April 1989.

13. Russell Chandler, "The Challenge is Acute; the Fields Ripe," *Evangelical Beacon,* 8 Jan. 1990, 10.

14. George Cornell, "Baptist Futurist Sees Fluid Religious Atmosphere Ahead," *Associated Press,* 4 May 1990.

15. Woodward, "A Time to Seek," 55.

16. Cornell, "Baptist Futurist Sees Fluid Religious Atmosphere Ahead."

17. Richard Cimino, "United Church of Christ Spirituality Incorporates Mystical Forms," *Religious News Service,* 11 April 1989.

18. Barna, *Frog in the Kettle,* 141.

19. Steve Turner, "Lean, Green, & Meaningless," 27.

20. Lawrence E. Adams, "The Greening of the Spirit," *Religion & Democracy,* Jan. 1991 (reprint).

21. "Despite the Great Return, All the Pews Aren't Full," *Newsweek,* 17 Dec. 1990, 54.

22. Victoria Balfour, "John Bradshaw," *People's Weekly,* 28 May 1990, 73–74.

23. Robert L. Randall, "The Road Peck Travels," *Christian Century,* 21–28 Nov. 1990, 1101–02.

24. John Wimber, "Facing the '90s," *Equipping the Saints,* Summer 1989, 21–22.

25. Woodward, "A Time to Seek," 56.

26. Kate Anders Marlin, "The Underground Ecumenist," *Christian Century,* 22–29 Aug. 1990, 757.

27. Ad from "The Shapes of the Spirit, Inc." PO Box 83939, San Diego, Calif., March 1990.

28. Marlin, "The Underground Ecumenist," 757.

29. David Neff, "Suckers for the Zodiac," *Christianity Today,* 15 July 1988, 15.

30. R. C. Sproul, "Faith and Astrology: Understanding Our Futures," *Eternity,* Sept. 1988, 84.

31. Irving Hexham and Karla Poewe-Hexham, "The Soul of the New Age," *Christianity Today,* 2 Sept. 1988, 21.

32. Andrew Miles, O.S.B., "The New Age Movement and Christianity," *Chariscenter USA Newsletter* 13, no. 8 (1988): 2–3.

33. Ken Bailey, "Crisis in Middle East," *Thesis Theological Cassettes,* audiotape, 1988.

34. Barna, *Frog in the Kettle,* 121, 146.

35. Hadden, author interview.

Chapter 19—Clashing Cosmologies

1. This chapter is an adaptation and expansion of a paper delivered by Russell Chandler, "Discerning Worldviews: Understanding the New Age," at the 41st annual meeting of the Evangelical Theological Society, San Diego, Calif., 17 Nov. 1989.

2. *USA Today,* 15 Nov. 1988, pt. A, p. 1.

3. David A. Reed, "Star Trek V Blasts 'God,'" *Gospel Truth* newsletter II, no. 3 (1989): 1.

4. "Witch Addresses San Francisco Seminary," *Presbyterian Layman* 22, no. 4 (1989): 1.

5. William M. Alnor, "Controversy Over Witchcraft Liturgy in Methodist Church Continues," *Christian Research Journal,* Winter 1991, 6.

6. Lewis Thomas, "Beyond the Moon's Horizon—Our Home," *New York Times,* 15 July 1989, pt. A. p. 25.

7. Jeremy P. Tarcher, "Here's to the End of 'New Age' Publishing," *Publishers Weekly,* 8 Nov. 1989, 36. Emphasis added.

8. Ibid.

9. Will Nixon, "The Flight from New Age," *Publishers Weekly,* 7 Dec. 1990, 21–32.

10. Don Lattin, "Mythologist's Sudden New Appeal," *San Francisco Chronicle,* 15 Aug. 1988, pt. A, p. 4.

11. Douglas Groothuis, "Myth and the Power of Joseph Campbell," *Genesis,* Summer 1988, 16.

12. Joseph Campbell with Bill Moyers, *The Power of Myth* (New York: Doubleday, 1988), 66.

13. Sine, *Wild Hope,* 126.

14. Sources unknown; cited in a textbook.

15. Chandler, *Understanding the New Age,* 26.

16. 1 Corinthians 1:21, 2:5.

17. Allan Bloom, *The Closing of the American Mind* (New York: Touchstone/Simon & Schuster, 1987).

18. Ibid., 25–26.

19. Reinhold Niebuhr, "Faith and Reason," *Thesis Theological Cassettes* audiotape, date unknown.

20. Campbell, *Power of Myth,* 31.

21. Groothuis, "Myth and the Power of Joseph Campbell," 20.

22. Brooks Alexander, "Back to the Garden," *Spiritual Counterfeits Project Newsletter* 13, no. 2 (1988): 6.

23. Ibid.

24. Quoted in Fergus M. Bordewich, "Colorado's Thriving Cults," *New York Times Magazine,* 1 May 1988, pt. 6, p. 37.

25. Donna Steichen, "Crystal Ball Catholicism: Welcome to the Wacko World of New Age Theology," *Crisis,* July–Aug. 1989, 21.

26. For a full presentation, see Russell Chandler, *Understanding the New Age,* especially chapter 2, "Prevalence of the New Age," 19–26.

27. Robert N. Bellah, interview with author, Berkeley, Calif., 25 Nov. 1987.

28. Genesis 1:26.

29. Søren Kierkegaard, *Philosophical Fragments* (Princeton, N.J.: Princeton Univ. Press, 1962).

30. Steve Turner, "Lean, Green, & Meaningless," *Christianity Today,* 24 Sept. 1990, 27.

31. Norman R. Gulley, "The Function of the Cross as a Strategy to Assert the Biblical Worldview," a response paper to Russell Chandler's plenary session paper, "Discerning Worldviews: Understanding the New Age," at the 41st annual meeting of the Evangelical Theological Society, San Diego, Calif., 17 Nov. 1989.

32. Stan Gaede, "Like Sampson, Strong Outside, but Pussycats Before Delilah's Wiles," *World,* 11 March 1989, 5.

33. Ibid.

34. Timothy J. Chandler, class notes, fall 1988.

35. Groothuis, "Myth and the Power of Joseph Campbell," 17.

Chapter 20—Shining the Pastoral Patina

1. Dethmer, author interview.

2. McKinney, "From the Center to the Margins," 28.

3. Carl F. George, "Church Trends in the '90s: Will We Survive?" Seminar at Azusa Pacific University, Azusa, Calif., 20 April 1989.

4. Richard Lee Olson, doctoral dissertation, cited in Schaller, "Megachurch!" 23.

5. Lynn, author interview.

6. Ibid.

7. Frank R. Tillapaugh, *Unleashing the Church: Getting People Out of the Fortress and into Ministry* (Ventura, Calif.: Regal, 1982), 118.

8. David Barrett, telephone interview with author, 19 April 1989.

9. George Barna, "The Challenge of the Church in the 90s," audiotape of talk presented at "Take Hold of the '90s" a conference in Ventura, Calif., sponsored by Gospel Light Publications, 3 May 1990.

10. Data compiled from additional sources by James M. Shopshire, Dec. 1990, "New Faces in Theological Education," *Christian Century*, 6–13 Feb. 1991, 142.

11. Barna, *Frog in the Kettle*, 130–40; *National & International Religion Report* 3, no. 13 (1989): 8; Linda-Marie Delloff, "New Roles, New Power for Women in the Church," *Progressions*, A Lilly Endowment Occasional Report 2, no. 1 (1990): 14.

12. Juanne N. Clarke and Grace Anderson, "A Study of Women in Ministry: God Calls, Man Chooses," *Yearbook of Churches 1990*.

13. Martin Marty, *Context*, 15 Aug. 1990, 4.

14. Robert Marquand, (untitled wire story), *Christian Science Monitor*, 16 May 1990.

15. Hadden, author interview.

16. George Barna, "Marketing the Church for the '90s"; Peter F. Drucker, "Developing Leadership to Take the Church into the 21st Century." Both were talks presented at "The 1990s: The Gateway into the 21st Century, Positioning the Christian Church for a New Era," a seminar in Ventura, Calif., 4–5 April 1989.

17. Barna, *Frog in the Kettle*, 145.

18. Loren Mead, telephone interview with author, 13 April 1989.

19. Gustav Spohn, "Episcopal Clergy 'Confused, Uncertain' About Role, Report Says," *Religious News Service*, 23 Oct. 1989.

20. Ibid.

21. "It's Now OK to Admit Clergy Get Stressed Out, Too," *Religious News Service*, 11 Feb. 1991.

22. Ibid.

23. Ibid.

24. Alban Institute, cited in Hank Whittemore, "Ministers Under Stress," *Parade Magazine*, 14 April 1991, 6.

Chapter 21—Making Dollars and Sense of Missions and Ministry

1. Gary O'Guinn, "Americans Miserly When Sizing Up the Preacher's Worth," *Religious News Service*, 17 Dec. 1990.

2. Cited in Hank Whittemore, "Ministers Under Stress," *Parade Magazine*, 14 April 1991, 5.

3. Spencer, author interview.

4. George Gallup, Jr., conversation with author, Los Angeles, 13 March 1990.

5. "Religious Faith: Firm Foundation for Charity," *Christianity Today*, 19 Nov. 1990, 63.

6. John Ronsvalle and Sylvia Ronsvalle, "Giving Trends and Their Implications for the 1990s," a paper presented at the North American Conference on Christian Philanthropy, Minneapolis, Minnesota, 24–27 Sept. 1990, 2.

7. Ibid., 1–6.

8. James Grant, *The State of the World's Children 1989* (New York: Oxford Univ. Press, 1989), 65.

9. Sylvia Ronsvalle, "Stewards into Consumers: Study Update Indicates Church Giving Down," news release from Empty Tomb, Inc., Champaign, Ill., 10 Oct.

1990; David E. Anderson, "Study Finds Drop in Religious Giving," *United Press International,* 26 Oct. 1990.

10. Engel, "We Are the World," 32.

11. Ibid., 32–33.

12. Cited in "Short-termers Increase," *Marketplace Urbana,* Winter 1991, 5.

13. Anderson, "Study Finds Drop in Religious Giving"; "Religious Faith," 63.

14. John Ronsvalle and Sylvia Ronsvalle, "The National Money for Missions Program," working draft, 13 Aug. 1990, 11.

15. "Religious Faith," 63.

16. Ibid.

17. "Money Magazine: High Marks to Religious Charities for Performance," *Religious News Service,* 26 Nov. 1990.

18. Barrett, author interview.

19. Barna, *Frog in the Kettle,* 135.

20. Quoted in *National & International Religion Report* 4, no. 18 (1990): 3.

21. J. Lee Grady, "New Missions Strategies for a Rapidly Changing World: A Sampling of Trends and Developments in Global Evangelism," *National & International Religion Report* 5, no. 3, 28 Jan. 1991, 1.

22. Ostling, "Those Mainline Blues," 95.

23. David Stoll, "Evangelicals Envision the World Through Computers," *Pacific News Service,* 22 Aug. 1990.

24. Ibid.; Grady, "New Missions Strategies for a Rapidly Changing World," 1.

25. Grady, "New Missions Strategies," 2–3.

26. Paul E. Pierson, "9 Trends for the 90s in World Missions," *Latin America Evangelist,* April–June 1990, 8.

27. Russell Chandler, "Freedom to Worship . . . and Make Money," *Los Angeles Times,* 1 Dec. 1990, pt. F, p. 16.

28. Viktor Reimer, Logos Biblical Training by Extension, correspondence with author, March 1991.

29. Bill Greig, "The Soviet Opportunity," *GLINT Focus,* Winter 1991, 2.

30. Barna, *Frog in the Kettle,* 144.

31. "The Hottest Product Is Brand X," *Fortune,* 25 Sept. 1989, 128.

Chapter 22—Goal Setting

1. Carroll, author interview.

2. Sine, author interview.

3. "ELCA Synods Seek Inclusiveness," news release, Evangelical Lutheran Church in America, 10 May 1990, 1–2.

4. Herbert W. Chilstrom, telephone interview with author, 19 April 1989.

5. "Church Council Adopts Mission 90," news release, ELCA, 19 April 1989, 2–3.

6. "Call to Mission in the '90s for the ELCA," working paper, 1989, 3–6.

7. Chilstrom, author interview.

8. David Briggs, "Liberals, Conservatives Battle for the High Ground," *Associated Press* series "Unholy Wars: Religion in Public Life," no. I, 19 Dec. 1990; Carolyn Lewis, telephone interview with author, 28 March 1991.

9. "Church Guides Corporate America," news release, ELCA, 14 Feb. 1991.

10. "ELCA Synods Seek Inclusiveness," news release, ELCA, 10 May 1990.

11. Jean Caffey Lyles, "Lutheran Meeting Highlights Goal of Outreach to Ethnic Minorities," *Religious News Service,* 7 July 1989.

12. Richard Walker, *Reuter,* "U.S. Lutheran Church Cuts Spending to Cope With Deficit," 17 March 1991.

13. "ELCA Income Short of Budget," news release, ELCA, 12 March 1991, 2.

Chapter 23—Drug Busting

1. DarEll T. Weist, telephone interview with author, 22 Aug. 1989.

2. "Ministry Strategy in the Los Angeles District for the 21st Century," *United Methodist Reporter,* 19 May 1989, 4.

3. Russell Chandler, "Churches Take Up Drug Fight," *Los Angeles Times,* 6 July 1990, pt. A, p. 1.

4. Kim A. Lawton, "Churches Enlist in the War on Drugs," *Christianity Today,* 11 Feb. 1991, 44–45.

5. Robert Lear, "1990: United Methodist Events Spanned the Global Parish, *United Methodist Reporter,* 14 Jan. 1991.

6. Chandler, "Churches Take Up Drug Fight," 1.

7. Ibid.

8. Lawton, "Churches Enlist in the War on Drugs," 49.

9. Sarah J. Vilankulu, "Churches Uniting Against Drugs," *Christian Century,* 14 Nov. 1990, 1052–53.

10. Chandler, "Churches Take Up Drug Fight."

11. Lawton, "Churches Enlist in the War on Drugs," 44.

Chapter 24—Perimeters and Satellites

1. Harry D. Williams, "Churches Must Offer Newer Options," *California Southern Baptist,* 17 May 1990, 6.

2. Elmer L. Towns, brochure from *Church Growth Institute,* Lynchburg, Va., 1991.

3. *Yearbook of Churches 1990* and *1991,* (1990) 89; (1991) 263.

4. Ibid.

5. Charles Dunahoo, interview with author, 4 April 1989.

6. Charles Dunahoo, telephone interviews with author, 20 April 1989 and 28 March 1991.

7. Towns, *Innovative Churches,* 90.

8. From a conversation Randy Pope had with John Haggai; cited in ibid, 91.

9. Ibid., 95–96.

10. Ibid., 239.

11. Ibid., 241–42.

12. Ibid., 243.

13. Ibid., 102.

14. Williams, "Churches Must Offer Newer Options," 6.

15. Ibid.

16. Towns, *Innovative Churches,* 251.

17. Ibid., 256.

Chapter 25—Willow Creek Community Church

1. This chapter is adapted and expanded from Russell Chandler, "'Customer' Poll Shapes a Church," *Los Angeles Times,* 11 Dec. 1989, pt. A, p. 1.

2. "The Ten Largest Churches," *Christianity Today,* 5 March 1990, 22.

3. Rob Shearer, interview with author, 14 Feb. 1991; "A Day in the Life, 5:41 p.m.," *Willow Creek* 1, no. 1 (1989): 26.

4. Correspondence with author, 14 Feb. 1991.

5. "April in Paris" International Pastors Conference, *Willow Creek* 1, no. 4 (1990): 9; Rob Wilkins, "Casting a Vision," *Willow Creek* 1, no. 6 (1990): 13.

6. Schaller, author interview.

7. Quoted in Tom Valeo, "The Drama of Willow Creek," *Daily Herald,* 19 May 1988, pt. 9, p. 4.

8. Marie Buscaglia, "How the Church Spends Money," *Willow Creek* 2, no. 2 (1990): 8.

9. Schaller, "Megachurch!" 22.

10. Barna, "Marketing the Church for the '90s."

11. Timm Boyle, "Three More for the Team," *Willow Creek* 2, no. 1 (1990): 7.

12. "2001, A Willow Creek Odyssey," *Willow Creek* 2, no. 2 (1990): 7.

13. Dethmer, author interview.

14. Bill Hybels, interview with author, 28 April 1989.

15. Fliers, Horizons Community Church, P.O. Box 1413, Glendora, Calif. 91740, John Ortberg, Jr., senior pastor, March 1991.

16. "Inside Notes," *Willow Creek* 1, no. 6 (1990): 10.

17. Anthony B. Robinson, "Learning From Willow Creek Church," *Christian Century,* 23 Jan. 1991, 69.

18. Hybels, author interview.

Chapter 26—All Saints Episcopal Church

1. This chapter is adapted and expanded from Russell Chandler, "Keeping the Faith at the Battlefront: Liberalism Combined With Creative Worship Has Resulted in Unusual Gains for All Saints Episcopal Church in Pasadena," *Los Angeles Times,* 12 Dec. 1989, pt. B, p. 1.

2. George F. Regas, interview with author, 3 June 1989.

3. Robert Franklin, telephone interview with author, 20 April 1989.

4. Donald E. Miller, "Bucking a Powerful Trend," *All Saints Church Every Member Canvass '90.*

5. Donald E. Miller, "Liberal Church Growth: A Case Study," a paper presented at the annual meeting of the Society for the Scientific Study of Religion, Salt Lake City, Utah, 27–29 Oct. 1989, 12.

6. *Voice,* All Saints Church Pro-Choice Newsletter, Feb. 1991; *Bulletin,* All Saints Church, 24 Feb. 1991.

7. *Bulletin,* All Saints Church, 24 Feb. 1991.

8. *Bulletin,* All Saints Church, 24 March 1991.

9. George F. Regas, "God, Sex and Justice," a sermon preached at All Saints Episcopal Church, Pasadena, Calif., 11 Nov. 1990.

10. *Bulletin,* All Saints Church, 17 Feb. 1991.

11. Miller, "Liberal Church Growth: A Case Study," 18.

12. George F. Regas, correspondence to author, 13 Feb. 1991.
13. Quoted in Anthony B. Robinson, "Learning From Willow Creek," *Christian Century,* 23 Jan. 1991, 70.

Chapter 27—St. John the Baptist Roman Catholic Church

1. This chapter is adapted and expanded from Russell Chandler, "Pastor Takes Dual Role as Spiritual Leader, Activist: Baldwin Park Parish Reflects Efforts to Keep Church Growing and Relevant, Improving Lives and Community," *Los Angeles Times,* 21 Oct. 1989, pt. B, p. 6.
2. Peter D. Nugent, interview with author, 13 July 1989.
3. Donald Wuerl, "Toward the Year 2000: Priests and the Laity," address at Mary Immaculate Seminary, Northampton, Pa., 8 March 1990.
4. Hemrick, author interview.
5. Frank Sotomayor, "State Shows 69.2% Rise in Latino Population," *Los Angeles Times,* Nuestro Tiempo section, 28 March 1991, 1.
6. Jane Redmont, "Communities of Service, Families of Faith," *Progressions,* A Lilly Endowment Occasional Report 3, no. 1 (1991): 14.
7. Jim Castelli, "The Church's Local Incarnation Thrives," *Progressions,* A Lilly Endowment Occasional Report 1, no. 2 (1989): 5–6.
8. Ibid., 6.
9. Ibid.

Chapter 28—True Vine Missionary Baptist Church

1. Mark Wingfield, "Oakland Church Forced to Postpone Revival"; Cameron Crabtree, "Church Runs Drug Dealers off Large Housing Project," both in *California Southern Baptist,* 29 March 1990, 1.
2. Newton Carey and Sallie Carey, interviews with author, Oakland, Calif., 28 Nov. 1990.
3. *Here's Hope: Jesus Cares for You,* New International Version New Testament (Nashville: Holman, 1988).
4. Denise Williams, "We Are About Winning People to Jesus!" a contribution submitted in 1990 to Newton Carey, Jr., pastor, True Vine Missionary Baptist Church, Oakland, Calif., for inclusion by the Sunday School Board of the Southern Baptist Convention in its book on Discipleship Training in Black Churches.
5. Ibid., 2–3.
6. Crabtree, "Church Runs Drug Dealers off Large Housing Project."
7. Carey and Carey, author interviews.
8. Williams, "We Are About Winning People to Jesus!" 6.
9. John Wierick, "Make-over in Motown," *Signs of the Times,* Jan. 1991, 16 (reprinted by permission of *World Vision* magazine).
10. *God, Help Me Stop: Break Free From Addiction and Compulsion* (Glen Ellyn, Ill., New Life Ministries). P.O. Box 343, Glen Ellyn, Ill. 60138. (312) 858-7878.

Chapter 29—Vineyard Christian Fellowship

1. This chapter is adapted and expanded from Russell Chandler, "Vineyard Fellowship Finds Groundswell of Followers: John Wimber's Merging of Super-

natural Power and Biblical Prophecy Has Led to a 'Boom Church,'" *Los Angeles Times,* 5 Oct. 1990, pt. A, p. 1.

2. *National & International Religion Report* 5, no. 23 (1991): 4.

3. John Wimber, interview with author, Santa Monica, Calif., 30 Aug. 1990.

4. C. Peter Wagner, *The Third Wave of the Holy Spirit: Encountering the Power of Signs and Wonders Today* (Ann Arbor, Mich.: Servant, 1988).

5. Les Parrott III and Robin D. Perrin, "The New Denominations," *Christianity Today,* 31; Robin D. Perrin and Armand L. Mauss, "Saints and Seekers: Sources of Recruitment to a New Evangelical Movement," a paper presented at the annual meeting of the Society for the Scientific Study of Religion, Salt Lake City, Utah, 27 Oct. 1989.

6. Anthony B. Robinson, "Learning From Willow Creek Church," *Christian Century,* 23 Jan. 1991, 69.

7. Richard Spencer, interview with author, Los Angeles, Calif., 4 Sept. 1990.

8. Ben Patterson, "Cause for Concern," *Christianity Today,* 8 Aug. 1986, 20.

9. Lewis B. Smedes, ed., *Ministry and the Miraculous: A Case Study at Fuller Theological Seminary* (Pasadena, Calif.: Fuller Theological Seminary, 1987), 76.

10. Kenn Gulliksen, interview with author, Anaheim, Calif., 29 Aug. 1990.

11. Parrott and Perrin, "The New Denominations," 32.

12. *National & International Religion Report* 5, no. 5 (1991): 4–5.

13. Kevin Springer, interview with author, Anaheim, Calif., 29 Aug. 1990.

14. Parrott and Perrin, "The New Denominations," 33.

15. Ibid.

Chapter 30—Other Models, Strategies, and Assessments

1. Win Arn, telephone interview with author, 3 May 1989.

2. Towns, *Innovative Churches,* 202.

3. Towns, "Changing Role of Leadership."

4. George Gallup, Jr., "Shape of Religion in the '90s," talk at the University Club, Los Angeles, Calif., 13 March 1990.

5. Towns, *Innovative Churches,* 76, 78, 84.

6. Ibid., 80.

7. Ibid., 81.

8. Ibid., 86.

9. Randy Knutson, telephone interview with author, 22 Nov. 1989; Chandler, "The Challenge Is Acute," 11.

10. Spiritual Gifts Inventory materials, Church Growth Institute, P.O. Box 4404, Lynchburg, Va. 24502, copyright 1986.

11. Olson and Leonard, *Ministry With Families in Flux,* 132–33.

12. Ibid., 134–35.

13. "Christian Group Holds Symposium on Dealing With Disabled Employees," *Evangelical Press News Service,* 8 March 1991, 9.

14. *Successful Churches: What They Have in Common* (Glendale, Calif.: Barna Research Group, 1990).

15. Ibid.

16. John Gallagher, *Jesus Doesn't Live in Brooklyn* (New York: copyright by Bill Wilson, 1989), 76.

17. "Metro Variety," video recording, 1990.

18. Judith Hill, "Not an Ordinary Farm," *Princeton Theological Seminary Alumni/ae News,* Winter 1991, 7–8.

19. Jon Trott, correspondence with author, 15 Jan. 1991.

20. Material sent author by Jesus People USA, Jan. 1991.

21. Associated Press, "Large Turnout Expected at Christian Rock Fest," *Charleston (W. Va.) Daily Mail,* 1 July 1987, pt. A, p. 3.

22. Material sent author by Jesus People USA, Jan. 1991.

23. John C. Long, "Three Congregations Discover Their Mission," *Progressions,* A Lilly Endowment Occasional Report 3, no. 1 (1991): 7–8, 10.

24. Ibid., 10.

25. Towns, *Innovative Churches,* 15.

26. Doug Murren, *The Baby Boomerang: Catching Baby Boomers as They Return to Church* (Ventura, Calif.: Regal, 1990), 189.

27. Ibid., 192.

28. Patricia Moir, "Entertainment Leads the Way," Bellevue, Wash., *Journal American,* 9 Dec. 1990, pt. A, p. 1.

29. Lorie Lund and Colin Lund, conversations with author, Woodinville, Wash., 20–22 Dec. 1990.

30. Jack W. Hayford, correspondence with author, 12 Sept. 1991.

Chapter 31—Anticipating the Next Age

1. Toffler, *Powershift,* xix.

2. Lance Morrow, "Old Paradigm, New Paradigm," *Time,* 14 Jan. 1991, 65.

3. Postman, *Amusing Ourselves to Death,* 139–40.

4. Ibid., vii.

5. Ibid., 138, 155–56.

6. Ibid., 163.

7. Morrow, "Old Paradigm, New Paradigm," 65.

8. Barbara Osborn, "Altered States: How Television Changes Childhood and Challenges Parents, an interview with Joshua Meyrowitz," *Media&Values,* Fall 1990/Winter 1991, 2.

9. Center for Media and Values, 1962 South Shenandoah, Los Angeles, Calif. 90034. (310) 559-2944.

10. Alan Jiggins, *Human Future? Living as Christians in a High-Tech World* (London: Scripture Union, 1988), 9, 19, 58.

11. David E. Sanger, "For a Job Well Done, Japanese Honor the Chip," *New York Times,* 11 Dec. 1990, pt. B, p. 1.

12. Willard Gaylin, "Fooling With Mother Nature," *Hastings Center Report* 20, no. 1 (1990): 20–21.

13. Martin Marty, "Women Make a Difference," and "Open for Debate," *Context,* 15 Aug. 1990, 4.

14. James U. McNeal, "From Savers to Spenders: How Children Became a Consumer Market," *Media&Values,* Fall 1990/Winter 1991, 4–5.

15. Quoted in Ronald K. L. Collins, "Sneakers That Kill: Kids and Conspicuous Consumption," *Media&Values,* Fall 1990/Winter 1991, 7.

16. McNeal, "From Savers to Spenders," 5.

17. Center for Media and Values. (See note 9 above.)

18. "Churches Die With Dignity," *Christianity Today,* 14 Jan. 1991, 69.

19. Donald E. Miller, "Liberal Church Growth: A Case Study," a paper presented at the annual meeting of the Society for the Scientific Study of Religion, Salt Lake City, Utah, Oct. 1989, 23–27.

20. "Christian Leaders Call for End to Anti-Christian Bigotry," *Evangelical Press News Service,* 15 March 1991, 1.

21. Cited in Martin Marty, "Why Is Everybody Always Picking on Evangelicals," *Context* 23, no. 6 (1991): 1–3.

22. Ibid., 3.

23. Quoted in George W. Cornell, Associated Press, "Most Americans Identify With Christian Faiths," *Los Angeles Times,* 13 April 1991, pt. F, p. 15; David E. Anderson, "Survey Shows Americans a Religious People," 3 April 1991.

24. George Gallup, Jr., speech made to the board of directors of Religion in American Life, 9 June 1988; excerpted in "People's Religion—America's Faith in the '90s," Joint Strategy and Action Committee *Grapevine* 20, no. 7 (1989): np.

25. Cited in Morrow, "Old Paradigm, New Paradigm," 66.

26. Buchholz, *New Ideas From Dead Economists,* 287.

27. Ephesians 6:11–14, *New English Bible* (New York: Oxford Univ. Press and Cambridge Univ. Press, 1970).

Index

C

R